ESSEX COUNTY DEEDS
1681–1684

ABSTRACTS OF VOLUME 6
COPY BOOKS
ESSEX COUNTY
MASSACHUSETTS

ESSEX SOCIETY OF GENEALOGISTS, INC.

HERITAGE BOOKS
2013

HERITAGE BOOKS
AN IMPRINT OF HERITAGE BOOKS, INC.

Books, CDs, and more—Worldwide

For our listing of thousands of titles see our website
at
www.HeritageBooks.com

Published 2013 by
HERITAGE BOOKS, INC.
Publishing Division
5810 Ruatan Street
Berwyn Heights, Md. 20740

Copyright © 2013 Essex Society of Genealogists, Inc.

All rights reserved. No part of this book may be reproduced or transmitted in any form or by any means, electronic or mechanical, including photocopying, recording or by any information storage and retrieval system without written permission from the author, except for the inclusion of brief quotations in a review.

International Standard Book Numbers
Paperbound: 978-0-7884-5502-5
Clothbound: 978-0-7884-6897-1

With special thanks to:

Essex County Registry of Deeds

And volunteers:

MaryAnn Ankiewicz
Barbara J. Beake
Marilyn Fitzpatrick
Polly Furbush
Rosalie Godfrey
Nancy Hayward

Although every effort has been made for accuracy by the volunteers, any deed of interest should be verified by consulting the original copy books.

Essex Society of Genealogists, Inc.
P.O. Box 313
Lynnfield, MA 01940
www.esog.org

Heritage Books by Essex Society of Genealogists, Inc.:

*Essex County Deeds, Abstracts of Volumes 1–4 (1639–1678)
Copy Books, Essex County, Massachusetts*

*Essex County Deeds, Abstracts of Volume 5 (1678–1681)
Copy Books, Essex County, Massachusetts*

*Essex County Deeds, Abstracts of Volume 6 (1681–1684)
Copy Books, Essex County, Massachusetts*

CD: *The Essex Genealogist, Volumes 1 and 2 (1981–1982)*

The Essex Genealogist, Volume 1 (1981)

The Essex Genealogist, Volume 2 (1982)

The Essex Genealogist, Volume 3 (1983)

The Essex Genealogist, Volume 4 (1984)

The Essex Genealogist, Volume 5 (1985)

The Essex Genealogist, Volume 6 (1986)

The Essex Genealogist, Volume 7 (1987)

The Essex Genealogist, Volume 8 (1988)

The Essex Genealogist, Volume 9 (1989)

The Essex Genealogist, Volume 10 (1990)

The Essex Genealogist, Volume 11 (1991)

The Essex Genealogist, Volume 12 (1992)

The Essex Genealogist, Volume 13 (1993)

The Essex Genealogist, Volume 14 (1994)

The Essex Genealogist, Volume 15 (1995)

The Essex Genealogist, Volume 16 (1996)

The Essex Genealogist, Volume 17 (1997)

The Essex Genealogist, Volume 18 (1998)

The Essex Genealogist, Volume 19 (1999)

The Essex Genealogist, Volume 20 (2000)

The Essex Genealogist, Volume 21 (2001)

The Essex Genealogist, Volume 22 (2002)

The Essex Genealogist, Volume 23 (2003)

The Essex Genealogist, Volume 24 (2004)

The Essex Genealogist, Volume 25 (2005)

The Essex Genealogist, Volume 26 (2006)

The Essex Genealogist, Volume 27 (2007)

The Essex Genealogist, Index to Volumes 1–15 (1981–1995)

The Essex Genealogist, Index to Volumes 16–20 (1996–2000)

The Essex Genealogist, Index to Volumes 21–25 (2001–2005)

ESSEX COUNTY DEEDS Book 6
"RECORDS OF SALEM 1681-1684"

ARON WAYE, SR. to ARON WAYE and WILLIAM WAYE – (6:1) Aron Waye, Sr. of Bostone upon due considerations and grounds and reasons gave unto two sons Aron Waye and William Waye, all that tract of land lying at the place comonly caled Wills hill within the bounds of Salem, that was formerly the Worshipfull Rich'd Bellingham's Esqr. & purchased by Bray Wilkins & John Gingen, the third of which farme was againe puchased by myselfe and my cozen William Ireland, as by deed doth appeere soe as the sixth pt of the farme is mine besides what is elce purchassed by me I give until my two sons Aron & William to be equally divided save only the housing & home lott that is inclosed which my sonn Aron now lives in & hath present possession of with all my portion of land that lyeth before the house in lieu of which my son William shall have that pr'cell of land that is mine next adjoining his house & that pt of mine upon the great neck. *Signed*: Aron Waye [mark]; Joane Waye. *Release of dower*: Joane, wife quittclaime dower. *Date*: 6 December 1680. *Witnesses*: Elias Maverick; Paul Maverick [aged about 24 yeares]. *Acknowledged*: 3 March 1680/81 by Elias Maverick aged about 39 yeares & Paul Maverick. *Recorded*: 9 May 1681.

FRANCES COLLENS to JOHN MASON – (6:2) Frances Collens of Salem (carpenter) sold to John Mason of Salem (brickmaker) for consideration of fower pounds, p'cell of land about one acre and a half formerly the land of Roger Conant & lately in the possession of Thomas Tuck & by him sold to me Frances Collins as per bill of sale bearing date 28:10mo:1659 situate in the township of Salem in the neck & bounded with the highway on west, the comon on east & a cove y^t branches in out of the north river on the north. *Signed*: Frances Collens. *Date*: 1 November 1660. *Witnesses*: Hilliard Veren; Joshua Turland. *Acknowledged*: 1 November 1660 & Hannah, wife gave consent. *Recorded*: 25 May 1681.

JACOB PUDEATER to JOHN GREENSLADE – (6:4) Jacob Pudeater (blacksmith) sold to John Greenslade of Salem (glover) for consideration of thirty pounds, a house & land lying & being in the towne of Salem, with the land the dwelling house now standeth upon, full five pole square of land, w'ch dwelling house is that which formerly Goodman Watson deceased his house, & land is also pt of that land which was Goodman Watson his land, which five pole square of land is bounded as followeth, house & land standeth upon being part of it southward toward Jacob Pudeaters barne, which he now hath. full five poles. viz: north and south five poles which is the front & from the highway which is the eastward bounds into the land of me Jacob Pudeater westward untill five poles square shall be fully completed. Wife Ann gives up right & dowry. *Signed*: Jacob Pudeater [mark]; Ann Pudeater [mark]. *Date*: 22 May 1681. *Witnesses*: Richard Prince; Frances Neale senr. *Acknowledged*: 23 May 1681 by both. *Recorded*: 23 May 1681.

JOHN NEWMAN to JOHN HULL, ESQ. – (6:6) John Newman of Bostone, Administrator to the estate of Antipas Newman late of Wenham deceased, with the consent of his mother, Mrs. Elizabeth Endecot of Salem, late relict & administratix to the estate of Antipas Newman aforesaid and Richard Wharton of Bostone, marchant, one of the overseers to said estate mortgaged to John Hull, Esq. of Boston for consideration of fifty pounds, one piece or p'cell of land within the bounds of Salem on a place comonly knowne by the name of Royall's side, containing about forty-fower acres butted & bounded on the northwardly by the Salem comon, & sotherly by Willistone river & easterly by Basse river. If John Newman, Elizabeth Endicott, or any other heirs of Antipas Newman should pay to John Hull the sum of fifty-three pounds before 21 May 1686, this present deed of mortgage shall be utterly voyde & cease. *Signed*: Elizabeth Endecott [mark]; John Newman. *Date*: 21 May 1681. *Witnesses*: John Endicott; Israel Milburne. *Acknowledged*: 21 May 1681. *Recorded*: 30 May 1681.

ROBERT BURGES to HENRY ROADES – (6:10) Robert Burges of Linn (bricklayer) sold to Henry Roades of Linn (Gent.) for consideration of six pounds & five shillings, one acre & one quarter of salt marsh ground, lying in the lower divission of lotts in Rumney marsh in the township of Linn, bounded easterly with the marsh that lately was or now is Andrew Mansfield's westerly with another divission of lotts, southerly with another division of lotts & northwardly with the marsh of the sd Henry Roades, which he formerly bought of sd Robert Burges. *Signed*: Robert Burges [mark]; *Release of Dower*: with the consent of Sarah his now wife in reference of surrendering up her thirds. *Date*: 2 August 1675. *Witnesses*: Joseph Roades; Ann Roades [mark]. *Acknowledged*: 25 April 1681. *Recorded*: 1 June 1681.

ROBERT BURGES to HENRY ROADS – (6:12) Robert Burges of Linn (yeoman) mortgaged to Henry Roads of Linn (gentleman) for consideration of one acre of salt marsh ground made over to him, which is part of his five acre lott which was formerly in the possession of John Lewis & lyeth in the lower divission of Rumny Marsh, lying all the bredth of the same lott of sd Robert & alsoe made over by him unto sd Henry Roads, being bounded by a small creeke, which runneth crosse sd lott into the lott of the sd Henry

Roads which is the southwardly bounds, eastward with the marsh of Andrew Mansfield and westward with the other range of lotts, and northward with the marsh the sd Robert Burges, Henry Roads lent unto the sd Robt. Burges five pounds sterling in current silver money of New England, for the space of one yeare next ensuing the date heareof fully to be compleated & ended, the which five pounds sd Robert Burges doth acknowledge receipt & alsoe doth heareby firmly make over above sd one acre of marsh unto the sd Henry Roads, as his security for the paiment of the aforesd five pounds in currant silver moneyes to him or to his order upon or before the second day of August 1676: this being to be understood that if the sd Robert Burges shall not pay or cause to be paid unto the sd Henry Roads the aforesd five pounds as abovesaid, then the aforesaid one acre of marsh shal be to the said Henry Roads, as his owne proper right and interest forever, & moreover sd Robert Burges doth heareby covenant, promise & grant to & with the sd Henry Roads that it shall & may be lawfull to & for sd Henry Roads to make use of the grass of the sd acre of marsh for this yeare: & in case sd five pounds be not paid unto the sd Henry Roads as abovesaid by the said third day of August 1676 the aforesd one acre of marsh shall bee to the only proper use & behoofe of him the sd Henry Roads, his heires & assignes forever. *Signed*: Robert Burgess [mark]. *Date*: 2 August 1675. *Witnesses*: Andrew Mansfield; Samuell Mansfield. *Acknowledged*: 14 August 1675. *Recorded*: 1 June 1681.

Robert Burges of Linn (yeoman) having received of Henry Roads of same towne (gent.) two pounds ten shillings promise to pay in same species betwixt day of date heareof & second August 1676 & for due p'formance make over unto sd Henry Roads halfe acre of salt marsh ground in lower divission in Rumney marsh athwart my five acre lott which joyneth to tenn acre lott of sd Henry Roades which halfe acre is bounded with one acre which I have made over unto said Henry Roads sotherly as in deed in this paper & northerly with my owne marsh which halfe acre is to be to sd Henry Roads forever upon non payment of the two pounds ten shillings. *Signed*: Robert Burges [mark]. *Acknowledged*: 25 April 1681.

SAMUEL VERRY SENIOR to THOMAS GOOLD – (6:16) Samuel Verry Senior of Salem (husbandman) sold to Thomas Goold of Salem (husbandman) for consideration of fifty pounds, a p'cell of land containing both upland & meddow ground, it being a pt of my farme at Seader pond soe caled & being the sothermost pt or end of sd farme, the sd p'cel of upland & meddow containing by estimation fifty acres, as it lyes butted & bounded as is heareafter exprest: firstly beginning at the southwesterly corner bounds, that is betweene my farme & Mr. Gedry's farme & is neere Redding highwaye & from that bounds runing easterly upon a straite line to the southeasterly corner bounds, which is the corner bounds between my farme & Mr. Johnsons farme, & from corner bounds northerly upon a straite line to or neere a black oake tree, soe farr as where my sonn Nursse & Robert Follett's land meets & is bounded, which is the northeasterly corner, & from thence westerly upon a straite line to a smale maple tree that stands toward the head of a brooke that runs into the meadow, joyning to some meadow that was formerly William Lord's & from thence sd brooke as it runs into river that comes out of Ceader pond to be the bounds westward, & then sd river to be the bounds untill you come to the first bounds that parts my farme & Mr. Gedny's farme, soe that bargained pr'misses as above described is bounded sotherly by Salem comon land, easterly by Mr. Johnson's farme, northerly by my sonn John Nurse his lands & west & west sotherly by brooke & aforesd river only excepting & by these pr'sents doe except & reserve a highwaye to go from Redding highwaye through the bargained premisses unto sd land of sd John Nurse, for our several uses that have land toward northerly end of the sd farme, & to make free liberty to pass & repasse with horse & cart from time to time forever. *Signed*: Samuel Verry [mark]. *Date*: 6 June 1681. *Witnesses*: Sara Parkman; Hilliard Veren. *Acknowledged*: 6 June 1681. *Recorded*: 6 June 1681.

JOHN GATCHELL and WIBRAH GATCHELL to JONATHAN GATCHELL – (6:19) John Gatchell of Marblehead with consent of wife Wibrah Gatchell guifted to Jonathan Gatchell for divers good causes known to us, one p'cell of ground, scituate, lying & being in Marblehead, that is to say, first bounds beginning at a cleft rock that lyeth northeast or east north east neere the corner of a stone wale that is joyning to dwelling house of sd John Gatchell and from the cleft of sd rock straite with a line to a brier bush that stands southward oppositt sd Jonathan Gatchell's porch of his dwelling house & from the midle of sd brier bush straite with a line toward the south west or west south west till you come even or abrest a small flat rock that lyeth within a pole or pole & halfe of a great rock that is southwest or to the westward of the small flat rockes & northward corner of those small rockes is the outside bound & as you runn straite with a line from sd briar bush, & com even with sd flatt rockes to run up square to sd flat rock & from sd small flat rock to run up toward the corner of sd Jonathan Gatchell's house & six foot behind sd Jonathan Gatchells house & soe home to the corner of sd John Gatchell's stone wale the back side of his house. *Signed*: John Gatchell; Wibra Gatchell. *Release of Dower*: wife Wibra giving up thirds. *Date*: 4 May 1681. *Witnesses*: William Furneax [mark]; Edward Humphryes. *Acknowledged*: 6 June 1681 by John Gatchell, sen'r. *Recorded*: 6 June 1681.

JONATHAN GATCHELL to WILLIAM FURNEUX – (6:21) Jonathan Gatchell of Marblehead (joyner) sold to William Furneux of Marblehead (tailor) for consideration of fifty pounds in hand paid or secured to be paid, all that my dwelling house with a shop or working house neere sd dwelling house with about one quarter of an acre of ground upon which sd housing doe stand which sd ground was lately given to me by my father John Gatchell, as by his deed of guift to me doe appeere, & is scituate & lying in Marblehead aforesaid, & is bounded in manner following, that is to say, the 1st bounds beginning at a cleft rock that lyeth north east or east northeast neere the corner of a stone wale that is joyning to dwelling house of my father John Gatchell, & from cleft of sd rock strait with a line to a briar bush that stands southward oppositt against me sd Jonathan Gatchell's porch of my sd dwelling house now bargained & sold & from the midle of sd brier bush strait with a line towards southwest or west southwest till you come even or abrest of a smale flat rock that lyeth within a pole or pole & a halfe of a great rock that is southwest or to westward of the small flat rocke & the northward corner of those small rocks is the outside bounds & as you runn straite with a line from sd brier bush & come even with the said flatt rockes to runn up square to sd flatt rock & from the sd smale flat rock to run up towards the corner of sd. John Gatchell's house & six foot behind my said house (now by these pr'sents sold) & soe home to the corner of the sd John Gatchell's stone wale the back side of his house: alsoe one cowes lease upon the comons belonging to the sd house. *Signed*: Jonathan Gatchell. *Date*: 1 June 1681. *Witnesses*: Hilliard Veren; John Pickering. *Acknowledged*: 6 June 1681. *Recorded*: 7 June 1681.

ZARUBABELL ENDECOTT and ELIZABETH C. ENDECOTT to WILLIAM BROWNE, JR. – (6:25) Zarubabell Endecott of Salem (Gent.) and Elizabeth C. Endecott sold to William Browne, Jr. of Salem for consideration of thirty pound sterling, a certaine p'cell of land containing about one hundred & fower rod or pole of ground, lying in length east & west seaventeene rod, & in bredth at the east end six rod, & at the west end six rod & a quarter, & is scituate in the towne of Salem, & is bounded on north with land of Leift. Thomas Putnam & on east with a lane that runns from north river to the corner of Mr. William Browne Sen'r oarchard, & on south with land of William Browne Junior & on the west with my owne land. *Signed*: Zarubabell Endecott; Elizabeth C. Endecott [mark]. *Release of Dower*: Elizabeth the wife of the sd Zarubabell Endecott yields dower. *Date*: 5 June 1679. *Witnesses*: Margarett Corwin; John Endecott. *Acknowledged*: 9 May 1681. *Recorded*: 10 June 1681.

WILLIAM BARTHOLOMEW – (6:27) For as much as the lands & hereditaments on the back side heareof made over, granted & confirmed unto Jacob Greene sen'r of Charlestown & especially to Mary his wife & her children are since sold by Jacob Greene & Mary his wife unto Daniell Huchins of Linne, as by an instrument of conveyance & sale dated the twenty fourth day of December one thousand & six hundred seaventy nine acknowledged & recorded (which hath alsoe my consent) & for that sd Jacob Greene hath otherwise made a p'ticuler assurance of part of his estate in moneyes &c. unto said Mary his wife & her children in leiu thereof to my full satisfaction William Bartholomew doe heareby make voyde & of none efect all & every pt. of the intaile or intailes made & written on ye back side heareof, of the lands & hereditaments therein granted & to every part thereof & as thereby secured or ought to have been secured. *Signed*: William Bartholomew. *Date*: 3 December 1679. *Witnesses*: William Killicupp; John Greene. *Acknowledged*: 5 December 1679. The above written relates to the sd deed & conveyance therein mention, on the back side as is exprest, which is recorded in booke ye 3rd, foll 104 & 105 in Salem records as ateste. Hilliard Veren Recorder. *Recorded*: 15 June 1681.

DANIELL HICHINS and ELLENOR HICHINS to RICHARD HAVEN JUN'R – (6:29) Daniell Hichins of Linne and Ellenor his wife sold to Richard Haven Jun'r for consideration of thirty pounds, a certaine tract of lands both upland & swamps to the quantity of thirty acres & was part of the farme that the said Daniell Hichens now dwelleth upon wch he lately purchased of Jacob Greene of Charlestowne lying on the easterly and southeasterly quarter of said farme, and begineth a little way from the now dwelling house of the sd Daniell butted and bounded as viz: on the westward by the lands of the sd Daniell Hitchins, from a stake sett downe in the plaine caled of old "Walkers plaine" for the north and by west corner, northward, by lands of sd Daniell Hutchins, being on that plain caled of old "Walkers plaine" eastward & southward facing towards farme now in the tennure & occupation of Richard George, the line being sett from a tree markett for the easterly & sotherly corner & soe the line runing from thence up through a plaine on easterne side of a brooke that runneth in sd thirty acres unto a black oake marked & standeth neere to the hills that ly above that plaine westerly & from that black oake leaving a sufficient cartwaye below those hills, unto a stake sett for the south & by west corner of this sd land & standeth over against the now dwelling of the said Daniell Hutchins. *Signed*: Daniell Hutchins [mark]; Elinor Hutchins [mark]. *Date*: 30 May 1680. *Witnesses*: John Wenborne; Oliver Purchas; Richard Haven sen'r. *Acknowledged*: 15 June 1681 & Ellenor rendering power of thirds. *Recorded*: 15 June 1681. The assignment of this deed is recorded in foll. 81 in this booke.

JOHN KITCHIN and ELIZABETH KITCHIN to RICHARD CROADE – (6:33) John Kitchin of Salem (cordwinder) and Elizabeth his wife sold to Richard Croade of Bostone (marchant) for consideration of one hundred & forty pounds in money & in goods, his now dwelling house in Salem aforesaid, with the ground on which it stands & adjoining to it, being by estimation neere one half acre, which sd house & ground is scituat & lying betweene land of the said Kitchin on the westward side & home to house & lands of George Deane on easter side, it butts upon the land of Thomas Robbins northerly & fronts upon the streete sotherly, the said land on the westward side of the house runing even with the front to sd Kitchins land, reserved to himselfe forty three foot or thereabouts, being bounded by the third mile post from the land of Richard Bishop & soe to runn upon an even line unto the extent of the sd ground butting upon Thomas Robbins his land as it is now markt out together with a pasture land on the south side of sd streete, as it is now fenced. being by estimation three quarters of an acre, & is bounded upon the land of sd Kitchin westerly & sotherly on the land of John Neale easterly & fronts upon the street northward. *Signed*: John Kitchin; Elizabeth Kitchin [mark]. *Date*: 9 July 1664. Since the above written instrument I doe acknowledge to have sold unto abovesd Croade for the sume of three pounds ten shillings the remainder of my ground above mentioned betweene Richard Bishop and the premises now sold. *Witnesses*: John Reves; Robert Graye. *Acknowledged*: by Elizabeth & shee doth owne that her husband did acknowledge same 4:4 mo:1679. *Recorded*: 23 Jun 1681.

WILLIAM EDMONDS SEN'R to JOHN DOWLETTEL SEN'R – (6:37) William Edmonds sen'r of Linn (taylor) mortgaged to John Dowlettell Sen'r of Rumney Marsh, alias Bostone (yeoman) for consideration of six pounds, two acres of salt marsh lying in the bounds of Linn butted & bounded viz: southwest by marsh of John Dowlettell, northeast by marsh of William Mirriam, southeast by marsh of Thomas Farrer sen'r, westward by marsh of Mr. John Browne of Redding.
The condition of this deed is such that if the abovesd William Edmunds do well & truly pay unto the abovesd John Dowlettell the full & just sume of six pounds in currant money of silver at or before the fifteenth day of June one thousand, six hundred and eighty & six, which wil be five yeares after the date of this instrument then this deed of mortgage to be voyd. *Signed*: William Edmonds. *Date*: 15 June 1681. *Witnesses*: John Floyd; Abraham C. Simes [mark]. *Acknowledged*: 17 June 1681. *Recorded*: 28 June 1681.

ELIZABETH CHATWELL to ALLEN BREAD – (6:40) Elizabeth Chatwell of Lynn sold to Allen Bread of Lynn, grandchild to Allen Bread, sen'r for consideration of six pounds, one acre of meddow with all privilidges belonging thereunto lying in the towne meddow lying in a square peece, at upper end of the said Elizabeth's meddow, & butting upon Allen Bread's land, father to abovesd young Allen, bounded north & south with Allen Bread his father's land & meddow & south the sd Elizabeth Chatwells meddow & west with William Crafts meddow. *Signed*: Elizabeth Chatwell [mark]. *Date*: 1 December 1680. *Witnesses*: Joseph Wheeler; Samuel Harte. *Acknowledged*: 1 December 1680 at Bostone. *Recorded*: 15 July 1681.

JOHN JEWETT and ELIZABETH JEWETT to SAMUELL JOHNSON – (6:42) John Jewett of Ipswich with his wife Elizabeth sold to Samuell Johnson for consideration of eleven pounds, two acres of salt marsh lying in towne marsh neere the place caled the two trees: being & lying with in the township of Lynn, bounded with a creek westerly parting betweene the sd marsh & the marsh of John Gillow & butting sotherly upon the sea & butting & bounded easterly & northerwardly upon marsh of sd John Jewett & Elizabeth his wife, & it is to be understood that his two acres of salt marsh was sold to pay some debts that the former husband of sd Elizabeth namely Benjamin Chadwell was indebted when he deceased. *Signed*: John Jewett. *Date*: 14 July 1681. *Witnesses*: Thomas Laighton sen'r; Ralph King. *Acknowledged*: 15 July 1681 by John Jewett & Elizabeth his wife as shee is administratrix of estate of Benjamin Chadwell. *Recorded*: 15 July 1681.

EDWARD RAWSON for JOHN KNOWLES to THOMAS LAUGHTON – (6:44) Edward Rawson of Boston (gent., aturney) for John Knowles cleark hearetofore pastor to the church of Watertowne in New England & since pastor of a church of Christ in Bristol in old England sold to Thomas Laughton of Lynn (gent.) for consideration of sixty pounds thirty in money, severall yeares since & the other thirty more lately in horses, all that the dwelling house of sd John Knowles in Linn aforesaid with all outhouses, gardens, yards, orchards, with a p'cell of upland thereunto adjoining, containing by estimation twelve acres, with all the fences, trees, woods, underwoods that are upon the same, & is bounded by land of late Mr. Edward Holioak northeast with land of Edward Richards northerly, which formerly was in the possession of Richard Whitney, & by the towne comon sotherly westerly & easterly. *Signed*: Edward Rawson, Attorney for Mr. John Knowles. *Date*: 27 March 1669. *Witnesses*: Thomas Marshall; John Saunders. *Acknowledged*: 20 September 1679. *Recorded* 16:5 mo: 1681. Looke foll: 90: where this assigned over.

ROBERT GOODELL to MARGARETT LAZENBY – (6:47) I Robert Goodell of Salem have made choyce of & by Gods pr'mition doe fully intend to take to my wife Margarett Lazenby, late of Exeter in New England (& by wh'ch being done) doe heareby covenant & promise to & with sd Margaret that in case shee outlives me to give & bequeath unto her for her comfortable subsistence after my decease during terme of her life the goods and chattells ensuing menticned, viz.: a new dwelling house which I doe intend God willing shortly to build, with what household stuffs therein God shall please to continue unto me untill my death: Item: two cowes & a horse or mare fitt for her to ride cn, alsoe my whole oarchard upon my farme, neere my dwelling house at bald hill, with six acres of the planting ground upon which the sd oarchard stands, the best of sd ground & fower acres of meddow ground neere to my sd orchard with a pasture plot of about two acres fenced in neere to my sd house & orchard & alsoe that shee shall have a competency of fire wood and timber for her use for building and fencing as she hath occasion upon some part of my aforesaid farme or som convenyent place neere unto it & after her decease my intent & mind is that pr'misses as aforesd given to my wife shall fale to my sonn Jacob Goodell and covenant with sd Margarett that in case shee outlive my sd sonn Jacob that then she shall have and injoy for her use & benefit that part of my estate which I shall and doe intend to leave unto my sd sonn Jacob during her life in like manner as the former & further if in case sd Margarett shall have child or children by me, then more amply to confirme the pr'misses if desired & take further care for her & their maintenance after me. *Signed*: Robert Goodell. *Date*: 30 August 1669. *Witnesses*: John Kitchin; Richard Croade. *Acknowledged*: 21:7 mo:1669. *Recorded*: 19 July 1681.

RICHARD LEACH, SARAH LEACH and JOHN LEACH to CHRISTOPHER WALLER – (6:49) Richard Leach of Salem with consent of wife & son John sold to Christopher Waller of Salem for consideration of one hundred pounds, one dwelling house & oarchard, together with twenty acres upland & medow thereunto belonging & appertaining, lying & being scituate within the township of Salem in a place caled the north field, & being bounded as followeth. viz: on the northeast with the river which runneth up toward the farme sometime belonging to the Worshipfull Jon. Endecott late Gov'r on the northwest with land sometime belonging to William Cantlebury southward with Nathaniell Felton's lott and westward with comon or highwaye. *Signed*: Richard Leach; Sarah Leach [mark]; John Leach. *Date*: 10 August 1667. *Witnesses*: Nathaniell Felton; John Hibburt [mark]. Possession was given of the land above mentioned by Richard Leach & his wife & his son John Leach & delivered by turf & twigg, as witnesseth. *Acknowledged*: 30 June 1681 Nathaniell Felton & John Hibbert made oath that they were pr'sent & saw Rich'd & Sarah Leach signe, seale & deliver this writing, as theire act & deed, alsoe Nathaniell Felton & John Felton made oath that they were pr'sent & saw Richard Leach give possession of the house & gave seizin & possession of the land hearin mentioned by turfe & twigg this 30th of June 1681 before me. Barthol. Gedney Assist. *Recorded*: 19 July 1681.

SAMUELL SOTHWICK to PHILLIP CROMWELL – (6:51) Samuell Sothwick of Salem (husbandman) mortgaged to Phillip Cromwell of Salem (slautherer) for consideration of 45 pounds silver, a dwelling house w'ch heretofore was dwelling house of John Sothwick the father of sd Samuell Sothwick with 2 acres of ground adjoining butting on streete at southwesterly end, on northeast side land of John Sothwick & Isaac Sothwick, to the farther end of barne next to house westerly from barne 10 poles upon John and Isaac Sothwick's land and soe runns strait away northerly to Isaac Cookes and Henry Cookes land, alsoe another piece of land in the same lott & inclosure w'ch is as was measured and bounded out by overseers of sd Samuel as heire to his fathers John Sothwick's estate containing by estimation 19 acres and a quarter of an acre bounded as hereafter exprest viz: on street westerly about 32 pole in front on northwest side on land of John Sothwick not yet shared about 106 poles at the head on northerne side upon land of Samuell Eborne sen'r 16 poles on east northeast side taperways on Isaac and Henry Cooks land and John Cooks and on land of John and Isaac Sothwick sotherly, provided if Samuell Sothwick pay sd Phillip Cromwell sum of 45 pounds in silver at or before the exspiration of terme of 5 yeares accounting from day of date heareof with interest after the rate of 20 pence in silver p'pound p'annum then this sale to be voyde. The one halfe of barne abovesd being likewise included in this deed of mortgage. *Signed*: Samuell Southwick [mark]. *Date*: 25 March 1680. *Witnesses*: John Cromwell; Richard Croade. *Acknowledged*: 19 July 1681. *Recorded*: 20 July 1681.

WILLIAM SWEATLAND to MR. PHILLIP CROMWELL – (6:56) William Sweatland of Salem (taylor) being indebted to Mr. Phillip Cromwell of Salem (slatherer) just sume of 70 pounds sterling which is for & in consideration of dwelling house bought of sd Phillip Cromwell & Edmund Bridges as by bill of sale bearing date with these presents, promise to pay to sd Phillip Cromwell viz: to say twenty pounds of current money of New England to be paid at or before ye twenty fifth day of December next ensuring date heare of & for second payment twenty pounds in like current money at or before ye twentyeth day of September 1681 & for the third payment twenty pounds in like current money at or before the twentyeth day of September 1682. & for the fourth & last payment ten pounds at or before the twentyeth day of September 1683 & sd Swetland is heareby obligated to pay interest for sd last three payments (which is in all fifty pounds) at the rate of twenty pence pr^{li} money yearly till the whole be paid every yeare for each payment untill the time of payment as is above exsprest. *Signed*: Will Swetland. *Date*: 18 September 1680. *Witnesses*: John Cromwell; Isaack Williams. *Recorded*: 20 July 1681.

WILLIAM DIXY to WOODBURY – (6:58) I William Dixy of Beverly did bargain with James Standish to buy his lott adjoining to mine in Bass river now caled Beverly, that I received of sd Standish a deed of sale bearing date 22 December 1652 yett soe that my sonn Woodbery did with mee pay halfe ye purchase to ye sd Standish when upon wee made a division & my sd sonn Woodberye hath now possessed & built upon his half & injoyed it as he still posseth it for sundry years I assigne over all right to all that pt of sd lott which is now in his possession together with all my right, title & interest in one halfe of the swamp mentioned in James Standish's deed & for conveniency of my said sonn Woodbury's house & lott above sd have given him a highway to the contry road from his said lott. I do heareby confirme sd highway as it is bounded between Edmund Gale & John Richards their lands unto ye sd Hugh Woodbury. *Signed*: William Dixy [mark]. *Date*: 27 July 1681. *Witnesses*: John Hale; Richard Stackhouse. *Acknowledged*: 1 August 1681. *Recorded*: 6 mo: 1681.

JOHN DEVORIX SENR. and ANN DEVORIX to VINSON STILSON JUNIOR – (6:59) John Devorix Senr. of Marblehead with free consent of Ann his wife sold to Vinson Stilson Junior of Marblehead (coardwinder) for consideration of a certain sum of money, one piece of ground lying & being in Marblehead adjoining on southwest side to land of John Hooper to his stone wall & towards northeast with Elias Henly's cove & towards northward or northwest to a great neck that is at the end of the stone wale next to the front or highway as it is fenced, being a quarter of an acre it runs toward the seaside & so all along from ye east toward ye southeast or southward by ye sea to the wall of John Hooper. *Signed*: John Devouix; Ann Devorix. *Release of Dower*: Ann wife yielded right. *Date*: 22 July 1678. *Witnesses*: Thomas Holeup; Edw. Humphrys. *Acknowledged*: 26:9 mo:1678 & Ann yielded thirds. *Recorded*: 2:6mo:1681.

NATHANIEL PUTNAM, SENIOR to JOHN PUTNAM – (6:61) Nathaniel Putnam, senior of Salem sold to John Putnam for divers good causes & considerations, especially for that love & natural affection which I have & beare unto my sonn John Putnam, a certaine tract or pr'cell of land containing one hundred acres, situate within limits of Salem and is bounded by Ipswich river northerly by land of Leift. Tho. Putnam, easterly the land of me sd Nathaniell Putnam southerly, & land of Job Swinterton ptly & of

William Sibly ptly westerly. I sd Nathaniell Putnam give & grant unto my sonn John Putnam for considerations as aforesaid to say about fower acres of meddow or low ground called by name of Massey's pond, lying on north side of Ipswich river, being bounded round with land formerly of Robert Prince, late deceased, now in the hands of Allexander Osbourne, which sd pr'cell I freely give to my sonn, over & above ye one hundred acres above mentions. *Signed*: Nathaniell Putnam. *Date*: 10 August 1681. *Witnesses*: Henry Renolds; Hilliard Veren senior. *Acknowledged*: 10 August 1681. *Recorded*: 10 August 1681.

ZAROBABELL ENDICOTT and ELIZABETH ENDICOTT to JONATHAN WALCUTT – (6:64) Zarobabell Endicott of Salem and wife Elizabeth Endicott of Salem sold to Jonathan Walcutt of Salem for divers cause & considerations especially for a valuable sume already paid, five acres & nine poles of medow lying within limits of township of Topsfield, being part of a farme given me by my honoured father, by deed of guift, this said meddow being bounded on north side with Ipswich river on the south side with a pr'cell of land called "the blind hole", on west end with a little brooke that runs into the river above exprist, on the east end alsoe with a little brooke running into ye river on ye southwest corner bounded with a stake upon the brooke, from thence on south side to a little tree, from thence on the south side bounded on the upland to the southeast corner to a stake. *Signed*: Zarobabell Endicott; Elizabeth Endicott [mark]. *Date*: first day of January 1678. *Witnesses*: Israell Porter; Henry Keny [mark]. *Acknowledged*: 10th of August 1681. *Recorded* 16 August 1681.

RICHARD HAINES to THOMAS HAINES – (6:67) Richard Haines of Beverly gave to kinsman Thomas Haines of Salem for ye love, good will & affection towards my kinsman Thomas Haines alsoe for divers other good & lawfull causes & considerations, all & singular my goods that doe belong unto me sd Richard Haines, not only all my land & tenements lying in Beverly or any other place whatsoever, but alsoe my dwellinghouse & household stuffs & all other estate either live or dead whatsoever, as well moveable as immoveable, whatsoever they be or in whose hands, custody or possession, the same of any of them or any pt thereof can or may be found. *Signed*: Richard Haines. *Date*: twenty ninth day of May 1679. *Witnesses*: James Bailey; Nathaniell Ingerson. *Acknowledged*: 12:11 mo: 79. *Recorded*: 16:August:81.

THOMAS HAINES to RICHARD HAINES – (6:68) Thomas Haines of Salem for the great love, respect & affection that I have & beare unto my uncle Richard Haines alsoe for & in consideration of a certain estate made over to me by deed of guift bearing date with these pr'sents bind & oblige myselfe to take care & provide for my sd uncle Richard Haines, all things necessary for his comfortable livelyhood during his life both in sickness & in health, not only in respect of meate & drink but apparell, washing, & lodging such as may be suitable for his age & comfortable for him during his naturall life.

It is to be understood that my unkle shall live with me in my house during his life & there be provided for according to the pr'misses. *Signed*: Thomas Haines. *Date*: twenty ninth day of May 1679. *Witnesses*: James Bailey; Nathaniell Ingerson. *Acknowledged*: 12:11 mo:1681. *Recorded*: 16 August 1681.

JOSEPH HUCHINSON to THOMAS HAINES – (6:69) Joseph Huchinson of Salem (yeoman) sold to Thomas Haines of Salem for a certain sum to me in hand paid, seaven acres of land, bounded with a smale red oake tree or heape of stones on southwest and from thence norwest upon the line of Nathaniell Putnam to a stake & heape of stones & from thence to northeast in a swamp the land of above said Joseph Huchenson lying to the norwest & from thence to southwest upon line of Jonathan Walcutt & soe to the bounds first named all of which lying in the township of Salem. *Signed*: Joseph Huchenson. *Date*: no date. *Witnesses*: Eleazer Gedney; Joshua Rea, senior. *Acknowledged*: 10:August:1681. *Recorded*: August the 9th, 1681.

JOHN TRASK to THOMAS HAINES – (6:71) John Trask of Salem sold to Thomas Haines of Salem for consideration of a certaine p'cell of land containing seaven acres lying & being as is exprest in his deed of sale to me bearing the date with these pr'sents, a certain p'cell of fresh medow ground containing five or six acres scituate & lying in bounds of Salem aforesaid, neere Ipswich river & is bounded sotherly with a brooke that runs down from the Widdow Pope's farme by south end of the premises & easterly it is bounded with a river that runs into Ipswich river, northerly with some meddow formerly of Elias Mason, now the widow of Caleb Buffum which bounds ye premises ptly on northerly side & on west with meddow of Josiah Sothwick. *Signed*: John Trask. *Date*: first day of March 1681. *Witnesses*: Eleazer Gedney; Joshua Rea senior. *Acknowledged*: 10th of August 1681. *Recorded*: 16:August 1681.

JOSEPH HOULTON to THOMAS HAINES – (6:73) Joseph Houlton of Salem (husbandman) sold to Thomas Haines of Salem for consideration of a certain sume to me in hand paid, three acres of land bounded on northeast & norwest upon dividing line as it was agreed upon by me abovesd Joseph Houlton & Nathaniell Ingerson, it now being within fence & improved by abovesd Thomas Haines, all which land lying in the township of Salem.

Signed: Joseph Houlton. *Witnesses*: Eleazer Gedney; Joshua Rea, senior. *Acknowledged*: 10: of August 1681. *Recorded*: August the 9th:1681.

JOHN DARLING and MARY DARLING to THOMAS MAULE – (6:74) John Darling of Salem with consent of wife Mary sold to Thomas Maule of Salem for consideration of a valuable sume of money to me in hand paid, my now dwelling house, where I now live in towne of Salem with all land, housing, barnes, buildings, gardens, orchards by estimation 20 poles of land bounded eastward land of Mr. Croade northerly land of Mary Darling formerly land of Richard Bishop deceased westerly Roger Darby his land sotherly with streete or highwaye. *Signed*: John Darling [mark]; Mary Darling [mark]. *Date*: 19: November: 1680. *Witnesses*: George Deane; Francis Neale, senior. I Mary Darling, wife to John Darling give my free consent to the above written bargaine & sale as witness my hand, this 19th November, 1680. *Acknowledged*: 19th of January 1680. *Recorded*: 16: August: 1681.

JONATHAN PRINCE to THOMAS MAULE – (6:77) Jonathan Prince of Salem (cordwinder) sold to Thomas Maule of Salem (shopkeeper) in consideration of a valuable sume to me in hand, a certain p'cell of ground lying in south feild in township of Salem by estimation about two acres as it is now bounded & is bounded by the sea easterly, by ye contry roade westerly, north and south upon land of Mr. Joseph Hardy senior. *Signed*: Jonathan Prince. *Date*: thirtieth day of July 1681. *Witnesses*: Deliverance Parkman; Hilliard Veren. *Acknowledged*: 2nd of August 1681. *Recorded*: 16: August: 1681.

JONATHAN PRINCE to THOMAS MAULE – (6:79) Jonathan Prince of Salem (cordwinder) mortgaged to Thomas Maule of Salem (merchant) in consideration of the full & just sume of eighty five pounds, which sd sume I doe acknowledge I stand justly indebted to Thomas Maule, a certaine dwelling house with the shop & outhouses, thereto belonging w'th land it stands upon & is adjoining & belonging thereto, containing twenty poles or rods being the house & ground I lately bought of sd Thomas Maule & is scituate in Salem & is bounded westerly with land of Richard Croade, easterly with land of George Deane, northerly with land of Thomas Robbins, southerly with streete & I Jonathan Prince covenant that pr'mises are free & cleere (except the paying fower shillings by the year into the town of Salem for which land is security & must be paid by possessors & owners of ye sd bargained premises & their successors for the time of 999 years next ensueing), provided if Thomas Maule pay sume of eight five pounds sterling, that is to say, eighty pounds in silver current money of New England & five pounds in good English goods, such goods as sd Maule shall or may have occasion for, at or before the late day of July in year 1682 then this bargain to be voyde. *Signed*: Jonathan Prince. *Date*: second day August in ye yeare 1681. *Witnesses*: Deliverance Parkman; Hilliard Veren. *Acknowledged*: 2nd day of August 1681. *Recorded*: 16:August:1681.

THOMAS ROBBINS to HANNA CROADE – (6:82) Thomas Robbins of Salem gifted to Hanna Croade for good causes & consideration & especially upon the affection & love I have unto Hanna daughter of Richard Croade, a piece of land out of my homestead in Salem next to the land of John Kitchin, George Deane, Thomas Maule & the land of sd Richard Croade bounded viz. that is to say to the oake being about five pole (mark't) from the exstent of the ground that I have sold to William King next to the lane easterly & to runn exactly square through my lott unto land that hearetofore was Richard Bishop's; alsoe an acre of salt marsh which lyes in northfeild almost over against my house, alsoe at my decease a living milch cow. *Signed*: Thos. Robbins. *Date*: twenty third day of August 1679. *Witnesses*: Zebulon Hill; Nathaniel Crynes; Richard Croade. Richard Croad and Zebulon Hill testified 27 April 1681 they saw Thomas Robbins signe above written instrument. Nathaniell Crynes testified that he did see Thomas Robbins signe this instrument 4th June 1681.

Furthermore I Thomas Robbins have upon real & absolute codiall meaning bestowed upon sd Hanna contence mentioned in deed upon second consideration thus I would have my meaning in p'misses to be explained that is to say I own Hanna Croad at the very hower of my decease to be the proper heire to the estate meaning if in case sd Hanna hath not issue before shee dyes then John Croade the brother of sd Hanna Croade shall be the proper heire to sd estate only in case sd Hanna should marry to any man & although shee hath noe child by him yet he her husband shall enjoy this estate now given by me to sd Hanna for the time of his naturall life & ye buildings that may be thereupon to that time but at his decease the sd estate shall fall to ye above sd John Croad. *Signed*: Thomas Robbins. *Date:* twenty fifth day of August 1679. *Witnesses*: Zebulon Hill; Nathaniell Crynes; Richard Croad. Zebulon Hill and Richard Croad made oath 27:April 1680 they saw Thomas Robbins sign; Nathaniell Crynes took oath 4:June 1681 that he did see Tho. Robbins signe.

The twenty fifth day of August 1679 I, Thomas Robbins, upon just considerations, best known to myself have seen cause to call in that will which I made bearing the date the 15th day of May 1679 not thinking it meet that y^t will in regard of my owne personall respect & alsoe of my successors should stand I doe therefore by these presents take of Docter Richard Knott from being my executor to my estate or any waies interested therein. I doe now in reality make & appoint Richard Croad of Salem senior & William Trask of Salem senior to be my proper executors to my estate John Trask & Edward Flint I doe appoint to be overseers to my concerns. *Signed*: Thomas Robbins. ***Witnesses***: Charles Phillips Junior [mark]; Elizabeth Croad; Zubelon Hill; Nathaniel Crynes. Zebulon Hill aged about 60 and Frances Croade aged about 50 years testify that upon the very day and about the hower when Thomas Robbins signed to a deed of guift which he had made to Hanna daughter of Richard Croade for piece of land in his homestead & something else as the sd deed makes mention of Thomas Robbins then went out from Richard Croad's house into his lott soe far as to a small white oak tree neare the land easterly & said to Richard Croad 'to this tree from your ground is the bounds of the lands here which I have given Hanna Croad' & soe Thomas Robbins went with his knife to mark the tree but by reason of his lamenes could not well doe it soe he had Richard Croad to doe it, aloe Thomas Robbins did that time after he had signed & sealed to ye deed of guift he had made to Hanna Croad take ye sd deed & give it into the hands of ye sd Hanna & kist her saying 'this my poor girl I freely give to thee' sworn: 27 Aprill 1681.

Thomas Robbins acknowledged that he did upon date of his instrument deliver estate by turf & twig in part for the whole unto Richard Croad father of Hanah Croad & John Croad & reason why sd Robbins did not mention it in deed of guift made by him afterward to William Pinson & his wife was because he had upon an honest & faithful intent & to his apprehension legally confirmed sd estate long before to Hanna Croad & John Croad. Acknowledgement recorded 2nd June 1691.

THOMAS ROBBINS to JOHN TRASK – (6:89) Thomas Robbins of Salem sold to John Trask of Salem (yeoman) in consideration of a valuable sume to me in hand paid, a certain p'cell of fresh meddow ground containing five or six acres, scituate & lying in bounds of Salem aforesaid neere Ipswich river bounded southerly with a brook that runs down from the Widdow Pope's farm by south end of premises & easterly it is bounded with a river that runs into Ipswich river, northerly with som medow formerly of Elias Mason now the meddoe of Caleb Buffum which bounds premises ptly on northerly side & on west with meddow of Josiah Sothwick, *Signed*: Thomas Robbins. *Release of Dower*: Mary my wife doe by these p'sents yield dower. *Date*: no date. *Witnesses*: Thomas Flint; John Bullock. *Acknowledged*: 28: 10 mo:1676. *Recorded*: 16:August 1681.

THOMAS HAINES to JOHN TRASK – (6:91) Thomas Haines of Salem sold to John Trask of Salem for consideration of a certain p'cell of fresh medow ground contayning five or six acres being as is exprist in his deed to me bearing the date with these presents as alsoe a young heifer already to me delivered, a certain p'cel of land lying within the bounds of Salem in common field comonly called the north field, the said land containing seaven acres being bounded on east side with land of John Massey, on west with land of Thomas Robbins & on north side with highway, on south side with the mill river. *Signed*: Thomas Haynes. *Date*: 1st day of March 1681. *Witnesses*: Eleazer Gedney; Joshua Rea, senior. *Acknowledged*: 10th of August 1681. *Recorded*: 16: August: 1681.

THOMAS MAULE to JONATHAN PRINCE – (6:94) Thomas Maule of Salem (shopkeeper) sold to Jonathan Prince of Salem (cordwinder) in consideration of a sale given to me of a quantity of upland lying & being in South field in towne of Salem given to him by will by his deceased father as alsoe for & in consideration of a bond given unto me by sd Jonathan Prince of eighty five pounds as is expressed in ye sd bond, my now present habition or dwelling place lying & being in towne of Salem viz: twenty polls of land, as it is now bounded & fenced & is bounded as followeth, westerly with Mr. Richard Croade, his land, easterly with George Dean, his land, northerly with the land of Thomas Robbins, southerly with streete, together with my now dwelling house & shop or shops with all other buildings of what nature soever standing or being thereupon ye dementions of land aforesaid & it shall be lawful for sd Jonathan Prince to hold pr'misses free & cleere except the paying of fower Shillings a year in money to towne of Salem for which land is security & must be paid by Jonathan Prince for 999 years & I Thomas Maule doe heareby empty myself of & from all other & former bargaines, claims, titles & interest to within mentioned pr'misses provided y^t I, Thomas Maule, with my family am to live in the above mentioned bargained premises until the one & twentieth day of July next ensueing. *Signed*: Thomas Maule. *Date*: this thirtieth day of July 1681. *Witnesses*: Deliverance Parkman; Hilliard Veren. *Acknowledged*: 2nd day of August 1681. *Recorded*: 16: 6 mo: 1681.

EDMOND HENFEILD to JAMES POWLAND – (6:97) Edmond Henfeild of Salem (marrenor) sold to James Powland of Salem (blacksmith) for & in consideration of fifteen pounds sterling, a certain p'cell of land scituate, lying in Salem containing about twenty seven rodd or pole of ground it being that p'cell of land my grandfather Mr. Joseph Grafton made over to me as pr deed of guift appeereth & is bounded easterly with land of Edward Wollan, northerly land of James Collens, southerly land of Venus Coldfox, a lane or p'ticular highway westerly. *Signed*: Edmond Henfeild. *Date*: fourteenth day of December 1680. *Witnesses*: Hilliard Veren, senior; Henry Scerry senior; Phillip Cromwell. *Acknowledged*: no date. *Recorded*: 16:August:1681.

HENRY BARTHOLOMEW, SENIOR to JOHN PILGRIM and ELIZABETH PILGRIM – (6:99) Henry Bartholomew, senior of Bostone (marchant) sold to John Pilgrim of Salem (march't) and his wife Elizabeth for divers good causes & considerations, especially for that love & natural affection which I have & beare unto my sonn in law John Pilgrim & to Elizabeth, his wife, my own natural daughter, a certain p'cel of land containing by estimation three quarters of an acre, & is scituate lying & being in Salem & is bounded northerly with streete & is in bredth abutting against sd streete fifty seaven foot and soe runns back sotherly abutting against the burying place comonly called burying point at which end it is in bredth forty six foot & is bounded on west side with ground of Mr. Timothy Lindall w'ch he lately bought of sd Henry Bartholomew & on easterly side it is bounded with land of Mr. Grove. *Signed* Henry Bartholomew. *Date*: twenty sixth day of August 1681. *Witnesses*: Nehemiah Willowby; Henry Bartholomew Junior. *Acknowledged*: 2d of September 1681. *Recorded*: 5 Sept: 1681.

JOHN LEMEN and EDWARD GROVE – (6:102) John Lemen of pr'cinct of St. Katherines neere the tower of London (saylemaker); whereas Edward Grove of pr'cinct of St. Katherines neere tower of London (sailemaker) by one obligation bearing date 8 August 1665 is bound to sd John Lemin in penalty of 10 pounds lawfull money of England with condition which is not pr'formed by reason whereof sd penalty is in law become forfeit, John Lemin have nominated, appointed my wel beloved friend Thomas Bartlett, comander of the good ship called the Herne to be true & lawfull Aturney & deputy for me & in my name & to my use to ask, demand, sue for leavy, recover & receive of aforesd Edward Grove the sd penalty or sum of ten pounds soe forfeited as aforesd & all other sume & sums of money, costs, charges, & damages whatsoever wh'ch shall or may accrue or happen to grow due or paiable by virtue of sd recited obligation & to compound & agree & upon any recovery or receipt of sume acquittance or acquittances or any other sufficient discharges for me & in my name to make seale & deliver & one aturney or more to make substitute & at his pleasure again to revoke & do whatsoever is necessary towards recovery. *Signed*: John Lemen. *Date*: 7th day of Feburary 1679. *Witnesses*: Samuell Rave: Solomon Lemen. *Recorded*: 5: September:1681.

[Entered as a memorandum to me Hilliard Veren] – (6:103)
TIMOTHY LASKIN is DR. to PAUL MANSFIELD:

	lb. s. d.
Impr'os for 15 months dyett pt'ly in yeare of our Lord 1680 & 1681	15:00:00

for keeping his cild one yeare	10.00.00
for house rent before his wife dyed	02:10:00
pd for you to Eleazer Giles	00:07:00
pd to Mr. Sam^{ll} Gardner Junior for halfe a btl of pork for you	01:15:00
a wheelebarrow	00:05:00
	29:17:00
Rec'd in pt of this acc't	lb. s. d.
A swine at	1:00:00
By a barrel macrell at	1:00:00
	2:00:00
Soe there rest due to me upon this 13:9 mo:1682	27:17:00

This is a tru acc't to this 13:9 mo:82; errors excepted pr me
Signed: Paule Mansfield

WALTER MOUNTJOY to RICHARD ROSE – (6:104) Walter Mountjoy of Salem (fisherman) with consent of wife Elizabeth sold to Richard Rose of Salem (marrenor) for consideration of the sume of twelve pounds in my hand paid, a small p'cell of square ground containing by estimation about fower or five pole in length or bredth scituate in Salem by the harbor or south river nere unto now dwelling house of sd Walter Mounjoy, bounded as followeth viz: northward with owne land, southward with land of Adam Westgate, west with land of Christopher Phelps and southeast with land of sd Richard Rose. ***Signed*** Walter Mountjoy [mark]. ***Date***: 22 day of Aprill 1678. ***Witnesses***: Edward Norrice; John Ingersoll. ***Acknowledged***: 19th of August 1681 & Elizabeth wife consented. ***Recorded***: 9:7 mo:1681.

JOSEPH HOLTON SEN'R to JOSEPH HOLTON JUNIOR – (6:106) Joseph Holton sen'r of Salem gave to Joseph Holton Junior of Salem, for divers good & lawfull causes & considerations especially for that fatherly love & affection that I have & beare my eldest sonn Joseph Holton Junior, a certain tract of land containing twenty acres lying within the bounds of Salem, being bounded as followeth viz: on south east with a swamp wit oake & upon a strait line to a red oake tree, marked over against northeast corner of sd Joseph Holton Junior's house, from y^t tree to a tree upon a hill westerly & upon a strait line to the line of Joseph Hutchenson & from thence butting upon sd Hutchenson's line three or fower pole from sd Joseph Holton Junior's saw pitt to a marked tree being southerly from sd saw pitt & from thence to the bound first mentioned. ***Signed***: Jos Holton senior. ***Date***: seaventeenth of January 1678. ***Witnesses***: Joshua Rea; Israell Porter. ***Acknowledged***: 7th October 1681. ***Recorded***: 7:8 mo:1681.

WILLIAM LORD, SEN'R and ABIGAIL LORD to STEEPHEN HASKETT – (6:108) William Lord, sen'r of Salem (yeoman) sold to Steephen Haskett of Salem (soape boiler) for consideration of ten pounds sterling to me in hand already paid, a certain p'cell of ground being pt of that ground on which the dwelling house sd William Lord standeth in Salem & is next adjoining to the water side or South river soe called, bounded on east next adjoining to some land of Mr. Elias Stileman, it begins at a stake drove down close to the rayles fower foot & two or three inches distant from outside of a stone wale of leantoo of John Coales house on ye north side & soe runs upon a straite line westward to a post where is a stake drove down against the middle of sd post which is hard upon or bout thirty foot & a half west of the westerne end of John Coale's house & from sd westerne stake to run southward upon a right line soe far into ye sd river as sd William Lord have any right or propriety. *Signed*: William Lord [mark]; Abigail Lord [mark]. ***Release of Dower***: Abigaile wife do freely yield up all her right of dower. ***Date***: 6th day of Aprill 1664. ***Witnesses***: Hilliard Veren; William Woodcock. ***Acknowledged***: Abigail White that was Lord acknowledged. Abigail White the late wife of William Lord within mentioned & executrix of ye sd William Lord's last will & testament declare deed was act & deed of husband William Lord 16th:7 mo:1681. ***Recorded***: 16 September: 1681.

Hilliard Veren made oath within written was signed sealed & delivered as act & deed of William Lord & Abigail his wife 16: September: 1681.

SAMUELL BENNETT to JOHN HATHORNE – (6:111) Samuell Bennett of Rumly marsh in the township of Boston (house carpenter) and Sarah his wife sold to John Hathorne of Linn (husbandman) for a valuable consideration to him in hand well & truly paid, a certain p'cell of land, meddow & pasture containing in all ten acres the which sd meddow & pasture mentioned is bounded as followeth lying within township of Linn butted & bounded with the land of John Gilloway southerly & by land of William Martin westerly & by towne comon of Linn easterly & a river running to the ironworks westerly. *Signed*: Samuell Bennett. ***Date***: twenty seaventh day of February in the year 1671. ***Witnesses***: Robert Potter; Thomas Newhall. ***Acknowledged***: 16:1 mo:76:7. ***Recorded***: 21:7 mo:1681.

DANIELL JEANVERIN to THOMAS MUDGETT – (6:113) Daniel Jeanverin of island of Jersey, now ressident in New England (marchant) sold to Thomas Mudgett of Salisbury (shipwright) for consideration of two hundred pounds sterling to me in hand, one eighth pt of the ship called the Daniell & Elizabeth of Jersey, burthen two hundred tunns or thereabout more or less, now being or riding in harbor of Salem in New England with one eight pt of all her masts, sails, sailyards, anchors, cables, roapes, tackle apparrell boat & furniture to sd ship any way belonging & all my right, title & interest. *Signed*: Daniell Jeaneverin. *Date*: twentieth day of October 1681. *Witnesses*: Hilliard Verin; William Hollingsworth. *Acknowledged*: 25:8:1681. *Recorded*: 25:8:1681.

JEREMIAH NEALE and MARY NEALE to CAPT. WILLIAM BROWNE JUNIOR – (6:115) Jeremiah Neale of Salem (carpenter) sold to Capt. William Browne Junior for a valuable consideration to me in hand paid, one acre of upland & salt marsh lying & being scittuate within township of Salem on the south side of the towne neere unto a place called Castle hill & being bounded eastward with the river which runeth from sd Castle hill down towards new mill & on other side with towne comon with fence which belongeth to sd land which I lately purchased of Samuell Beadle. *Signed*: Jeremiah Neale; Mary Neale [mark]. *Release of Dower*: Mary, wife doth yield up dower. *Date*: twentieth day of August 1681. *Witnesses*: Joseph Neale; William Murray. *Acknowledged*: 5th of September 2 1681 by Jeremiah & Mary. *Recorded*: 22:7 mo:1681.

LOTT GOURDING to JOHN HATHORNE – (6:117) Lott Gourding of Bostone (marrenor) sold to John Hathorne of Salem (merchant) for consideration of the sume of sixty five p'ds of current money of New England, a certain p'cell of land upland & meddow containing by estimation five acres & scituate in Salem & is bounded on north with streete or highway, easterly with land of partly of said John Hathorne & ptly land of John Pickering southerly with milne pond & westerly with land of said John Hathorne. *Signed*: Lott Gourding. *Date*: first day of October in ye year 1681. *Witnesses*: John Price; Edward Morrle; William Veren. *Acknowledged*: first of October 1681; *Recorded*: 3:October:1681.

JOHN MASSEY to PHILLIP CROMWELL – (6:120) John Massey of Salem sold to Phillip Cromwell of Salem (slatherer) for consideration of 35 pounds, p'cell of upland & marsh in Salem by estimation three acres & halfe bounded to westward on comon contry roade to northward on land which was hearetofore Mr. James Browns on eastward to cove and sotherly to land of Francis Skerry. *Signed*: John Massey. *Date*: 14 Aprill 1680. *Witnesses*: Thomas Robbins; Richard Croade. *Acknowledged*: 19:2 mo:1680. *Recorded*: 4:October 1681.

WILLIAM BOWDITCH to PHILLIP CROMWELL – (6:123) William Bowditch of Salem (march't) mortgaged to Phillip Cromwell of Salem (slaughterer) for consideration of sume of fourer hundred pounds in silver in hand paid, land by me bought of Samuell Pickman, lying at the burying poynt in Salem soe called with my ware house & housing standing upon sd land & also the sellar and wharfe, this being the one halfe that piece of land that lyes betweene John Pickman's garden fence & the water side & as the garden fence stands: to begin at the lane next George Keaser's & soe to take in halfe the bredth of sd land. & soe to runn down the same bredth to the water soe farr as the proprietie of the land goes (only excepting) & it is hearby excepted, the privilidge of a convenient waye for horse & cart, from the other halfe which is sd John Pickman's land to sd lane next George Keaser's which sd land is to be a convenient highwaye for the use & benefitt of sd Phillip Cromwell, John Pickman, & Samuell Pickman, from water side to the towne streete soe y^t sd one halfe of said p'cell of land now sold to said Cromwell lyes bounded to garden fence of sd John Pickman to the north & the other halfe being alsoe sd John Pickman lying to the west & the water or south river & the sd lane or highwaye left between bargained pr'misses & George Keasers to the east: alsoe said William Bowditch hath by these pr'sents sold unto aforesd Phillip Cromwell two ketches, being of about twenty six tunn apiece, with their boates &c & as they are now in equipage & furniture that is to say with all ye appurtenances now belonging to sd ketches & boates. the one of which ketches is now at sea, Pasco Foot master & she called by name Bettee, the other called by name William, now lying in Salem at wharf abovesaid provided if William Bowditch pay the full & just sume of fourer hundred pounds in silver, with the usuall allowance for interest, within the space of fourer years from the date heare of. then this above written instrument with everything therein contained is to be voide. *Signed*: William Bowditch. *Date*: twentieth of November 1679. *Witnesses*: John Cromwell; Richard Croade. *Acknowledged*: 9:10 mo:1679. *Recorded*: 18:8 mo:1681.

WILLIAM BOWDITCH to PHILLIP CROMWELL – (6:126) William Bowditch of Salem (marchant) sold to Phillip Cromwell of Salem (slautherer) in consideration of ye sume of one hundred & forty pounds in silver, my brew house & copper, oven & wharfe upon which said brew house, brewing coper & oven stands, scituate & bordering the south river, neere ye burying place in Salem. In witnes whereof I have sett my hand & seal & alsoe all the land I lately purchased of towne of Salem at eight shillings pr yeare for one thousand years with all buildings that are on may be upon same & alsoe my fish house upon Winter Island. *Signed*: William Bowditch. *Date*: twenty sixth day of August 1680. *Witnesses*: John Corwin; Patience Denison. *Acknowledged*: February 1:1680. *Recorded*: 18:8:1681.

ELIZABETH BREADE to NATHANIELL BALLARD – (6:129) Elizabeth Breade, of Linne, late wife of William Knight deceased as alsoe executrix, upon good considerations and divers good causes by deed of guift gave unto wel beloved sonn Nathaniel Ballard, that p'cell of land bought by my first husband William Ballard, father to sd Nathaniell Ballard, that is to say five acres of upland bounded easterly upon highwaye, northerly with land of Allen Bread senior and sotherly with land of Samuell Hart and Benjamin Chadwell, westward with land of John Ballard. *Signed*: Elizabeth Bread. *Date*: no date. *Witnesses*: John Bennett; John Bread. *Acknowledged*: 3:1 mo:1673. *Recorded*: 18:8 mo:1681.

DANIELL BACON to PHILLIP CROMWELL – (6:130) Daniell Bacon of Salem (shipwright) mortgaged to Phillip Cromwell of Salem (slautherer) for consideration of sume of twenty five pounds & one shilling, my dwelling house in Salem together with the outhouse thereunto p'taining & all my land on which my sd dwelling house & other housing standeth, the whole continent of land being by estimation of about seaven or eight pole, & is bounded northerly towards or upon land of John Ruck, easterly upon land of Benjamin Ganson, westerly towards or upon land of John Norman & sotherly upon the river called south river provided if Daniell Bacon pay Phillip Cromwell the just sume of twenty five pounds & one shilling in silver money at or before second of June next ensuing date heareof this mortgage to be voyde. *Signed*: Daniell Bacon. *Date*: twenty eighth day of June 1681. *Witnesses*: John Cromwell; Richard Croade. *Acknowledged*: 18 day of October 1681. *Recorded*: 18:8:1681.

RICHARD HUTCHENSON to JOHN PUTNAM – (6:133) Richard Hutchenson of Salem (yeoman) sold to John Putnam of Salem (yeoman) for a valuable consideration to me in hand alreddy paid, a certain p'cell of land containing eighteen acres or thereabouts, bounded with land of Capt Lothrop's on southeast & land of Nathaniell Putnam on north side all which sd land lying within township of Salem. *Signed*: Richard Huchenson [mark]. *Date*: 16 day of February 1668. *Witnesses*: John Porter junior; Samuell Archer. *Acknowledged*: 22:1 mo:71/2. *Recorded*: 4:9 mo:1681.

JOB INDIAN, KATE INDIAN and MARY INDIAN to HENRY SEAWELL – (6:134) Job Indian, grandson, Kate Indian and Mary Indian, daughters to old Will Indian of Newbery Fales, deceased, sold to Henry Seawell of Newbery (gent.) for good causes especially in consideration of six pounds thirteene shillings, & fower pence in hand paid to each & every one of them (considerating what sd Sewell hath formerly purchased), a tract of land part of which is known by the name of the Indian field, lying at Newbery & is buttelled and bounded as followeth viz: on northerly side with great brooke which runneth along the side of the greate field, on westerly side with a line runn by said Seawell from head of sd farme unto Newbery river at or neare the upper fales & on ye southerly side with said river, as alsoe all right they have to land at or nerne Indian hill or anywhere else within the township of Newbery as heires to old Will Indian. *Signed*: Job Indian [mark]; Kate Indian [mark]; Mary Indian [mark]. *Date*: fourteenth daye of June 1681. *Witnesses*: Daniell Quinsey; Samuell Cleark. *Acknowledged*: June 14th 1681 by Kate & Mary Indians & also Widdesgin whoe Kate sd was her Sannop was present & consented to what said Kate did; June 25th 1681 by Job Indian. *Recorded*: 18:8 mo:1681.

ELIZABETH BREAD to NATHANIELL BALLARD – (6:137) Elizabeth Bread of Lynn sold to Nathaniell Ballard of Linn (taylor) for divers good causes especially in consideration of nine pounds to her in hand paid, three acres of salt marsh lying in towne marsh of Linn, bounded easterly with land of John Newall senior and northerly with land of Allen Bread S'r. & westerly & southerly with a creeke. *Signed*: Elizabeth Bread. *Date*: Indenture made 12: of August 1672, but signed 3:1 mo:1673. *Witnesses*: Henry Skerry; John Bennett. *Acknowledged*: 18:8 mo.:1681. *Recorded*: 3:1 mo.:1673.

ELIZABETH CHADWELL to NATHANIELL BALLARD – (6:138) Elizabeth Chadwell of Lynn, widow & admistratrix to the estate of Benjamin Chadwell, lately deceased, sold to Nathaniell Ballard of Lynn (taylor) for consideration of twenty seaven pounds to her in hand paid in current moneyes, fower acres & an halfe of planting ground scituate & being in town of Lynn in Howseneck. bounded easterly with highway, westerly with land of Samuell Hart, southerly with land of Joseph Hall, northerly with land of sd Nathaniell Ballard. *Signed*: Elizabeth Chadwell. *Date*: twenty ninth day of July 1679. *Witnesses*: John Ballard; Allan Bread. *Acknowledged*: 8:7 mo.:79. *Recorded*: 18:8 mo.:1681.

SAMUELL BEADLE and HANNAH BEADLE to JOHN FOSTER, JUNIOR – (6:141) Samuell Beadle of Salem (turner) sold to John Foster, Junior of Salem (planter) in consideration of seaventy pounds in money to me in hand paid or secured to be paid, a quantity of land of upland & meddow by estimation twenty acres & is the land I formerly bought of Nicholas Manning & is lying together in township of Salem in the field comonly called the north field wch sd land was comonly called or known by the name of Goodells lotts & is bounded on the east side with land which was formerly land of Mr. Peters, now in possession of Deacon Horne, on ye west with land of Job Swinerton, on the north with land of Robert Pease & on south with land of John Neale & Nicholas Potter. *Signed*: Samuell Beadle; Hannah Beadle. *Date*: twenty fourth day of October 1681. *Witnesses*: Jeremiah Neale; Hilliard Viren. *Acknowledged*: 26:8 mo:1681 by Samuell Beadle & wife Hannah. *Recorded*: 26:8 mo:1681.

JOHN FOSTER JUNIOR and MARY FOSTER to SAMUELL BEADLE – (6:143) John Foster Junior of Salem mortgaged to Samuell Beadle of Salem (turner) for divers good causes & considerations with several conditions, hearafter expresst and more especially for & in consideration of sume of seaventy pounds sterling, which sd John Foster doe owe in moneyes unto Samuell Beadle, quantity of upland & meddow ground by estimation twenty acres & is lying together in township of Salem in the feild comonly called north feild & was formerly caled & known by name of Goodells lotts & is bounded on east side with land that was formerly Mr. Peters, now in possession of Deacon Horne, on west with land of Job Swinerton, on north with land of Robert Pease, on south with land of John Neale & Nicholas Potter provided if John Foster pay seaventy pounds in current money unto sd Sam'll Beadle in manner & forme following that is to say fourteen pounds for the first payment in current moneyes as aforesd at or before the first day of December in year 1682 & for the remainder fourteene pounds yearly to be paid at or before first day of December every yeare successively by fourteene pounds a year until whole abovesd sume of seaventy pounds be well & truly paid, that then this bargaine & sale is & stand voyd & none effect force proven or virtue but in case of defect in any of payments in part or in whole to stand in full power according to condition hearafter expresst viz. it is provided that in case sd land mortgaged by forfeited for want to payment as abovesd, in part or in whole that notwithstanding sd John Foster, his heirs & assigns shall have, hold, occupy, possess & injoy forever soe much of sd land or such part of it by an equal proportion & just value amounts to soe much of sd seaventy pounds as is before such forfeiture paid, by any of former payments upon an equall division or otherwise to repay sd Foster back again soe much as I shall have paid towards or in pt of sd seaventy pounds & provided in case of failure in pt or in whole that this mortgage become forfeite & sd Beadle reposses sd land or soe much of it as is not paid sd Foster shall pay as rent fower pounds in moneye, to sd Beadle as rent for the next before or pr'ceading yeare before such default of payment or forfeite shall happen & in case sd Foster shall not survive till severall payments be made then heirs shall not cut downe or make use of any of the growing wood or timber, upon any part of said land until all & every of the sd payments be fully & truly paid. **Signed**: John Foster; Mary Foster [mark]. **Date**: 26 October 1681 by John Foster and Mary wife. **Witnesses**: Jeremiah Neale; Hilliard Veren. **Acknowledged**: 26:October 1681. **Recorded**: 26:8 mo.:1681.

JOHN HILL to DELIVERANCE PARKMAN – (6:147) Barbadus: John Hill of Island of Barbadus appoint trusty & wel beloved friend Mr. Deliverance Parkman of Salem (marrener) true & lawfully aturney, in my name to ask, receive, recover, demand of & from all manner of p'son or p'sons whatsoever but more especially of & from Mr. John Cole of New England, all & all manner of sums of money, debts, dues & demands whatsoever of or belonging to me granting to my sd aturney full power & authority to recover all such sum & sums of money as should be due & owing unto me from sd Cole or any p'son or p'sons also give full power & authority unto my sd aturney or aturney or more under him. *Signed*: John Hill. *Date*: third day of August 1682. *Witnesses*: John Sanders; Richard Croade. *Acknowledged*: Richard Croade made oath that he was pr'sent & saw John Hill sign the 25th November 1682. John Sanders acknowledged [no date]. *Recorded*: 25:9 mo:1682.

NATHANIELL PICKMAN to JOHN SANDERS – (6:148) Nathaniell Pickman of Salem (house carpenter) sold to John Sanders of Salem (marrenor) for divers good causes & considerations especially for & in consideration of a valuable sume to me in hand, all that my farme or p'cell of land lying in Salem bounds at the head of Forrest river soe caled, containing one hundred acres & is bounded northerly by Frost fish brooke so caled & from thence sotherly to an elme tree that was marked & is lately cut downe & now a great heap of stones lying about the stump & from y^t corner bounds it runs upon a strait line easterly to a great red oake marked & standing neere to George Darling's house. From there & from that tree to the cold spring with all the meddow belonging to sd farme adjoining thereto being about five acres. *Signed*: Nathaniell Pickman senior. *Date*: 29 of October 1681. *Witnesses*: Phillip Cromwell; Hilliard Veron. *Acknowledged*: 30th of October 1681. *Recorded* 1: November:1682.

JEREMIAH NEALE – (6:151) Whereas there was a conveyance of house & land to Jeremiah Neale by Capt. Nicholas Maning by instrument dated first of September 1675 and recorded – Jeremiah Neale for divers good causes and considerations quitt right & interest in house & land emptying myself of & from any right in & to same or any part thereof & by these presents declare sd instrument & all my right thereto or in or to the pr'mises or any part thereof to be null and voyd from the date of these pre'sents. *Signed*: Jeremiah Neale. *Date*: 4th day 9th mo:1681. *Witnesses*: Daniel Turrell, Jr.; Hilliard Veren. *Acknowledged*: 11:9 mo:1681. *Recorded*: 4:9:1681. [This refers to deed recorded in the 5 book page 77.]

THOMAS MARSHALL and REBECKA MARSHALL to JOHN EDMONDS – (6:152) Thomas Marshall of Linn (captaine of the foot company-here) with consent of Rebecka wife in reference to her free surrendering up of her thirds according to law of dowers sold to John Edmonds of Lynn (yeoman) for consideration of twenty pounds sterling, 20 acres Linn w'ch was formerly Mr. Edward Tomlins and bought by sd Thomas Marshall of Mr. Jonathan Palme of Ireland aturney of sd Edward Tomlins bounded eastwardly with land of Joseph Kitchen, westwardly with land of Edward Baker southwardly with highwaye northwardly with towne comon. *Signed*: Thomas Marshall; Rebecka Marshall [mark]. *Date*: 16 August 1680. *Witnesses*: Thomas Stocker [mark]; John Severnie. *Acknowledged*: 10:September 1681. *Recorded*: 2:9:1681.

JOSEPH NEALE to THOMAS MALE – (6:155) Joseph Neale of Salem (joyner) sold to Thomas Male of Salem (marchant) for consideration of 64 pounds, one acre and fower & half pole of ground Salem on south side of the broad street that goes from meeting house westward to townes end, the p'cell is to be in bredth next ye street according to square line seaven pole or rod & to run the same bredth to the uper end next to Jonathan Pickerings on south end, so that sd land is to be seaven pole broad throughout from the streete to the further end next sd Pickering's fence and lyes bounded by streete northerly, land of sd Joseph Neale westerly, land of Jonathan Neale easterly, and land of Jonathan Pickering southerly & alsoe y^t ye sd Thomas Maule from first day of December next ensueing have above granted pr'mises provided Thomas Maule sett up a good & sufficient fence & maintain same for and duering the terme of forty three yeares next following from the date of these pr'sents on westerne side being p'tition fence betweene pr'mises and sd Joseph Neale. *Signed*: Joseph Neale. *Date*: seventh day of July 1681. *Witnesses*: Jeremiah Neale; Hilliard Veren, Sr. *Acknowledged*: 5th October 1681. *Recorded*: 2:9 mo:1681.

JONATHAN NEALE to THOMAS MAULE – (6:158) Jonathan Neale of Salem (cordwinder) sold to Thomas Maule of Salem (marchant) for consideration of 35 pounds in money in hand paid in part & the other part secured by bill to be paid, halfe acre in Salem bounded northerly with streete or highwaye easterly in part with land of Benjamin Marstone which he lately bought of me & the other part with my land & southerly with land of me sd Joseph Neale & westerly with land of sd Thomas Maule which he lately bought of Joseph Neale containing in bredth next streete and fronting to sd streete three and a halfe poles nearest being all ground I have there lying betweene sd Marston's and & Maule's land there and soe to runn the same bredth back sotherly soe farr as sd Thomas Maule's land runn which he lately bought of sd Joseph Neale provided sd Thomas Maule is to be at charge of setting up & maintaining a sufficient p'tition fence for & during the terme and time of tenn yeares next following date of these pr'sents betweene now land of Jonathan Neale & sd Thomas Maules own land where it joynes together. *Signed*: Jonathan Neale. *Date*: 6 October 1681.

Witnesses: Hilliard Veren; Jeremiah Rogers. *Acknowledged*: 6 September 1681. *Recorded*: 2:9 mo:1681.

THOMAS MAULE and NAOMY MAULE to JOSEPH NEALE – (6:162) Thomas Maule of Salem (marchant) sold to Joseph Neale of Salem (joyner) for consideration of 62 pounds, dwelling house and twenty pole of ground part upon which house stands upon and is adjoining thereto with all out housing in Salem & is that house out housing & land I lately bought of John Darling as by deed of sale bearing date 19th November 1680 & is bounded easterly with land of Richard Croad northerly land y^t was late Mary Darlings and before in time past Richard Bishop's deceased westerly land of Roger Darby sotherly with streete alsoe p'cell more adjoining halfe acre lately bought of Mary Darling daughter of John Darling as by bill of sale from her dated 19 November 1680 & is bounded sotherly with land now lately bought of sd John Darling & partly with land of Roger Darby easterly with land of Richard Croad, northerly land of Thomas Bishop in reversion now in possession of Thomas Robbins, westerly with land that was formerly Widdow Spooner's deceased together with all housing outhousing, garden, oarchard, fences, pr'vileges & appurtenances, also all deeds, writings, evedences, minuments concerning same. *Signed*: Thomas Maule; Naomy Maule [mark]. *Date*: 17 July 1681. *Witnesses*: Jeremiah Neale; Hiliard Veren. *Acknowledged*: 5:8 mo.:1681 and Naomy Maule acknowledged her hand freely giving up power of thirds 3:9 mo:1681. *Recorded*: 2:9 mo:1681.

ROBERT GOODELL to SARA BACHELOR – (6:166) Robert Goodell of Salem guifted to daughter Sarah Bachelor of Wenham wife of John Bachelor, 32 acres upland & two p'cells of meddow about eight acres in Salem being part of the eleven hundred acres granted by towne of Salem to severall proprietors on south side of Ipswich River having on north side of it land of Isaack Goodell, adjoines brook caled Mr. Norrice's brook, the meddow one p'cell of it being all the meddow that lyes between Tho. Flints bound and aforesd upland on east side of brook called Mr. Norrice's brook, the other p'cell being an acre & halfe of meddow lying upon other side of brooke aforesd bounded by Isaack Goodell's meddow east & west & on south upon commons. *Signed*: Robert Goodell. *Date*: 20 September 1665. *Witnesses*: Job Swinerton, Jr.; Lott Killum. *Acknowledged*: I Robert Goodell owneth that I have given John Bacheler my son in law a firm deed of guift of 40 ackers of land & about eight acres of meddow, attest. William Hathorne. Marshall Scerry made oath that he was pr'sent & heard Robert acknowledg the above written & that Major Hathorne took the acknowledgment as above written this 7:9 mo:1681. *Recorded*: 1:9 mo:1681.

THOMAS CROMWELL – JOHN CROMWELL – HUGH JOANES – (6:168) These pr'sents are to certifie unto whome it may concerne that wee Thomas Cromwell & John Cromwell whoe have beene long inhabitants heare in the towne of Salem doe testifie that we have known Hugh Joanes as one coming from England in same ship with us in to the contry above thirty yeares agoe (& as wee understood abord Mr. Strattons ship) that he came from Vincanton & was servant to Mr. Robert Gutch & his sister & Elizabeth Due & Margarett White & James Abbott & John Vinning as we understood came from the same place & the same Hugh Joanes that came along with us into contry is row living. Taken upon the corporall oaths of sd Thomas & John Cromwell in court at Salem 27:June:1682 & alsoe sd Hugh Joanes then personally appeared in Court being in health attests. *Signed*: Hilliard Veren Cler.

GRIFFEN EDWARDS, JOHN MYLES, and ANN MYLES to SAMUELL JOHNSON – (6:168) Griffen Edwards of Boston (gent. & aturney & admistrator on behalfe of his mother in law Mrs. Ann Miles whoe is reputed only heire surviving of Collonell John Humphrey's Esq. deceased & shee is now wife of Mr. John Myles minister of Swansy a plantation in the colloney of Plimouth) sold to Samuell Johnson of Linn for consideration of thirteene pounds current money, three acres salte marsh in Rumney marsh in the first division within township of Linn to be the full halfe of a six acre lott that did formerly belong to Collonell John Humphrey's Esq. deceased, bounded southwest with marsh aforesd Samuell Johnsons & northeast with marsh of Serg't Thomas Marshall butting sotherly upon marsh of aforesd Thomas Marshall & northerly upon towne comon. *Signed*: Griffin Edwards; John Myles; Ann Myles. *Date*: 25th October 1681; *Witnesses*: William Bassett; Ralph King. *Acknowledged*: 29th October 1681 by all three. *Recorded*: 2:9ber:1681.

JOHN BECKETT and MARGARETT BECKETT to PHILLIP CROMWELL – (6:172) John Beckett of Salem (ship wright) with free consent of Margarett wife sold to Mr. Phillip Cromwell of Salem (butcher) for consideration of sum valuable in hand paid, the benefit & privilidg of a cart highwaye from the comon towne streete in Salem begining & having its enterance from house & ground of Michaell Combes on westerne side & Thomas Sollas his house & ground on easterne side & alsoe from thence to runn through the land of sd Beckett home to land which was formerly land of Goodman Harwood & since the land of Jeremiah Booteman but now in possession sd Cromwell. *Signed*: John Beckett; Margarett Becket [mark]. *Date*: 1 February 1675/6. *Witnesses*: Wm. Bowditch; Richard Croade. *Recorded*: 7:9 mo:1681.

Phillip Cromwell doe assigne & make over to Edmond Bridges of Salem blacksmith all my right in within bargained pr'mises & p'vilidg of the highway to use, benefitt & behoofe of sd Edmond Bridges according to tennour of within written. *Signed*: Phillip Cromwell; Mary Cromwell [mark]. *Date*: 22 September 1680. *Witnesses*: John Cromwell; Isaack Williams. *Acknowledged*: 22:7 mo:1680.

PHILLIP CROMWELL and MARY CROMWELL to EDMOND BRIDGES – (6:174) Within mentioned Phillip Cromwell for consideration of about fiftie pounds in money, pd by Edmond Bridges of Salem (blacksmith) assigne over within deed with all right in within bargained pr'mises to sd Edmond Bridges and warrant ag'st all manner of p'sons laying claim by or under me or sd Jeremiah Booteman. *Signed*: Phllip Cromwell; Mary Cromwell [mark]. *Release of Dower*: Mary wife yields right of dower. *Date*: 21 September 1680. *Witnesses*: John Cromwell; Isaack Willliams. *Acknowledged*: September 1681 by both. *Recorded*: 7:9mo:1681.

MARY DARLING – (6:176) Whereas there was a bequest or legacy (given to Mary the daughter of John Darling by Mary his wife daughter of Richard Bishop deceased) by sd Richard Bishop in his will as appeered by testimony in writing from his owne mouth upon his death bed, approved and allowed by the county court held at Salem as by records of sd court may appeere and sd Mary Darling being com to age of 18 yeares and having ocasion to improve her sd grandfather's guift and bequest in consideration whereof as in discharge of our bounden duty wee Thomas Bishop & John Darling adminstrators of estate of sd Richard Bishop deceased have laid p'cell of land halfe acre out to said Mary Darling to be to her use according to our best understanding to the mind of sd Richard Bishop and lay out and bound in manner following: taking in the whole front next streete betweene land of Richard Croade on east & land of sd John Darling on west & from the streete to extend backward northerly on easterne side next said Richard Croade eight poole seven foot & halfe to stake there now drive & on the westerne side next land of Widow Spooner deceased beginning at northerly bound of Roger Darby's land he late bought of John Darling & from his bounds or fence to run northerly back on that westerne side next said Spooner's land tenn poole fourtene foot & three inches & so to take in the whole bredth of Richard Bishop's land backward to make up full halfe acre. *Signed*: Thomas Bishop [mark]; John Darling [mark]. *Date*: 7 November 1680. *Witnesses*: Robert Fuller; Frances ___ [mark]. *Acknowledged*: 9 November 1681 by both. *Recorded*: 17:9 mo:1681.

JOSEPH NEALE to THOMAS MAULE – (6:178) Joseph Neale of Salem (joyner) sold to Thomas Maule of Salem (marchant) for consideration of tenn pounds in silver currant money which is for & in consideration of the faling short in measure a considerable quantity or severall poles of land belonging to house & ground I bought of sd Maule which he lately bought of John Darling I say I have received the sd tenn pounds in full satisfaction for what fales short of measure of land according to deed of sale & doe fully acquit & discharge sd Thomas Maule from any claim or demand in reference to land that fales short by computation is about fourteene poole. *Signed*: Joseph Neale. *Date*: 17 November 1681. *Witnesses*: Hilliard Veren; Jeremiah Neale. *Acknowledged*: no date. *Recorded*: 17:9 mo:1681.

JOHN PEASE, SR. and ANN PEASE to WILLIAM OSBOURNE – (6:179) John Pease, Sr. of Salem (yeoman) sold to William Osbourne of Salem (husbandman) for consideration of fourteen pounds, two acres in north feild Salem part of my home lott bounded: upon lane or highwaye to westward upon land of Robert Pease, Jr. to northward upon land of Samuell Eborne, Sr. to eastward upon land of myselfe John Pease to southward. *Signed*: John Pease [mark]; Ann Pease. *Release of Dower*: Anne wife signs in testimony of giving up thirds. *Date*: 24 October 1681. *Witnesses*: Frances Croad [mark]; Richard Croade. *Acknowledged*: 25 October 1681 by both. *Recorded*: 19:9 mo:1681.

JOHN PEASE, SR. to WILLIAM OSBOURNE – (6:182) John Pease, Sr. of Salem sold to William Osbourne of Salem for consideration of three pounds p'r acre, three or fouer acres Salem in northfeild bounded on westerly side with land of Henry Trask on easterly side with highwaye on northerly end with land of Robert Stone and on sotherly end with land of Josiah Southwick. *Signed*: John Pease, Sr. [mark]. *Date*: 20 January 1680. *Witnesses*: Nathaniell Felton, Sr.; Samuel Eborne [mark]. *Acknowledged*: 26 January 1680. Recorded: 19:9 mo:1681.
Memorandum: Robert Pease, Sr. having formerly had a grant of three quarters of an acre of land above specified to enjoy during his aboad in Salem the sd three quarters of an acre he is still to injoy as aforesd by consent of both parties above specified. I doe give up my right in this land. *Signed*: Ann Pease the wife of John Pease, Sr.

THOMAS ROBBINS to LOTT KILLUM – (6:184) Thomas Robbins of Salem sold to Lott Killum of Salem for consideration of three pounds tenn shillings, p'cell meddow Salem bounded westerly upon upland of Widdow Pope & northerly upon meddows of Isaack Cook easterly upon Norrice brook sotherly upon meddow of Henry Renols and is in all two acres &

halfe. *Signed*: Thomas Robbins [mark]. *Date*: 17 November 1681. *Witnesses*: Robert Kitchin; Stephen Small. *Acknowledged*: 20th 9mo:1681. *Recorded*: 22:9 mo:81.

William Pinson manefest consent to above written sale of two acres & halfe of meddow it being formerly sold unto Lott Killum by my Unckle Robbins but no deed of sale given untill date above written. I hereby release unto said Killum my right thereto. *Signed*: Willliam Pinson. *Date*: 20 November 1681. *Witnesses*: Stephen Smale; Elisha Kebbe. *Acknowledged*: 20:9 mo:1681.

LOTT KILLUM to ELISHA KEBBY – (6:186) I Lott Killum resigne within written deed of sale unto Elisha Kebby and sell unto sd Elisha Kebby the within mentioned two acres & halfe acres of meddow & as it is there bounded. *Signed*: Lott Killum. *Date*: 21 November 1681. *Witnesses*: Benjamin Smale; Steephen Small. *Acknowledged*: 21 November 1681. *Recorded*: 22:9 mo:1681.

ELISHA KEBBY to STEEPHEN SMALE- (6:187) Elisha Kebby of Salem sold to Steephen Smale of Salem for valuable consideration in hand paid, two acres & halfe fresh meddow Salem neere unto pound meddow according to tenour and bounds mentioned in within written deed of sale. *Signed*: Elisha Kebby. *Date*: 21 November 1681. *Witnesses*: Lott Killum; Benjamin Smale. *Acknowledged*: 21:9 mo:1681. *Recorded*: no date.

ALEXANDER MACKMANING to SAMUELL BEADLE and HANNA BEADLE – (6:187) Indenture made 1 November 1677 witnesseth Alexander Mackmaning sonn of Alexander Mackmaning inhabitant of Salem hath of his free & voluntary will & with consent of his father put himselfe apprentice unto Mr. Samuell Beadle of Salem turner & his wife Hanna the science or trade which he now useth to be taught and with him after the maner of apprentice to dwell & serve from the day of date hereof untill the full end & terme of 9 years from date hereof shal be fully exspired, by all which terme of time the sd apprentice sd Samuell Beadle well and truly shall serve his secreats shall keep close, his comandements lawfull and honest everywhere he shall willingly doe, hurt to his master or Mrs. he shall not doe, nor suffer to be don, to the value of twelve pence or more by the yeare, but lett it if he may or cann the goods of sd master he shall not inordinatley wast nor them to any body, lend, at dice or any unlawful game he shall not play, fornication in house of sd master or any where elce he shall not comit, matrimony he shall not contract, taverns or ale houses he shall not frequent, from the service of his sd master day nor night he shall not absent or prolong himselfe, but in all things as a good & faithfull apprentice shall beare & behave himselfe toward his sd master &

Mrs. & his during terme aforesd and the sd Samuell Beadle to his sd apprentice the science or art which he now useth shall teach & informe, or cause to be taught & informed the best way he may or cann, the apprentice capable to learn, & shall teach or cause to be taught sd apprentice to read English as alsoe to write & cast accounts & alsoe shall find to his sd apprentice meat drink beding & apparel & all other necessaries meete & convenient for an apprentice both in sicknes & in health & at the expiration of the sd time shall give unto his sd apprentice doble sute of apparell as alsoe the value of twenty shillings in tooles fitt for his trade & in witness of truth heareof the p'ties hearein concerned viz: Samuell & Alexander Mackmanning, Jr. have heareunto interchangeably sett to their hands & seales the first day of November 1677. This indenture being drawne by the other indenture word for word & compared therewith, that pt that was signed by sd Alexander being stolne & gonn this counterpaine is drawn in steed thereof by consent of p'ties & whereas sd Alexander have left his masters service at times & ocasioned trouble & charge to his master, in consideration whereof the sd Alexander doe by these pr'sents agree to discharge his sd master from his ingagement of the value of twenty shillings in tooles or pay his master twenty shillings in money in steed thereof at the exspiration of sd time exspressed in first above indenture. *Signed*: Alexander Mackmaning [mark]. *Date*: Signed sealed & delivered this 12th December 1681 being the time when this new counterpaine was drawne, the memorandum being underwritten. *Witnesses*: Richard Pritharrch; John Baxter; Hilliard Veren. *Recorded*: 14:10 mo:1681.

GEORGE HODGES and SARAH HODGES to THOMAS ROOTES –

(6:190) George Hodges of Salem (marrenor) sold to Thomas Rootes of Salem (weaver) for consideration of divers good causes especially valuable sum in hand paid, my dwelling house with all land adjoyning about one quarter acre in Salem bounded with street sotherly, house and ground of Richard Roberts easterly, creeke or town common northerly, house and ground of Wm Cash westerly. & George Hodges doe covenant to quit claim all interest to ten acre lott in Beverly side of sd Thomas Rootes his &c. & whereas there was a former writing & covenant & contract drawne betweene sd George & sd Thomas dated twelfth day of April 1680, it being mutually agreed upon between p'ties above mentioned upon this our collaterall agreement to make null & voyde the sd writing & doe by these pr'sents declare sd writing & all articles & agreements to be wholy null, voyde & of none effect from date of these pr'sents. **Signed**: George Hodges; Sarah Hodges [mark]. **Release of Dower**: Sarah wife yielded dower. **Date**: 3 November 1681. **Witnesses**: Samuell Gardner, Sr.; Samuell Gardner, Jr.. **Acknowledged**: 14:9 mo:1681 by both. **Recorded**: 28:9 mo:1681.

WILLIAM MIRRIAM, SR. to SAMUELL EDMONDS – (6:193) William Mirriam, Sr. of Linn (husbandman) sold to Samuell Edmonds of Linn (joyner) for divers & waity considerations, upland & meddow Linn containing in whole six acres bounded easterly Joseph Edmonds lands, sotherly the comon, westerly William Mirriam, Sr. his land as it is marked out with a heape of stones to a little blacke oake tree & thence to a walnutt tree & soe along by the highwaye to a black oake tree on other side of bridg in fresh marsh to white oake tree that stands by a great rock, notherly to stake in midle of fresh meddow adjoyning to Joseph Edmonds land. *Signed*: William Mirriam. *Date*: 30th second month 1678. *Witnesses*: Thomas Marshall; Richard Haven. *Acknowledged*: 7:3 mo:1678. *Recorded*: 10:10 mo:1681.

EZEKIELL CHEEVER – (6:195) Ezekiell Cheever of Bostone (scoolemaster) for divers good causes have constituted loving sonn Thomas Cheever of Malden true and lawfull aturney in my stead & name to enter and come into & upon all housing & lands left by Capt. Thomas Lothrop late of Beverly deceased, any & every part & p'cell thereof in hands soever any or every pt or parcel shal be found, & of them & any & all of them in whose hands any & every part & p'cell of sd estate of housing & land shal be found to ask for & demand giveth & peaceable possession of all & every part & p'cell of pr'mises & with them & any or all of them to treate, compound & agree by himselfe or other meete p'sons whome my sd aturney shall nominate, choose & impower to arbitrate & determin any differences that now or heareafter may arise betweene my sd aturney or any other p'son or p'sons, about bounds of forenamed pr'mises, or any other waies whatsoever relating to title of all or any of the pr'misses or appurtenances & pr'vilidges in way thereunto belonging & for want of a speedy & redy compliance in y^m or any of them that now have or heareafter shall lay claime, right, title or interest in or unto premises, or any or every pt & p'cel thereof, y^m or any or all of y^m to arrest, sue, implead, prosecute, cast & condem in any court or courts whatsoever & upon satisfaction had & obtained, them & any or all of them, to release, acquit & discharge & to answer & defend all or any case or cases, action or actions, sute or sutes at law that shall be comenced by any & every person whatsoever in anything relating to the premises or any or every pt thereof to demise, grant & to farme lett the housing & lands lying in Beverly to Robert Cobourne paying the yearely rent of eight pounds to my sd aturney or his orders or for a longer terme to demise grant & to farme lett the same & any or every part of premises to him sd Robert Cobourne or any other p'son by indenture of lease or otherwise for such yearely rent as shall be indented & covenanted for by & betweene my sd atturney & any person to whome pr'misses or any pt thereof shall be demised & granted as alsoe power to sell & alienate same to him or any other p'son whomsoever giving & by these pr'sents granting to my sd aturney my full power, strength & authority all & every act or acts, thing or things, device or devices, whatsoever needfull & requissit to be don in or about pr'mises for me & in my name to do, execute & p'forme as fully, largely & amply in all respects as I myselfe might or could doe if p'sonally pr'sent, ratifying, allowing & holding firme whatever my sd aturney shall lawfully doe or cause to be don in or about the execution of pr'misses by these pr'sents. *Signed*: Ezekiell Cheever. *Date*: 2 May 1681. Ezekiell Cheever signed sealed & delivered instrument & acknowledged same 2 May 1681 - Humphrey Davy. *Recorded*: no date.

THOMAS ROOTES to GEORGE HODGES – (6:198) Thomas Rootes of Salem (weaver) sold to George Hodges of Salem (marrenor) for divers good & lawfull consideration especially in consideration of valuable sum in hand paid, all that my now dwelling house where I now live with all land belonging thereunto about four acres containing the orchards, garden, yards, moeable & planting land, with all the fences, out housing, pr'fits, privilidges & appurtenances thereto belonging in Salem now in tenure & occupation of sd George Hodges & is bounded by the sea or salt water easterly, & land of Mr. Henry Bartholmew in part & the other part with comon sotherly & comon westerly & with land of Samuell Gardner, Jr. ptly & other part by salt water northerly.
Memorandum: & it is to be understood & is true meaning of these pr'sents & it is heareby excepted, a lane or highwaye of the town's which runns through pr'misses from creeke or cove on south to creek or cove on north of bargained pr'misses & it is to be understood not included in afore bargain & sale. *Signed*: Thomas Roote. *Date* 3 November 1681. *Witnesses*: Samuell Gardner, Sr.; Samuell Gardner, Jr. *Acknowledged*: 14 November 1681. *Recorded*: 10:10 mo:1681.

JAMES STANDISH for WILLIAM EVERTON to WILLIAM PITT – (6:201) James Standish of Manchester in the behalfe & for the use & by the order of William Everton sold to William Pitt of Boston all that pr'cells of land, 6 or 7 acres, whereof 3 acres was bought of Benjamin Parmiter & ye other 3 acres or thereabout given him by Townsmen of Manchester, joyning to Abraham Whittyeares land. *Signed*: James Standish [mark]. *Date*: 29 Oct 1657. *Witnesses*: Pasco Foott; William Allen [mark]. *Recorded*: 19:10 mo:1681.

William Everton doth rathifie & allow of the sale of ye sd lands by James Standish, abovesd being about 11 acres as ye town's book of Manchester appeareth. *Signed*: William Everton. *Date*: 14 Dec 1651. *Acknowledged*: by

William Everton that sale of land on ye other side by James Standish was with his consent & he ownes it as his act & deed. 27 Jul 1665.

William Pitt doe assign over all my right interest I have of ye within lands, that is expressed in ye sd instrument unto Nicholas Woodberye of Beverly, his heirs & assignes & I have rec'd full satisfaction. *Signed*: William Pitt. *Date*: 3 Mar 1674. *Witnesses*: Hilliard Veren; Thomas Cromwell.

Nicholas Woodberry Senr do aliene, assigne, sett over unto Richard Maine of Manchester his heirs & assignes all my right, title in ye premises within these sales & alienations written. *Signed*: Nicholas Woodberye. *Date*: October 30 1680. *Witnesses*: Samuel Hardie; Paule Thorndike. *Acknowledged*: Nicholas Woodberye ackn this instru. to be his act & deed & y^t all his rights he have conveyed to Richard Maine this 16:10 mo. 1681.

I Richard Maine do hereby assign unto Jenckin Williams of Manchester all my right & interest in this deed & ye contence thereof. *Signed*: Richard Maine [mark]. *Date*: 17:10 mo: 1681. *Acknowledged*: 17:10 mo:1681.

BENJAMIN FELTON to JEREMIAH ROGERS – (6:203) Benjamin Felton of Salem sold to Jeremiah Rogers of Salem for consideration of 60 pounds, a certaine pr'cell of land and a dwelling house scittuate & lying in ye bounds of Salem, containing 40 rods or one quarter of an acre, bounded by the contry road, north & east by land in possession of Mr. John Hathorne south & west with all waies, easements, comons, liberties & privilidges & also all estate right title of said Felton. *Signed*: Benjamin Felton. *Date*: 29th Nov 1681. *Witnesses*: Mannaseth Marstone; Nehemiah Jewett. *Acknowledged*: 1 Dec 1681. *Recorded*: 21:10 mo:1681.

Whereas it is expressed in the within deed forty pole or one quarter of an acre, & the land faling short a considerable quantity, the sd Jeremiah Rogers doth ingage not to molest or compell ye sd Benjamin Felton to make good or secure unto him any more land then is in pr'sent possession within fence on ye westerly side of the house, with the land ye house stands on & with ye land fronting before it towards ye meeting house that belongs to it, thats not inclosed, with all pr'vilidges as is above. *Signed*: Jeremiah Rogers. *Witness*: Hilliard Veren. *Acknowledged*: Jeremiah Rogers this 21:of December 1681.

THOMAS CHEEVER for EZEKIELL CHEEVER and ELLEN CHEEVER to THOMAS WOODBERY – (6:206) Thomas Cheever of Maulden (Gentleman Attorney to Ezekiell Cheever of Boston, schoolmaster & Ellen his wife heires of the estate of Capt. Thomas Lothrop) sold to

Thomas Woodbery of Beverly (marrenor) for consideration of 300 lbs sterling, current money of N.E., all the lands & housing thereupon or any part thereof, with all ye comonages & privilidges that ye sd Capt. Tho. Lothrop dyed possessed of, lying & being in the township of Beverly, or of right did belong to him. viz: his home lott containing about 10 acres with ye dwelling house, barne & all out housing standing thereupon, with the orchards, gardens & fences thereto belonging which sd tenn acre lott is bounded by ye land of ye sd Thomas Woodbery easterly, ye plains belonging to ye sd Capt. Thomas Lothrop, northeasterly, the land of ye sd John Black, westerly & ye sea sotherly: alsoe all that pr'cell of land caled the plaine adjoining to the home lott, which bounds ye sd land caled the plaine, sotherly, which sd pr'cell of land containes about twenty three acres, is also bounded easterly with ye land of Isaack Woodbery in part & ye other part by ye land of John Black. westerly by ye land of Humphrey Woodbery, Senr & northerly by som land of John Pride, alsoe one pr'cell of land now lying by "Snake Hill" containing about twenty acres, bounded sotherly with ye land of Mr. Thorndike westerly in part by some land of Isaack Woodbery & the other part by comon land & easterly & northerly alsoe by ye comon land: alsoe about six acres of meddow lying by Cornishes Farm, which was the meddow of William Dodg's Senr. *Signed*: Thomas Cheever as aturney as alsoe in owne name. *Date*: 28 October 1681. *Witnesses*: Benjamin Browne; John Atwater. *Acknowledged*: 28 October 1681. *Recorded*: 29:8 mo:1681.

THOMAS WOODBERY to THOMAS CHEEVER for EZEKIEL CHEEVER and ELLEN CHEEVER – (6:209)

Thomas Woodbery of Beverly (marrenor) mortgaged to Thomas Cheever of Maulden (gent,. attorney to Ezekiel Cheever of Bostone & Ellen his wife) for consideration of 300 pounds sterling current money which I doe owe & stand indebted unto Thomas Cheever of Mauldon gent. atturney to Ezekiel Cheever of Boston & Ellen his wife, all the lands with the housings thereupon, in Beverly that were formerly housing and lands of Capt. Thomas Lothrop deceased that he dyed possest of & which sd Thomas Woodbery the day of ye date of these pr'sents bought of sd Thomas Cheever as atturney, before the sealing & delivery of these pr'sents, as may appear by a deed of sale then made from ye sd Thomas Cheever bearing dates with these pr'sents, provided that if said Thomas Woodberry do well or truly pay or cause to be paid unto the sd Thomas Cheever the full sum of three hundred pds sterling currant money of New England in manner and forme following, fifty pounds on or before the first of May which shall be one thousand six hundred eighty & five & fifty pounds more thereof on or before the first day of May one thousand six hundred eighty six, & fifty pounds more thereof on or before ye first day of May: one thousand six hundred eighty seaven &

fifty pounds more thereof, on or before the first day of May one thousand six hundred eighty and eight as the last paiment & full remainder of sd sume of three hundred pounds provided the one hundred pounds in two paiments to be made are otherwise secured to be paid, the 4 last paiments being made in form & manner as aforesd, that then this bargain & sale shall be voyd, but if default shall happen to be made in 4 paiments above mentioned, within the times above limitted, in pt. or whole, then to remaine in full power & for the paiment of sd sume of three hundred pounds, the said Thomas Woodbery have given six bills, two of which are with ye security before expressed. The other 4 payable at the time limitted as above written. *Signed*: Thomas Woodbery. *Date*: 28 October 1681. *Witnesses*: Benjamin Browne; John Atwater. *Acknowledged*: 28:of October 1681. *Recorded*: 29:8 mo:1681.

JOHN BARTON and LIDEA BARTON to JOHN SANDERS – (6:213) John Barton of Salem (cherurgeon) sold to John Sanders of Salem (marrenor) for consideration of twenty pounds in money, a certain pr'cell of land containing by estimation twenty five pole of ground as it is now bounded out & is scituate in Salem being that pr'cel of land formerly bought of John Gardner, as pr deed of sale appeareth & is bounded on ye north with land of John Sanders, easterly with land of Humphrey Coomes, sotherly with land of sd John Gardner, & westerly with a lane or highway: the sd pr'cell of land extends from land of sd John Sanders into ye lands of sd John Gardner, soe far as the south end of sd Humphrey Coomes land runns. *Signed*: J. Barton; Lidea Barton. *Date*: 17 October 1681. *Witnesses*: Edward Grove; William Hirst. *Acknowledged*: 30 Dec 1681. *Recorded*: 30:10 mo:1681.

NATHANIELL HAYWARD to JEREMIAH NEALE – (6:215) Nathaniell Hayward of Salem sold to Jeremiah Neale of Salem (carpenter) for consideration of twenty shillings in money, a certain piece of land containing about fower poles scituate in towne of Salem viz that house plott, which yet is well known y^t my father Nicholas Hayward did live in when he did live in Salem towne being bounded northerly with the contry roade, which goeth from Salem meeting house to the ferry & easterly & southerly with ye lands of Jonathan Hart and westerly with land which aforesd Nicholas Hayward exchanged with towne of Salem, for land where he now dwelleth. *Signed*: Nathaniell Hayward. *Date*: 14 Dec 1681. *Witnesses*: John Leach; Richard Thistle. *Acknowledged*: 14 Dec 1681. *Recorded*: 30: 10 mo:1681.

The deposition of Edward Gaskin aged about 70 years saith that Nicholas Hayward had to his knowledge a house plott on which he sd Hayward did

live uppon when he came first to Salem the sd house plott scituate & being in Salem upon the west corner of John Neales land, which lyethes as I goe from Salem Ipswich ward on the righthand: this abovesd pr'cell of ground or house plott being bounded on the east or southest corner with the well which was in sd house plott & westerly neare upon a square home to sd Neales now standing fence by road & from said well neere upon a square to said Neales now standing fence by road & from said well neere upon a square to said Neales now standing fence southerly & further saith not.
Taken upon oath 22:3 mo:7/4

The deposition of Frances Skerry aged 66 yeares or thereabouts saith y^t Nicholas Hayward had to his knowledge a house plott, on which he ye sd Hayward did live upon when he came first to Salem, this sd house plott scituate in Salem, upon west corner of John Neales land which lyeth as I goe from Salem Ipswich ward on the right hand, this abovesd pr'cell of ground or house plott being bounded on east or southeast corner with the well which was in this sd house plott & westerly neere upon a square home to sd Neales now standing fence by road & from said well neere upon a square to said Neales now standing fence southerly & further saith not.
Taken upon oath 22:3 mo:7/4

WILLIAM BROWNE SENR to ROBERT FOLLETT – (6:218)
William Browne Senr of Salem in ye N.E. (marchant) sold to Robert Follett of Salem (fisherman) for consideration of eighty pounds, all that my farme or pr'cell of land containing two hundred & seaven acres of ground, as it was granted & laid out to me sd William Browne by towne of Salem & is scituate within township of Salem & is bounded southerly with the land of Mr. Frances Johnson & westerly with the land of Samuel Ferry & northerly ptly with some land of John Roapes part by land of John Smale partly the lands of Elisha Kebe, & partly with land of ye John Hill & easterly with som land of sd Robert Follett. *Signed*: William Brown. *Date*: 21 Sept. 1678. *Witnesses*: Edward Morrle; Benjamin Browne. *Acknowledged*: 28 December 1681 by William Browne Esq. *Recorded*: 30:10 mo:1681.

JOHN GOULD to MAJOR GENERAL DANIELL DENISON – (6:220)
John Gould of Topsfield (yeoman) sold to Major General Daniell Denison of Ipswich for divers good causes especially ye sum of fifty pounds to me in hand paid & secured to be paid, one whole sixteenth part of Iron works, lately erected in or near Topsfield, now in occupation of Henry Leonard, together with a sixteenth part of all the buildings, dams, water courses, land implements & tools, stock of coales & mine, with all privilidges, rentes, profits or appurtenences and waies belonging or appertaining to the same & ye sd John Gould doth further covenant to & with ye sd Daniell that sd John

shall & will at his owne proper costt & charge finish & pr'fect all ye buildings, dams & water courses & furnish the workers with so much stock of coale & mine belonging to said sixteenth pt of sd ironworkes, as by agreement betweene the pt'iners, owners of the sd ironworkes & (sd Mr. Leonard whoe hath hired sd workes & stock for the space of eight yeares, as more largely appeareth in a lease made to sd Leonard) the sd works ought to be furnished with & as they ought to be finished & compleated, & delivered to sd Leonard to take charge thereof according to the covenents and agreements betweene sd. owners of sd ironworkes & sd Leonard & sd John Gould doth further covenant & promise to & with sd Daniell to give & make any assurance of sixteenth part of sd ironworks, houses, lands, stock, myne, coales, with the rents profits & appurtenances there unto belonging, as the learned in ye law shall judge necessary as alsoe to cause his wife to surrender up her thirds or dower. *Signed*: John Gould. *Date*: 1 May 1671. *Witnesses*: Thomas Baker; Amos Gednie. *Acknowledged*: 7 August 1671 & Sarah his wife yielded dower. *Recorded*: 30:10 mo:1681.

JOHN GOULD and SARAH GOULD to SIMOND BRADSTREETE, JOHN RUCK and THOMAS BAKER – (6:223) John Gould of Topsfield (yeoman) sold to Simond Bradstreete of Andover (gent.), John Ruck of Salem (marchant) and Thomas Baker of Topsfield (yeoman) and the rest of the part owners of ye ironworkes, whereof myselfe am one for consideration of twenty two pounds, tenn shillings paid by owners of ye ironworkes at Rowly village, all that pr'cel of upland & arable ground, lying & being within tract of land comonly called Rowly village by estimation eighty acres on pt whereof the said ironworkes now standeth bounded by a walnut tree growing by the brook, comonly caled the fishing brook, soe up to a bastion tree bounded with land of Samuel Simonds on the south east & from bastion tree upon a straite line to a poplar tree standing west or to the northward of the west bounded with land of sd John Gould & from the poplar tree upon a straite line to a popler stake & heape of stones by it east or to the norward of the east, bounded with land of sd John Gould & John Newmarsh & soe downe as the pond goeth to the walnut tree again. *Signed*: John Gould; Sarah Gould. *Date*: 25 December 1670. *Witnesses*: John How; Rebecka Smith [mark]. *Acknowledged*: Decem:23:1673. *Recorded*: 30:10:1681.

DANIEL DENISON ESQR and PATIENCE DENISON to JOHN RUCK SEN'R – (6:225) Daniell Denison Esqr. of Ipswich sold to John Ruck Sen'r of Salem (marchant) for consideration of a valuable sume to him in hand already paid, one sixteenth part of all the housings, buildings & water workes, dames, water courses, lands wood, timber, tooles, instruments, with all the stock of coales, provissions of every kind that now belongs or in any will belong or appertaine to sd works & all appurtenances w'sover or right is thereto belonging or ap'rtaining to ye sd bloomery or ironworkes with appurtenances. *Signed*: Daniell Denison; Patience Denison. *Release of Dower*: Mrs. Patience Denison wife of sd Daniell gives up dower. *Date*: this seaventeenth of February, one thousand sixteen hundred & eighty one. *Witnesses*: John Ruck Jun'r; Daniell Denison Jun'r. *Acknowledged*: 11:November 1681. Patience, my wife surrendered her thirds & signed this writing with her hand. *Signed*: Daniell Denison. *Recorded*: 30:10 mo:1681.

GRIFFEN EDWARDS for MRS. ANN MILES and MR. JOHN MYLES to RICHARD HUDD – (6:228) Griffen Edwards of Boston (gent. & atturney & administrator on behalfe of his mother in law Mrs. Ann Miles, who is the reputed only heire surviving of Col. John Humphries Esq., deceased & she is the now wife of Mr. John Miles minister at Swansey a plantation in colloney of Plimouth) & Mr. John Myles & Mrs. Ann Miles his wife sold to Richard Hudd of Lynn for consideration of one hundred pounds, current money in hand paid, one dwelling house & barne & barnes, with all outhouses & twenty acres of land, adjoining to sd dwelling house & barne & barnes, with all fences, timber, trees or underwood standing & growing upon sd twenty acres abovesd; the sd housing & land being & lying within the township of Lynn aforesd, which house & land did formerly belong and appertaine to Col. John Humphreys Esq. deceased bounded with town comon southwest, & easterly & northerly with remainder of land which did belong to the abovesd John Humphries, which is the remainder of sd twenty acres. *Signed*: Griffin Edwards; John Myles; Ann Myles. *Date*: twenty seaventh of October 1681. *Witnesses*: John Smith; John Lewis; Jacob Knight. *Acknowledged*: 29:day of October 1681 Griffin Edwards; Mr. John Myles & Ann, his wife. *Recorded*: 24:11 mo:1681.

MR. JOHN MYLES and ANN MYLES to WILLIAM BASSETT JUN'R – (6:232) Mr. John Myles of Swansea (minister in the colloney of Plimouth) & Mrs. Ann Myles, wife to sd Mr. Miles abovesd & who is reputed to be the only heire of Collonell John Humphries Esq. deceased, sold to William Bassett Jun'r of Lynn for consideration of thirty & fower pounds of currant money in hand pd, tenn acres of upland, being bounded with land of Robert Ingalls Jun'r & the remainder of the land that this tenn acres did belong unto on the northeast & with land of Richard Hudd, on other pt. of same land that formerly the tenn acres did belong unto on the southwest butting northerly upon land of said William Bassett, being his owne & sotherly upon the salt sea, the sd land lying and being, within township of Lynn aforesaid which is part of that land which was formerly belonging to abovesd John Humphries Esq. *Signed*: John Myles; Ann Myles. *Date*: the last of October in one thousand, six hundred eighty one. *Witnesses*: William Griggs; John Hayward. *Acknowledged*: 1:November:1681 Mr. John Myles & Ann his wife. *Recorded*: 24:11 mo:1681.

PHILLIP CROMWELL and MARY CROMWELL to WILLIAM HIRST – (6:235) Phillip Cromwell of Salem (slautherer) sold to William Hirst of Salem (marchant) for consideration of sixty pounds of currant money, a certain pr'cell of land, containing by estimation one acre & a halfe, or one acre & three quarters, as it now lyes bounded scituate, lying & being in towne of Salem & is bounded sotherly with the main streete, easterly, with land that now is or late was land of Hilliard Veren, northerly by north river or highwaye that runs betweene it & the north river & westward pr'tly with some land of Edward Gaskin & pr'tly with some land of Belknaps, now sd to be Thomas Maules. *Signed*: Phillip Cromwell; Mary Cromwell [mark]. *Date*: fourteenth day of March, one thousand six hundred seventy nine. *Witnesses*: Edward Grove; John Hathorne. *Acknowledged*: 23:11 mo:1681 by Mr. Phillip Cromwell and wife Mary before me William Browne Assistant. *Recorded*: 24:11 mo:1681.

BENJAMIN SMALL to WILLIAM OSBOURNE – (6:239) Benjamin Small of Salem (sayle maker) sold to William Osbourne of Salem (husbandman) for consideration of 3 pounds 16 shillings, certaine p'cell of ground bought of John Cromwell slautherer lying in Salem containing fowerteen foot square being at the northeast corner of ground belonging to now dwelling house of sd John Cromwell in Salem as at full appears by deed of sale given for the sd land bearing date twentieth day of March 1678:79 acknowledged and recorded in book of records with all right & priviledge unto same & unto lane or highway thereby as appropriated by virtue of sd John Cromwell's bill of sale. *Signed*: Benjamin Small. *Date*: 25 January 1681:82. *Witnesses*: Jeremiah Neale; Richard Croade. *Acknowledged*: 25 January 1681:2. *Recorded*: 24:11 mo:1681.

THOMAS TUCK and JOANE TUCK to JOHN TUCK – (6:241) Thomas Tuck of Beverly with consent of wife Joane sold to John Tuck for divers good causes as namely a debt of thirteene pounds & fifteene shillings pd by my son John Tuck for me to Mr. William Browne Senr of Salem & other debts paid by my said son for me, all that my pr'cell of land scittuate & lying in Beverly, aforesd with the pr'viledges & appurtenances thereunto belonging as it now bounded on south & east with the sea & on north with land of Joseph Rootes & on west with a parcel of land of Mr. William Brown's. *Signed*: Thomas Tuck [mark]; Joane Tuck [mark]. *Date*: 21:9

mo:1677. *Witnesses*: Walter Fairefeild; Hugh Woodberrye. *Acknowledged*: 22 June 1680 by Thomas and Joane. *Recorded*: 9:12 mo:1681.

EDMUND BATTER and MARY BATTER to STEEPHEN SEWALL – (6:242)   Edmund Batter of Salem (march't) sold to Steephen Sewall of Salem (marchant) for a valuable consideration to me paid, a certaine pr'cell of land, containing twenty eight rod or pole of ground, scituate, lying & being in Salem & is bounded with the highway or streete sotherly, the ground of John Mascoll westerly, the ground of Mr. Daniell Weld, northerly, the land of sd Edmund Batter easterly: the sd ground now bargained & sold being in bredth fronting against the highwaye or streete three pole & six foot, & abutting upon ground of sd Weld to the north in bredth there four pole from John Mascoll's ground eastward & soe from thence to runn upon a straite line on the easterne side to the street to three pole distance eastward in bredth from that end of John Mascoll's ground. *Signed*: Edmund Batter; Mary Batter. *Release of Dower*: Mary wife yields up dower. *Date*: this day of October in one thousand six hundred eighty & one. *Witnesses*: William Dounton; Henry West. *Acknowledged*: December 2d. 1681. *Recorded*: 24:11 mo:1681.

THOMAS PUTNAM SEN'R to NATHANIELL PUTNAM – (6:245) Thomas Putnam Sen'r of Salem (yeoman) sold to Nathaniell Putnam of Salem (yeoman) for consideration of the value of about five pounds paid, in a pr'cell of land containing five acres (which sd five acres Mr. James Baily had), five acres of land, scituate & lying in bounds of Salem, at south end of little hill soe called which said five acres of land lyes in the forme of a acute angle, having at the westerly corner a bound tree, formerly the bound tree of Mr. Phillip Cromwell, at the sotherly corner a bound tree formerly John Hathorne, at the easterly corner bounded with a heap of stones & a stake, & it is bounded east northerly with ye land of sd Thomas Putnam & by land of sd Nathaniell Putnam on other two sides. *Signed*: Thomas Putnam Sen'r. *Date*: twenty one day of November on thousand six hundred eighty & one. *Witnesses*: Richard Knott; Eleazer Gedney. *Acknowledged*: 21:9 mo:1681. *Recorded*: 24:11 mo:1681.

WILLIAM DIXY to HENRY HARWOOD – (6:248) William Dixy of Salem sold to Henry Harwood of Salem house which sd Willliam Dixy now live in with an acre of ground thereunto adjoining, lying betwist John Jackson and John Black, with five acres of ground lying on Darby Fort side, which house & ground aforesd. Henry Harwood is to have full possession uppon nine and twentieth day of September, next to come after the date hereof.   *Signed*: William Dixy [mark]. *Date*: twenty day of April

Anno:Dom:1640. *Witnesses*: Thomas Warrin; John Black; John Jackson [mark]. *Acknowledged*: 13 February:1681:2. *Recorded*: 13:February:81.

JOHN NEALE SEN'R to NATHANIELL PUTNAM – (6:249) John Neale Sen'r of Salem (yeoman) administrator of estate of Frances Lawes late of Salem, deceased sold to Nathaniell Putnam of Salem (yeoman) for consideration of a valuable sume to me in hand already paid, a certaine pr'cell of land, containing thirty acres, it being formerly a grant by towne of Salem to the said Frances Lawes, it is laid out, scituate & is lying in bounds of Salem, aforesd & is bounded with land of Thomas Putnam & Robert Prince on southwesterly, the land of Joseph Huchenson west, the land of Thomas Fuller north & land of ye sd Nathaniell Putnam & partly river east. *Signed*: John Neale [mark]. *Date*: thirteenth day of September one thousand six hundred & seaventy. *Witnesses*: William Hathorne; Elizabeth Hathorne. *Acknowledged*: 16:11 mo:1681. *Recorded*: 24:11 mo:1681.

ZARUBBABELL ENDICOTT to JOSEPH WILLIAMS – (6:250) Zarubbabell Endicott of Salem sold to Joseph Williams of Salem for consideration of sixteene pounds secured to be paid, a certaine tract of land, being about twenty acres, which was granted & given unto sd Zarubabell Endecot by towne of Topsfield being part of first devission & bounded on the south side with land of Mathew Stany, & on north side with land given to Thomas Browning by sd towne of Topsfield. *Signed*: Zarabbabell Endecott. *Date*: first of May one thousand, six hundred seaventy. *Witnesses*: Nathaniell Felton sen'r; Samuell Phippen. *Acknowledged*: 17th September 1679. *Recorded*: 24:11 mo:1681.

EDWARD WOOLLAN SEN'R to THOMAS SEARLE – (6:252) Edward Woollan Sen'r of Salem (fisherman) sold to Thomas Searle of Salem (fisherman) for consideration of tenn pounds five shillings sterling in hand paid, a certaine p'cell of land containing one sixth pt of an acre scituate lying & being in Salem & is pt of that land lying behind sotherly of my now dwelling house & is in length nearest east & west, five pole & six foot & in bredth north & south five poles wanting thirteene inches or there abouts, soe much as to make up the full of one sixth pt of an acre & is bounded easterly with land of William West, northerly with land of Richard Simons, sotherly with land of sd Edward Woolan & westerly with a lane or highwaye, left for the use of the propietors & it is to be understood sd Thomas Searle, his heires & assigns is to leave out towards highwaye or lane, seaven foot in bredth through the front of sd p'cell of land in pt of highway, unto which sd Edward Woolen, my heires & assignes are hereby ingaged to leave out soe much of my ground, as to make it a convenient highwaye to pass & repass from streete with a cart for the use of sd Thomas

Searle, his heirs & assigns forever, together with the rest of the proprietors. ***Signed***: Edward Wolland [mark]. ***Date***: seaventeenth day of February one thousand, six hundred, eighty one:1681:2. ***Witnesses***: Hilliard Veren; Christopher Babbiddge. ***Acknowledged***: 18th of February 1681. ***Recorded***: 18:12:1681.

ANN NEALY to WILLIAM BROWNE JUN'R – (6:255) Ann Nealy of Salem, administratrix to ye estate of John Neale sold to William Browne Jun'r of Salem (marchant) for consideration of forty five pounds, a certain p'cell of upland ground being one acre & halfe or thereabouts, it being in towne of Salem, being sixteen pole & a halfe on the east side next to Mr. John Gedney's pasture, twenty pole on the west side, & fourteene pole on north & south, the sd land is butted and bounded northerly with land of me said Ann Neale, easterly with land of Mr. John Gedney sen'r sotherly partly with land Jacob Pudeater purchased of Mr. Edmond Batter & partly with land of Jeremiah Neale & westerly with a strip of land of Jeremiah Neales, or howsoever sd p'cel of land or any part thereof otherwise is butted & bounded or reputed to be bounded, which sd land was lately my husband John Neale's given him by his father by his will, together with all ye appurtenances, profits & privileges what soever thereunto belonging & all my estate, right & title & interest, of, in & to ye sd bargained pr'misses or any part or p'cel, thereunto, with all original deeds, writings & evedences touching & concerning same faire & uncancelled. ***Signed***: Ann Neale [mark]. ***Date***: sixteenth day of February, one thousand, six hundred, eighy one. ***Witnesses***: Benjamin Browne; Jeremiah Neale; Charles Redford. ***Acknowledged***: first of March 1681:2. ***Recorded***: 10:March:1681:2.

PHILLIP CROMWELL and MARY CROMWELL to ELENOR HOLLINGWORTH – (6:258) Phillip Cromwell of Salem (slauterer) sold to Elenor Hollingworth of Salem widdow & relict of William Hollingworth Sen'r deceased for consideration of two hundred & fifty pounds in money & goods in hand, that house, housing & land in Salem, now in possession & use of sd Ellenor Hollingworth bounded on east with land formerly Curwithies land, now the land of Phillip English on north with land of Robert Storr, on west with land of John Clifford, on south with Salem harbour, the pr'misses bargained for & by these pr'sents sold, being the same & all the same which sd Ellenor sold unto me, as p her bill of sale, given unto me for the same recorded, dated the first day of June in one thousand, six hundred & seaventy two. ***Signed***: Phillip Cromwell; Mary Cromwell [mark]. ***Release of Dower***: Mary wife yielded thirds. ***Date***: fourth day of March one thousand six hundred, eighty one/82. ***Witnesses***: John Corwin; Richard Croad & possession given by turfe & twigg.

Acknowledged: 13th of March 1681:82 Phillip & Mary Cromwell. *Recorded*: 13:March 81/2.

JOHN HILL and ABIGAILE HILL to PEETER WOODBERY – (6:261) John Hill of Beverly (cooper) sold to Peeter Woodbery of Beverly (yeoman) for consideration of a valuable sum in hand paid, all the land, as well meddow as upland ground, now in possession of aforesd John Hill, that is to say all his pt of the farme formerly John Woodbery's now deceased, father-in-law unto said John Hill that is five & twenty acres of upland ground, scituate & lying in towne of Beverly, aforesd & is bounded easterly with land of John Woodbery & sotherly with land of William Dodge & westerly with the highwaye or comon roade, & northerly with land of Benjamin Balch sen'r & land of John Balch & likewise a pr'cel of meddow ground lying & being pt of the meddow comonly caled "the great marsh" with all land or p'cells of land whatsoever lying in Beverly aforesaid or elsewhere appertaining unto sd John Hill, as pt. or which was part of sd John Woodberry's farm (now deceased.) *Signed*: John Hill; Abigaile Hill [mark]. *Release of Dower*: Abigaile ye wife of John Hill doe by these pr'sents freely yield up all her right. *Date*: 15 June one thousand, six hundred & eighty one. *Witnesses*: Thomas West; John Pickad. *Acknowledged*: 25 January, 1681 John Hill & Abigail, his wife. *Recorded*: 13:March:1681:2.

JOHN GREENE and MARY GREENE to PETER WOODBERRY – (6:264) John Greene of Salem (husbandman) sold to Peter Woodberry of Beverly (yeoman) for consideration of a valuable sume to me in hand paid, two certaine p'cels of land, containing thirty acres or thereabouts both p'cells scituate, being & lying in township of Salem, the one p'cell thereof is twenty five acres of upland, bounded easterly with land of John Giles, sotherly with land of John Leach, westerly with land of Jacob Barny, and northerly with highwaye or comon road, the other p'cell of sd thirty acres, is five acres of meddow ground, bounded easterly with land of Benjamin Porter, sotherly with meddow ground of Nathaniell Putnam, & westerly with a smale piece or strip of upland, being & lying betweene ye bargained pr'mises & meddow sometime Rich'd Huchenson's & northerly with a brooke. *Signed*: John Greene [mark]; Mary Greene [mark]. *Release of Dower*: Mary wife freely yield up all her right, title, dower. *Date*: second day of January one thousand, six hundred & seaventy nine. *Witnesses*: Andrew Eliott; Joseph Dodge. *Acknowledged*: 15:June:1681 John Greene & Mary his wife. *Recorded*: 13:March:1681:2.

JOHN HAWKES to JOHN BREAD – (6:267) John Hawkes of Linn (yeoman) sold to John Bread of Linn (yeoman) for consideration of a valuable sume of money or moneys worth to him in hand paid, a certaine p'cell of land lying scituate & being in township of Lynn aforesd, lying eastwardly of ironworks containing two acres & one hundred & six poles which is part of the lott was Thomas Arington's, on which his dwelling house did stand, which dwelling house did formerly stand upon pt of abovesaid two acres one hundred & six poles, the whole lott being bounded northerly with a tenn acre lott of John Breade which he bought of sd John Hawkes sotherly with lott formerly William Edwards, abutting easterly on the swamp caled Edwards Swamp. *Signed*: John Hawkes. ***Release of Dower***: with consent of Sarah his now wife in reference to her surrending up her thirds. *Date*: first day of December, 1673. *Witnesses*: John Bennett; William Hathorne. *Acknowledged*: 3:1mo:73:4. *Recorded*: 17:March:1681:2.

SARAH HEALY to ABRAHAM BROWNE – (6:269) Sarah Healy wife to William Healy of Cambridge, doe give liberty and full power to my son Abraham Browne to take into his possession & make sale of that piece or p'cell of land in Salem given him by his father's will. *Signed*: Sarah Healy. *Date*: 9th day of August 1681. *Witnesses*: Joseph Noyce; John Ireland. *Acknowledged*: 18th of 12th mo:1681. *Recorded*: 3: Aprill:1682.

JOHN HAWKES to JOHN BREAD – (6:270) John Hawkes of Linn (gent.) sold to John Bread of Linn (husbandman) for a valuable consideration in hand paid, a tenn acre lott lying & being in Linn aforesd, adjoining to a lott of land formerly Thomas Errington's lying to westward of sd lott, it was also in former time given unto Thomas Talmadge of towne of Lynn. *Signed*: John Hawkes. *Date*: tenth day of July one thousand, six hundred, seaventy & two. *Witnesses*: John Hathorne; Ebenezer Hathorne. *Acknowledged*: 3:1 mo:73:4. *Recorded*: 17:March:1681:2.

SAMUELL EBORNE SEN'R to JOSEPH HOLTON JUN'R. – (6:271) Samuell Eborne sen'r of Salem (yeoman) sold to Joseph Holton Jun'r (son-in-law) for a valuable consideration in hand paid, a p'cell of meddow containing three acres or thereabouts, bounded at the northeast corner with a spring, neere to the resting tree lying to the southward of a little brook which is the deviding bounds between my meddow & Banjamin Pope his meddow lying neere to the bounds deviding betwixt Salem & Lynn: all w'ch meddow being my owne meddow & bound with upland to bounds first named. It is to be understood before ye enstealing hereof, that one acre of the three expressed in abovesd deed, is to be to the use of the granter during his life time, & after his decease to be to use of abovesd. Joseph Houlton Jun'r. *Signed*: Samuell Eborne senr [mark]. *Date*: 2d March

1681:2. *Witnesses*: Joseph Houlton; Joseph Huchenson; Sarah Holton [mark]. *Acknowledged*: 20 March 1681:2. *Recorded*: 20 March 1681:2.

JOSEPH HUTCHENSON to NATHANIELL INGERSON – (6:273) Joseph Hutchenson of Salem (husbandman) sold to Nathaniell Ingerson of Salem for consideration of a certaine sume in hand paid, five acres of upland, & swampy ground, bounded at the deviding line at south east of my pasture to a post & heape of stones, in the dividing line betwixt Nathaniell Ingersons land & my land & from thence to a white oak tree standing to the north east, marked on two sides standing about three or four pole in the swamp, which is the deviding bounds betwixt brother Hadlock & my land, to the head of a litle brook, the brook being the bounds to north side of the oarchard that was formerly Mr. John Endecotts, all the land that I have lying to the west side of the dividing line & the brooke to the deviding line of Joseph Houltons & Nathaniell Ingersons land, that is my land lying & being in township of Salem aforesd. *Signed*: Joseph Hutchenson. *Date*: February 28:1677. *Witnesses*: Thomas Haines; John Cheas [mark]. *Acknowledged*: 21:of November 1681. *Recorded*: 20 March:1681:2.

ELIZABETH LEACH to RICH'D LEACH – (6:275) Elizabeth Leach of Salem, widow, executrix unto ye estate of Laurance Leach deceased sold to Rich'd Leach of Salem for consideration of fourteene pounds secured to be paid unto daughter Rachell Golthwright, all my part of meddow, being fifteene acres that lyeth in the greate fresh meddow comonly caled Leach's meddow, lying & being betweene land of Joseph Porter & great pine swamp (only five acres excepted.) *Signed*: Elizabeth Leach [mark]. *Date* two & twentieth of January a thousand six hundred & seaventy. *Witnesses*: Nathaniell Felton; Nathaniell Putnam. *Acknowledged*: 16:3mo:71. *Recorded*: 4:Aprill:1682.

JOHN SMALE, SEN'R to JOHN LEACH JUN'R – (6:276) John Smale, sen'r of Salem (planter) sold to John Leach Jun'r of Salem (yeoman) son of Richard Leach for consideration of therteene pounds, tenn shillings in hand paid, one acre & halfe of salt marsh, scituate lying & being on Ryall's side soe caled in township of Salem, aforesd, & is lying in two p'cells the halfe acre, more or less, one parcell lying betweene a half acre of marsh of ye Leach's on north side & a halfe acre of Capt. Dixes lying on sotherly side, the upland bounds it easterly & river westerly: & the acre, more or less, being the other pr'cell, joyning to & lying on sother side of aforesaid Capt. Dixe & sotherly, bounded with som marsh of Goodman Rayes & the upland, easterly & sd river westerly John Leach, Jun'r son of Richard Leach. *Signed*: John Small [mark]. *Date*: twentieth day of March in ye yeare of our Lord, God, one thousand six hundred & eight one 1681:2.

Witnesses: Henry West; Hilliard Veren. *Acknowledged*: 20th of March, 1681. *Recorded*: 20:March:1681:2.

JOHN TAULY to BARTHLOMEW GEDNEY ESQ. – (6:278) John Tauly of Salem (marenor) owe & justly stand indebted unto Barthlomew Gedney Esq. of Salem the full & just sume of one hundred, seaventy & one pounds, sixteene shillings & tenn pence which is for & in consideration of one halfe of a new catch of late bought of sd Barthlomew Gedney Esq. caled content which sd sume of one hundred seaventy one pounds sixteen shillings & ten pence in current lawful money of New England. I said John Tauley doe covenant & promise to pay or cause to be paid to sd. Barthlomew Gedney, Esq. or to his executors, administrators or assignes, at or before fifteenth day of October, next ensuing date of these pr'sents, unto which payment well & truly to be made I bind myself. I also doe by these pr'sents bind over my now dwelling house in Salem, all ground thereto adjoining belonging thereto with all my other estate, reall & pr'sonall for further security of paiment of said sume abovesaid & upon non paiment as aforesd sd Gedney to have occupy possess & injoye same forever. *Signed*: John Tawley. *Date*: this first day of Aprill, in ye yeare of our Lord one Thousand, six hundred eighty & two. *Witnesses*: Hilliard Veren; John Croade. *Acknowledged*: 1 day of April 1681. *Recorded*: 4:Aprill:1682.
12 December: Then rec'd as pt of within written bill ninety & one pound & 8d. 91^{lb}:0^s:8^d. p me Barthlomew Gedney.
9:May:1683 – Rec'd by goods now on catch content: bound to Newfoundland. The full remainder of within written bond p me. Barthlomew Gedney.

ISAAC MEACHUM to MARY VOEDEN – (6:280) Isaac Meachum of Salem (weaver) stand justly indebted to Mary Voedon of Salem (widdow) the sume of two hundred pounds, lawful money of New England to wich paiment to be made I bind me firmly by these pr'sents the condition of this obligation is such that if Mary Voeden shall & may forever peaceably & quietly have hold use occupy possess & injoy all measuage or tenement, containing one dwelling house & twenty six pole of land thereto belonging, except the reserve of a highway of tenn foot broad on eastward side thereof, scituate, lying & being in Salem, aforesd, & every pt & p'cel thereof, mentioned to be bargained & sold, by above bounded Isaac Meachum, to sd Mary Voeden as appears by a certain bill of sale bearing date the day of date of these pr'sents cleerelye discharged or otherwise sufficiently saved & kept harmless of & from all manner or estates, titles, intailes, troubles, changes & incumbrances, at any time heartofore made by Isaac Meachum & to keep harmless sd Mary Voeden in peaceable injoyment & possession of sd measuage or tenement as her right in fee simple against the claime or molestation that may arise forever hearafter by sd Isaac Meachum or by or under the heires, executors or administrators of Thomas Browning, late of Salem, deceased y^t then this obligation to be voyd & of none efect, otherwise to be & remain in full power force & vertue. *Signed*: Isaac Meachum. *Date*: twenty seventh day of March, one thousand, six hundred & eighty two:1682. *Witnesses*: Hilliard Veren; Thomas Mould. *Acknowledged*: 27th of March 1682. *Recorded*: 17:Aprill:1682.

JONATHAN PICKERING with JONATHAN NEALE and JOSEPH NEALE – (6:282) Jonathan Pickering of Salem (shipwright) contracted with Jonathan Neale and Joseph Neale of Salem sons of John Neale of Salem elder deceased, notwithstanding all & every former contract made between any and every of the pr'decessors of sd Jonathan & Joseph Neale & Jonathan Pickering aforesd, or his pr'decessors concerning a gutter & water passage through land of the sd Jonathan Pickering, which is the pertaining lott to sd Jonathan Pickerings now inhabited dwelling house in Salem now notwithstanding whatsoever is obliged unto in any former contract by any of the pr'ties aforesd, with respect to pr'misses or any under them, or either of the pr'ties aforesd under them, allowed or empowered, we, the aforesaid by these pr'sents covenanting, & now only & imediately concerned in premisses as having the only right, title, interest & claime in & unto pr'misses, & likewise to anihilate & nullifie as we may see cause, all former bargains, promises or contracts, by any our ancestors or rights by them with respect to pr'misses, doe now by this pr'sent agreement had, and, made between us, thus, determin, agree upon & conclude betweene ourselves viz: that said Jonathan Pickering for & in consideration of his being by these pr'sents bound, his heirs, executors & administrators, at his sd Pickerings cost & charge, to make up a good and sufficient fence of stone wall against all ordinary orderly cattell, at northerne end of p'tion fence, between sd Jonathan Pickering & land of the abovesd Jonathan Neale, that is to say, & it is hereby to be understood that one halfe of sd fence is aforesaid Jonathan Neale: alsoe Joseph Neale aforesd, his heirs, executors, adminstrators & assigns are forever to have the liberty & benefitt of cleering the gutter in said land of sd Jonathan Pickering by these pr'sents – intended & granted unto sd Joseph Neale for the freedom & benefitt of his sd Joseph Neales, his heires, & assigns. forever freeing & passing awaye water from of his sd Joseph's land, adjoining as he sd Joseph, his heires, executors or assignes may have ocasion at all time & times from hence for & forever (provided there be noe renewall of covenents) doeing as little damage as may be possible to sd Jonathan Pickering, his heires, executors, adminstrators & assignes and the considerations alowed & granted unto the sd. Jonathan Pickering, his heires, executors, adminstrators, is a certaine strip of land lying on west side of Jonathan Neales land, containing ten foot upon front to comon southwest, & soe to run backward to a poynt tapering to the now corner northen bounds of sd Jonathan Pickering's land: for & unto the due faithfull p'formance of convenanted pr'mises betweene p'tie & p'ties herein concerned, according to a true faithful intent & meaning for they themselves the p'ties aforementioned in this covenant: they the aforesd p'ties by these pr'sents as aforesd covenanting for & unto the true & faithful p'formance of & on each part respectively one & to ye other doe have & hould pr'misses according to the reall intent & meaning, & to each other p'ties abovesd respectively concerned, theire heires, executors, adminstrators & assignes forever, and doe by these pr'sents acknowledge themselves to be firmly bound. **Signed**: Jonathen Pickering [mark]; Jonathan Neale; Joseph Neale. **Date**: fourth day of Aprill one thousand, six hundred & eighty two. **Witnesses**: Jeremiah Neale; Richard Croade. **Acknowledged**: 4:Aprill:1682 by Jonathan Pickering, Jonathan Neale & Joseph Neale. **Recorded**: 7:Aprill:1682.

SAMUELL SHATTOCK SENR. and SAMUELL SHATTOCK JUNR. to HILLIARD VIREN – (6:285) Samuell Shattock Senr (hatter) and Samuell Shattock Junr. of Salem (hatter) & the aturneys (jointly & severally) of George Wharton of the Tower of London, yeoman the executor or administrator of his late brother, Edward Wharton late of Salem in New England aforesd, decease'd sold to Hilliard Viren of Salem aforesd (scrivner) for consideration of twelve pounds in money currant of New England for the use of the said George Wharton, as executor or administrator, aforesd, before ye sealing & delivery of these presents, the receipt whereof we do acknowledge & therewith ourselves fully & satisfied & paid, as true & legell aturneys joyntly & severally, that p'cell of ground which was lately bought by Edward Wharton of Stephen Haskett, & by the said Haskett formerly bought of William Lord sen'r deceased, as may appear by their severall bills of sale recorded,: the sd parcell of land being scituate & lying in Salem by south river side, & is pt of land y^t did belong to dwellling house & ground of sd William Lord, deceased, & is bounded by a stake that was formerly drove down close to the fence of Capt. Elias Stileman, adjoining to his ground on east, which sd stake or bound is fower foot & two or three inches distance northerly from backside of the lentos stone wale, of the house formerly built by John Coale, & soe to carry that breath of fower foot & two or three inches westerly, on northside of sd lentos stone wale, till it come fower foot and halfe westward of end or back of chimly of said John Coles house, & then to run right downe into river, & from that first easterly stake or bounds against Mr. Stileman's fence, to runn westerly fower foot & two or three inches distance from sd lentos wale, straite to a stake formerly downe neere the back side of a little warehouse lately built by William Godsoe, which line just takes in stone wale, & is from that easterly, bounds to westerly bounds at Godsoe's warehouse, to be fifty foot & a halfe & soe to runn bredth from fower foot & a halfe west of Coale's house, to the said Godsoe's esterly end of his warehouse, running right down into river sotherly, soe farr as ever sd William Lord first possessor had a legall right & pr'vilidges into river. To have & hold sd parcell of land with wharfe & stone wale unto sd Hilliard & sd Samuell Shattock sen'r & Samuell Shattock Jun'r as aturneys have full power to sell as alsoe by vertue of an order of a county court held at Salem, the 26 of November 1678. *Signed*: Samuel Shattuck srnr; Samuel Shattuck Junr. *Date*: eight day of Aprill in one thousand, six hundred eighty two. *Witnesses*: John Tawley; Abigaile Browne. *Acknowledged*: 8:April:1682. Recorded: 12:Aprill:1681.

There is recorded in foll:82 the making over of this sale to Deliverance Parkmon in this booke.

ISAAC MEACHUM to MARY VOEDEN – (6:289) Isaac Meachum of Salem (weaver) sold to Mary Voeden of Salem (widdow) for consideration of sume of fifty five pounds in currant money of New England in hand paid, a certaine p'cel of land with a dwelling house standing there upon, scituated lying & being in Salem, the sd p'cell of land contains full twenty six rod or pole, only there is excepted & by these pr'sents do except & reserve, for part of or towards a highwaye, which is agreed upon to be left ten foot in bredth on east side of sd land, & soe to run sume bredth from streete back sothward to my other land & is in bredth I say ten foot from eastward end of sd dwelling house to some land formerly sold to Christopher Babage, which sd highwaye or part of highwaye is left for my comon use, together with sd Mary Voeden her heires & assignes forever, the sd house and whole peice of land is bounded northerly with sd streete, with said land of Christopher Babadge easterly, the land of sd Isaac Meachum sotherly, & lands of Steephen Daniell 'westerly. *Signed*: Isaac Meachum. *Date*: twenty seventh daye March, one thousand six hundred, eighty & two. *Witnesses*: Hilliard Veren; Thomas Mould. *Acknowledged*: 27: of March, 1682. *Recorded*: 17:Aprill:1682.

RICHARD SALTONSTALL vs. MICHAELL FARLY, Sen'r – (6:292) Thursday ye 27 of Aprill, 1682 – A protestation against Michaell Farly sen'r & c. made by Richard Saltonstall in order to his process & proceeding at law against Michaell Farly sen'r.

At a meeting which hapened on Munday last, (within ye bounds of Ipswich) Richard Saltonstall of Wenam, of ye Marrachusetts colloney, being then & there pr'sent asked, Michaell Farly sen'r some necessary questions for the cleering of a case depending betweene ye sd Richard and Michaell, the scope & true intent of which question was the ending of all controversys in the most amicable way y^t neither the one nor the other of them, nor yett the case itselfe might be taken up into the lips of talkers: —

for better understanding of that which followes, it is necessary to pr'mise that Michael Farly Senr. by a covenant, w'ch comenced June 24:1675, he & his son Michael Farly Jun'r were the covenant servants of Richard Saltonstall & from time to time have received their wages of ye sd Richard according to theire covenant comencings aforesd, that is to say, according to theire covenant respecting the quantity of their wages (as in charity he would hope) but not according to their covenent respecting the time maner & quality of theire wages, in w'ch respects ye sd Richard hath beane greatly trespassed & damnified by ye sd Michael Farly sen'r & Michael Farly Jun'r as shall be easily demonstrated to our p'p' judges, when the case shall come before them: – This covenant of June 24 did exspire & determine upon ye 29 of March, 1682: on which day ye sd Richard & Michael Farly sen'r made a covenant intituled articles of agreement & c. & this covenent took its rise from Michael Farly sen'r whoe had told ye sd Richard, that his sonns (Michaell & Misheck) were greatly discontented at their pr'sent condition, & this he atributed to the counsell of such p'sons as frequented the mills whereunto he added, that in respect of himselfe, as well as of his sons, he desired a new covenant might be made betweene ye sd Richard and Michaell Farly sen'r for himselfe & for his sons: including his son Misheck as well as Michael Farly Jun'r –

This covenant of March:29:1682 being made, & that of June 24:1675 being thereby abrigated, the sd Richard then told ye sd Michaell Farly sen'r that if he judged himselfe under any disadvantage, by his covenent of March 29:1682, he would give him leave to return unto his covenent of June 24:1675: the sd Michaell returned this answer before the witnesses then pr'sent, that he prefered his covenant of March 29:1682 before that other Covenant of June 24:1675: – The day following wee (the sd Richard & Michaell) went to Dorchester, to the house of ye worshipful William Stoughten Esq. & there ye sd Richard, read the covenent of March 29:1682 & at the same time told ye sd Michaell as formerly, in ye same words, that if he judged himselfe under any disadvantage by the covenant now read. (bearing date 29, March 1682.) ~~before that other covenant of June 24:1675~~ The sd Richard then & there declared y^t he should have free leave & liberty to returne unto his covenant of June 24:1675 his answer was as before that he preferred his covenant of March 29 1682 before that of June 24 1675 – Hearupon the Munday. following was appoynted & agreed to be the day of our meeting with ye sd Michaell Farly sen'r & his two sonns, for the further confirmation or rather methodising the & establishment of our last covenant in som particuler respects: which day ye sd William Stoughton Esq. & ye sd Richard did duly & pr'cisely attend, but ye sd Michaell & his sonns neither came nor sent until ye day after, & then ye sd Richard received a letter from ye sd Michaell Farly sen'r which letter is directly repugnant to all that he had done upon ye 29:March:1682 & repugnant to what he had declared at Dorchester on ye day following, before Wm. Stoughton Esq. – heareupon ye said Richard by the advice of his ever honor'd & absolutely intrusted friend, thought it necessary to take his chests, trunks & other goods out of Codmen's sloop bound for Long Island & ingaged to put ye sd Richard & his goods on board of Joalesis ship: this passage for England he hath now lost, to his great pr'judice, meerely & only by ye sd Michaell's breach of covenant with him (namely of y^t covenant bearing date 29:March, 1682) having thus lost his passage with Joales he imediately went to Ipswich where he had a meeting with Michael Farley sen'r & there his question to ye sd Michael was by what covenant do you hold possession of Ipswich Mills mill house &c his answer was by his covenant of June 24:1675 against which answer ye said Richard then protested as now he doth at this instant: unto which sd protest the sd Michaell did imediately subjoyne these following words (directing the same unto ye sd Richard saying): You cannot pr'forme your articles of agreement with me because the towne of Ipswich will not give you leave to build a mill at the rockes or falls having granted ye same place unto Mr. Wade, with leave & liberty to erect a corne mill at the rockes or fales for the service of the towne & your articles of agreement with myself & sonns doe confine you to this place aforesd, (at the rockes or falls) to this the said Richard offered & returned, saying "I will give you bond with good sureties to performe every title of my contract with you, contained in that covenant of Mch 29:1682, & I likewise the like I require of you for p'formance of all promises & covenants w'ch are thereby due unto myselfe." (& this is nothing else but what wee are directly led, unto by ye sd articles of agreement) this offer was then absolutely refused & rejected by ye sd Michaell Farly, sen'r who then told ye sd Richard, that his articles of agreement were voyde & of non efect, & that he would not be ingaged by them, untill his speciall freind Mr. Thomas Berry shall returne from the Barbadus, nor then neither, unless ye sd Mr. Berry shall upon a new deliberation approve ye sd articles of agreement, and joyne with him ye sd Michaell for ye term of years & for the yearly rent, expressed in ye same: – Since this time Samuel Parrell Newell Esq. upon a speciall service of the colloney, being at Ipswich, spoke with Michaell Farley sen'r concerning his abovesd trespasses ag'st his covenant of March 29:1682, but obtained noe sattisfaction from him, either as a man or as a Christian.

And this was the true state of the case, betweene ye sd Richard & Michaell Farly sen'r upon Fryday the 28th of April, 1682 at which time ye sd Richard left Ipswich & returned to Boston, with respect to his voyage for England in Mr. Foye.

The pr'misses considered: The sd Richard Saltonstall hath & doth heareby solomly protest against ye sd Michaell Farly & his sd sonns, for all costs, damages, charged, losses, detriments, wrongs, injuries, inconveniences, pr'judices, sufferences & spoyles already done or shall hereafter be don or suffered, for or by reason of ye sd Farly & his sd sonns, denying, refusing or non p'formance of cover ant on theire parts as above expressed. This 28th:Aprill 1682 the sd Rich'd Saltonstall Esq. gave oath that the ye above written is a true narrative & upon which he grounds protest as abovesd before me. **Signed**: Bartho: Gedney, Assistant. Recorded: 28:2 mo:1682.

JOSEPH PROCTER to ANTHONY NEEDHAM – (6:298) Joseph Procter of Ipswich sold to Anthony Needham of Salem for consideration of two neate cattle already received & tenn shillings in money to be paid before delivery heareof, a certaine tract of land being the third part of twenty three acres of land (formerly ye land of John Hurd) lying & being in ye township of Salem, the sd twenty three acres of land being bounded on northerly side with land of ye sd Anthony Needham on south with highway, on west with land of sd Anthony Needham & on east with lands now in occupation of John Proctor. **Signed**: Joseph Proctor. **Date**: fifth of November, a thousand, six hundred, eighty one. **Witnesses**: Corporall Thomas Cleark; Samuel Gidding. **Acknowledged**: by Joseph Proctor & Martha his wife 27 of Aprill 1682. **Recorded**: 28 Aprill:1682.

EDMOND NICHOLLS to PHILIP DORY – (6:299) Edmond Nicholls of Sainteleyre in Jersey (merchant) to Philip Dory of Salem (marrenor) doe owe & am indeted sume of eighteen pound sterling in lawful money of England to be paid to sd Phillip Dory, his executors, administrators or assignes, or is lawful aturney, upon demand, at Sainteleur in Jersey or at Salem in Sterling money, to w'ch paiment well & truly to be made, I bind myselfe, my heires, executers & administrators in the penall sum of thirty six pounds like lawful money, firmly by these pr'sents. **Signed**: Edmond Nicholls. **Date**: twenty first day of April:1682. **Witnesses**: Richard Chamberlain; Johabad Rogers. **Acknowledged**: 27:of Aprill, 1682. **Recorded**: 8:May:1682.

EDMOND BRIDGES SENIOR to MRS. ELIZABETH TURNER – (6:303) Edmond Bridges senior of Salem (blacksmith) mortgaged to Mrs. Elizabeth Turner of Salem (widdow) for consideration of sum of one hundred & sixty pounds in hand, my dwelling house & shop & wharfe with sixty poles of ground with it & all things thereunto belonging, being bounded easterly with land of John Beckett senior, sotherly with the water side or river, westerly with land of Richard Flinder & northerly with land of

Edmond Bridges Junior provided if Edmond Bridges shall pay the sume of sixty pounds in iron work & fish within a yeare after the date heareof & fifty pounds a yeare for two next yeares heareafter & it is to be understood that fifty one pounds, fifteen shillings is to be paid in ironworke at five pence pr pound & all ye rest at six pence pr pound. *Signed*: Edmond Bridges. *Date*: twelfth day of April 1682. *Witness*: William Andrews. *Acknowledged*: 15:May:1682. *Recorded*: 15:May:1682.

SAMUELL BENNETT to ROBERT MANSFEILD – (6:306) Samuell Bennett of Boston (carpenter) sold to Robert Mansfeild of Linn (yeoman) for consideration of sume of fower pounds in hand paid in a yoake of oxen at the time of sealing & delivery, fower acres of salt marsh scituate lying & being in Lynn, three acres of which lying in the first divission in Rumney marsh bounded westerly with the marsh of John Fuller & easterly with marsh of Capt. Bridges butting sotherly upon second divission & northerly upon upland, which three acres was lately in possession of Edmund Burchum alsoe one acre of salt marsh lying in second divission in same marsh lately in possession of John Fuller bounded easterly with the marsh of Mr. Laighton & westerly with marsh of Thomas Newell butting sotherly upon Mr. Willis marsh northerly upon first division: the two p'cells of marsh be either of them more or less & sd Robert Mansfeild after the twenty fifth day of second month next ensuing date heare of upon which day or before sd Samuell doth by these presents bind himselfe in the full sume of tenn pounds to sd Robert Mansfeild to invest, possess & interest sd Robert of or into the sd p'cells of marsh. *Signed*: Samuell Benett. *Date*: twentieth of the third month 1650. *Witnesses*: Thomas Townsend; George Taylor [mark]; Andrew Mansfield. *Acknowledged*: 21:3 mo:50. *Recorded*: 15:May 1682.

CAPT. THO. MARSHALL to THOMAS WHEELER SENIOR – (6:308) Capt. Tho. Marshall of Lynn (gent.) sold to Thomas Wheeler senior of town and county of New London in New England (yeoman) for sum of tenn pounds & tenn shillings in current money, two acres of salt marsh lying in Lynn in first divission of lotts in Rumney marsh, bounded easterly with lands of Daniell Hitchin, westerly lands of Daniell Gott, sotherly with lands of Thomas Newall senior, northerly with towne comon & Thomas Marshall covenant that pr'mises is free & cleere & freely discharged of & from all incumbrances by him or from, by, or under Edmond Tomlins formerly of Linn. *Signed*: Thomas Marshall. *Date*: first day of November 1681. *Witnesses*: John Fuller; Clement Coldum. *Acknowledged*: 28:9 mo. *Recorded*: 15:May:1682

JEREMIAH NEALE to WILLIAM BROWNE JR. – (6:311) Jeremiah Neale of Salem (carpenter) sold to William Browne Jr. of Salem (marchant) for consideration of a valuable sume to me in hand paid, a certain strip of land in Salem lying & adjoining to west or southwest side of the land sd Browne lately bought of my sister in lawe An Neale & with land lately bought of Jacob Pudeater & with highway on the southwest side of it, it being about halfe a pole wide at the northwest or norther end of it & about one pole three quarters at the southeast or souther end of it; and alsoe a certain p'cel of land at northeast end of sd land sd Brown lately bought of sd Pudeater containing in length fower pole & two pole in bredth at northwest end, the sotherne end being an angle which sd Neale had of towne of Salem in pt of satisfaction for about three quarters of an acre of land the towne of Salem had of my father John Neale, deceased, for a highway which sd land joined to land that was formerly Thomas Watsons, as doth more at large appeere in towne book of records for lands granted. *Signed*: Jeremiah Neale. *Date*: 25:of Aprill 1682. *Witnesses*: Daniell Webb; Charles Redford; William Murry. *Acknowledged*: 25:of Aprill. 1682. *Recorded*: 15May:1682.

EDMOND FARRINGTON to MATHEW FARRINGTON – (6:314) Edmond Farrington of Lynn (yeoman) sold to Mathew Farrington of Linn for consideration of a valuable sume of money & current pay of new England, the one half of all & singular my tide mill at Linn aforesd with the hoysen, barne & severall p'cells of land thereto belonging or in any mesure appertaining with the dame water, water cources, pr'vilidges & appurtences: them & every of them to be and remaine with all other utensells. *Signed*: Edmond Farrington [mark]. *Date*: 3rd day of December one thousand six hundred sixty & nine. *Witnesses*: Joseph Armitage; Thomas Newhall; William Howard. *Acknowledged*: third day of December Anno: Dom: one thousand six hundred sixty & nine. *Recorded*: 15:May:1682.
In consideration of sale of pr'mises as on other side in respect of my age & inability of travill for the more compleating & sure making of pr'misses to sd Mathew Farrington I have requested, deputed & authourized my well beloved friend Thomas Marshall of Lynn to be my lawfull attorney.

JONATHAN NEALE to SAMUELL SHATTOCK JUN'R – (6:316) Jonathan Neale of Salem (cordwinder) son of John Neale deceased & heire to the estate of Frances Lawes sold to Samuell Shattock Jun'r of Salem (hatt maker) for consideration of a sum of money in hand paid, a certain p'cell of land lying in Salem bounded upon land of Samuell Shattock to north runing in bredth three pole, 13 foot & halfe bounded upon land of William Lord to east, running in length by land of aforesd Lord south, fower pole ten foot & bounded upon land of Samuell Wakefield to west running in length by land of sd Wakefield three pole & three foot south & bounded upon land of me Jonathan Neale to the south runing in bredth three pole, thirteen foot & halfe being thirteen pole of land. *Signed*: Jonathan Neale. *Date*: fifth day of June one thousand, six hundred, eighty two, 1682. *Witnesses*: Abraham Cole; Thomas Adams. *Acknowledged*: 12:of June:1682. *Recorded*: 12:June:1682.

EDMOND BRIDGES to EDMOND BRIDGES – (6:319) Edmond Bridges of Salem (blacksmith) for fatherly love & affection unto son Edmond Bridges as being my oldest sonn & now by God's p'mission with my free consent & approbation upon marriage with Elizabeth, the daughter of Richard Croade give & bestow one halfe pt of that my land in Salem which I lately bought of Mr. Phillip Cromwell being between land of Richard Flinder & John Beckett sen'r & this land which I now give devision is to be made between us for both our conveniency & benefitt with respect to the improvement of ye land & alsoe for a highwaye for us both to the water side & wharf of mine now built of which my sd son & his after him are to have an equall pr'viledge with myselfe & mine succeeding me alsoe I doe convenant & promise & with my sd sonn Edmond & his pr'sent intended wife to build at my owne cost for them upon land aforesd, within the space of twelve months from date hereof a dwelling house & lentoo to it & seller to it, all to be in time aforesd, compleately finished both within doare & without from top to bottom, both house, lentoo & cellar, to be of the same proportion, demensions & manner as my dwelling house, lentoo & cellar which now I am speedly to set on my land & that the house which I give sonn Edmond I shall at my cost & charge build chimbyes & oven thereto as mine hath, alsoe I am to build & give him my sd sonn a convenient smithshop for his trade, finished for that use within ye space aforesd & to give him a necessary sett of tooles for that his smith's trade to work with all, a chaldron of sea coles & five hundred of barr iron soe soone as he setts up & begins to worke distinctly for himselfe & see cause to take a servant or apprentice to work with him: however & in the mean time in my fatherly love & kindnes to him he shal have privilidg of working in my shop with myself & servant & servants & shall have the benefitt of the gains produced by his labor according to his proportionable due, considering the charges of coale iron, utensells & whatsoever elce necessary for carring an end of our smithery trade, asoe he shall have the pr'viledge of my pr'sent wharfe and wharfing as his ocasions shall needfully & in reason require & to inlarge the same for his owne halfe part for future as he may see cause, & as wee may soe cause for our p'ts respectively heareafter for our coveniences & alsoe shall at my owne cost allow unto my sd sonn Edmond & his wife a convenient house to dwell in from the day of their marriage until such time as house above mentioned by me to be given them be finished which is to be done in space of twelve months from the date but in case extraordinary providences or disapoyntments should hinder & interpose my pr'sent intent, then my sd sonn & daughter with my paying for their house rent must be content to tarry for theire sd house one year or more unless I can with out my great damage accomplish it sooner. Alsoe I will give my sd sonn at time aforesaid when he sett up for himselfe a bar of steele but in case Elizabeth Croade lyes before her marriage with my above sd sonn Edmond then above written & every thing theirin contained is to be voyde & of none affect. *Signed*: Edmond Bridges. *Date*: second day of Aprill 1681. *Witnesses*: Edmond Bridges Jun'r; Thomas Daby; Judith Croade [mark]. *Acknowledged*: May 2;1681. *Recorded*: 7th of the 5th mo:1682.

EDMOND GROVER to NEHEMIAH GROVER – (6:322) Edmond Grover of Beverly (yeoman) for the love & natural affection w'ch I beare unto my sonn Nehemiah Grover alsoe for divers other good causes & considerations, me thereunto moving have given & granted & by these pr'sents due give sd Nehemiah Grover five acres of land or my house lott bounded on east and south with the roade waye to the mill & Drapers poynt as it is called, on west with land of John Dodge & on north with land of Andrew Elliott, alsoe twenty acres of land that lyes next the farme that was formerly Roger Hascalls upon the rockes bounded on east with comon, on north with land of Roger Hascal his children, on south with land of Edward Gale & John Stone alsoe five acres of land lying on east side of Beaver pond bounded on northwest with land of Mr. Thorndike; alsoe two acres & halfe of meddow lying neere Beaver pond bounded on the west with the smale farmes soe called, on east with land of Josiah Rootes viz his meddow as alsoe with meddow of Edward Bishop. *Signed*: Edmond Grover [mark]. *Date*: twenty third day of July in the year of one thousand six hundred seaventy & seaven. *Witnesses*: Exercise Conant; William Rayment. *Acknowledged*: ye 22nd day of Aprill 1678. *Recorded*: 19:July:1682.

JONATHAN PRINCE and MARY PRINCE to MATHEW ESTES – (6:324) Jonathan Price of Salem (cordwinder) sold to Mathew Estes of Pascattaque (marrenor) in consideration so ye sume of one hundred & one pounds to me in hand paid & secured to be paid by Mathew Estes from ye one & twentieth day of July next, all that my dwelling house & shop or shops thereunto adjoining & belonging with all outhouses & ground said housing stands upon & is thereto adjoining belonging thereunto as now it is fenced in & bounded which land contains about twenty pole or rod of ground & is that house and ground I lately bought of Thomas Maule scituate, lying & being in Salem being bounded westerly with land of Richard Croade, esterly with land of George Deane, northerly with land of

Thomas Robbins southerly with streete to have pr'misses from one & twentieth day of July next ensuing & further warrant against all persons laying claime from or under me or said Thomas Maule. *Signed*: Jonathan Prince; Mary Prince [mark]. *Release of Dower*: Mary wife do yield up dower. *Date*: twenty fifth day of May one thousand six hundred & eighty two. *Witnesses*: Hilliard Veren; Samuell Shattock senior. *Acknowledged*: 19:July:1682 by both. *Recorded*: 19:July:1682.

THOMAS CHADWELL to MATHEW FARRINGTON SEN'R – (6:328) Thomas Chadwell of Charlestowne (shipwright) sold to Mathew Farrington sen'r of Lynn (yeoman) for consideration of the sum of three pounds in money in hand paid, p'cell of land lying in Lynn usually caled by name of "Fox hills" they being two acres bounded with Lynn river upon northeast, upon southwest with lands of George Keaser & southeast with lands of Joseph Belknap, & northwest with sd Belknap lands. *Signed*: Thomas Chadwell. *Date*: fift of July one thousand six hundred & eighty one. *Witnesses*: John Fuller; Sarah Farrington. *Acknowledged*: June:23:1682. *Recorded*: 26:July:1682.

JOHN BACHELER and SARAH BACHELER to LOTT KILLUM – (6:330) John Bacheler of Wenham sold to Lott Killum of Wenham for and in consideration of land sold by aforesd Lott Killum to John Bacheler according to a bill of sale, all that his right in & to a p'cel of upland containing or being by estimation about thirty two acres, as alsoe two parcells of meddow being about eight acres, lying within limits of Salem being that land which I had of my father Goodell, the upland being bounded by John Pease his land east & north & by Isaack Goodell his land on the south & by the brooke on northwest: & aforesd meddow lyeth in two p'cells, the one being all that meddow betwixt Thomas Flint's bounds & aforesd upland, the other parcel being an acre & a halfe lying on the other side of brooke, bounded by Issack Goodell his meddow east & west & on the south upon comon. *Signed*: John Bacheler; Sarah Bacheler [mark]. *Release of Dower*: Sarah wife do consent. *Date*: 16th dayof the ninth month one thousand six hundred sixty & six. *Witnesses*: Mark Bachelor; Daniell Gott. After John & Sarah sign: I Robert Goodell acknowledge the abovesd upland & medow to be a free gift unto John Bacheler with his wife Sarah, my daughter, at her mariage & doe aprove of the sale as it is specified in this deed as witness by hand. *Signed*: Robert Goodell. *Acknowledged*: 7th November 1681. *Recorded*: 7:9 mo:1682.

RICHARD HOOD to MATHEW FARRINGTON JUNIOR – (6:332) Richard Hood of Lynn (husbandman) with the consent of Mary his now wife sold to Mathew Farrington Junior of Lynn (yeoman) for consideration of divers causes thereto moving especially in consideration of ye sume of fifty six pounds in current money, one dwelling house & all that p'cell of land scituate & lying in Lynn, sometime in possession of Anthony Newhall, deceased. viz: fower acres or two thirds of a six acre lott where the house standeth with orchard bounded westerly with lands of John Gillow, easterly with land of John Hathorne, northerly with land of Robert Potter senior, southerly with country highwaye that lyeth in mill streete, likewise fower acres of upland lying upon Hudson's hill that is to say one third of a six acre lott formerly in tenure of Anthony Newall deceased one piece which was formerly in tenure of John Gillow being two acres bounded northerly with highway by the fresh marsh, southerly with lands of Jonathan Hudson, easterly with lands of John Gillow, westerly with lands of John Newall Junior & covenant same is free from all incumbrances made or don by sd Richard Hood or Anthony Newall sometime of Lynn or John Gillow sometime of Lynn. *Signed*: Richard Hood [mark]. *Release of Dower*: Mary released dowryes 26th of July 1682. *Date*: seaventh day of July one thousand six hundred eight two. *Witnesses*: William Bassett; Samuell Cobbett. *Acknowledged*: 26th of July 1682. *Recorded*: 26:July 1682.

GRIFFEN EDWARDS, JOHN MILES and ANN MILES to JOHN BURRELL SENIOR – (6:336) Griffen Edwards of Boston (gent & aturney & adminstrator on behalfe of his mother in law Mrs. Ann Miles whoe is the reputed only heire surviving of Col John Humphryes Esq'r deceased & shee is the now wife of Mr. John Miles, minister of Swazsy a plantation in coloney of Plimouth) & Mr. John Miles & Mrs. Ann Miles sold to John Burrell senior of Lynn in consideration of one & twenty pounds & five shillings current money, a certain p'cell of meddow land lying & being in a certain meddow called Rumsey marsh belonging to the towne of Lynn aforesd containing four acres & a halfe by estimation, accounted the one halfe pt of nine acres soe accounted that did formerly belong & appertaine to Col. John Humphrys Esq., deceased butted & bounded by the marsh that doth or did formerly belong or appertaine to Wm Edmonds on westward & joyneth upon a creek comonly called Bennet's creek on northward & by the maine river that vessel pass to & froe in & paiteth between Lynn & Boston on southward & by marsh belonging to Benjamin Farr of Linn which he hath purchased on eastward & was the other halfe part of the nine acres aforesaid. *Signed*: Griffin Edwards; John Myles; Ann Myles. *Date*: eight day of October, one thousand six hundred eighty & one. *Witnesses*: William Bassett; Daniell Johnson. *Acknowledged*: 29th day of October 1681 by all three. *Recorded*: 26:July:1682.

ROBERT PRINCE to HENRY KENY – (6:339) Robert Prince of Salem with consent of my wife sold to Henry Keny of Salem for a valuable consideration to me in hand alredy paid, one p'cell of meddow ground, containing by estimation six acres lying & being scituate within township of Salem amongst the farmes and being bounded as followeth, viz: upon north east bordering upon upland & bounded with a great old tree upon southwest with an iland having an old tree upon it being between land of sd Henry Kenny & Corporall John Putnam, being bounded alsoe upon the southwest with a brooke runinge between land of sd Henry Kenny & John Putnam's meddow, & lastly being bounded upon southeast with meddow of sd Robert Prince & upon northwest with upland. *Signed*: Robert Prince. *Date*: nineteenth day of November in one thousand six hundred sixty & eight. *Witnesses*: John Horne; Edw. Norrice. *Acknowledged*: 14 mo.:10:1668 [sic]. *Recorded*: 26:July:1682.

JOHN LEACH JUNIOR and MARY LEACH to JOHN GREENE – (6:341) John Leach Junior of Salem & Mary, my wife sold to John Greene of Salem for consideration of ye sume of twenty pounds to be paid upon demand according to agreement, twelve acres of land scituate & being in township of Salem on west end of land of John Leach sen'r adjoyning to land of Joseph Herrick on southwest, & to a piece of comon next to Wenham on other side & to land of sd John Leach senior on all other quarters round, on the comon next Wenham the bound is a black oake & bounded with two stakes next sd Herrick's land & with one stake next land of sd John Leach senior. *Signed*: John Leach Junior; Mary Leach [mark]. *Date*: sixth day of September one thousand six hundred seventy five. *Witnesses*: John Swinerton; Mathew Woodwell. *Acknowledged*: 1:11 mo:1677 by John Leach & Mary did release dowery 1 September 1682. *Recorded*: 2:7 mo:1682.
Rec'd ninth day of October in year 1677 by me John Leach Junior of Salem the fill & just sum of twenty pounds mentioned within this written bill being the consideration & in full sattisfaction of & for all that twelve acres of land, now bargained & sold as is exspresed within this written bill bearing its date the 6th Day of September 1675.

JOHN LEACH and MARY LEACH to JOHN GREENE – (6:343) John Leach of Wenham (carpenter) and my wife Mary sold to John Greene of Salem (yeoman) in consideration of ten pounds, ten shillings to me in hand paid, a p'cell of land, upland & swamp, containing nine acres or there abouts scituate & lying in Wenham & is bounded easterly with land of me sd John Leach & with Wenham comon, southerly, with land of sd John Greene and with Wenham comon, westerly with land of sd John Greene, northerly with land of me sd John Leach & with land of aforesd Greene. *Signed*: John Leach; Mary Leach [mark]. *Date*: this last day of August in the yeare of our Lord one thousand six hundred eighty & two. *Witnesses*:

John Bennett Jr.; Robert Kitchin. ***Acknowledged***: this first day of September 1682 by John & Mary wife did release dowry. ***Recorded***: 2:September:1682.

JOSEPH ELWELL to JOHN TURNER – (6:345) Joseph Elwell of Cape Ann (fisherman) mortgaged to John Turner of Salem (marchant) in consideration of thirty pounds to my good content to me in hand paid, all that my dwelling house, messuage & out housing thereunto belonging, scituate & standing in Cape Ann aforesd, & alsoe land thereunto appertaining, being three pole & halfe in bredth & nine pole & halfe longe or in length bounded northerly on land of my father Osmond Dutch & southerly on land of William Ellerly: alsoe a piece of upland being by estimation fower acres scituate & lying in Cape Ann aforesd bounded westerly on land of John Collins, sotherly on land of William Ellery, northeasterly on said Ellery's land & sotherly on land of my father Osmond Dutch & alsoe two acres of Bastard marsh as it lyes according to the towne record scituate & lying in township of Cape Ann aforesd. It is heareby to be understood that in case abovesd Joseph Ellwell shall well & truly satisfy & pay or cause to be satisfied & paid above sd sum of thirty pounds in silver, fish or other pay to content of sd John Turner, at or within the space of one yeare & a day, accounting from the day of date heareof, then this above written instrument & every thing hearein contained is to be voide & none effect, otherwise to stand in full power force & vertue. ***Signed***: Joseph Elwell. ***Date***: twelfe day of December in ye yeare of our Lord one throusand six hundred seaventy & nine. ***Witnesses***: Nath: Wallis; Richard Croade. Acknowledged: Richard Croade made oath he saw Joseph Elwell sign 17 June 1681 & Nath: Wallis made oath 30 June 1681. Joseph Elwell p'sonally appeared & acknowledged within written instrument to be his free act & deed 5:March 1682/3. ***Recorded***: 18:August:1682.

WILLIAM PORR to MRS. ELIZABETH TURNER – (6:349) William Porr of Marblehead (fisherman) mortgaged to Mrs. Elizabeth Turner of Salem administratrix to estate of John Turner, deceased in consideration of ye sume of forty five pounds, two shillings & fower pence, my dwelling house and garden & all land thereunto appertaining, scituate & standing in Marblehead aforesd, being bounded with the townes land all round & nigh unto house of John Card & Richard Normans. It is hearby to be understood that if in case abovesaid William Porr shall well & truly satisfy & pay or cause to be satisfied & pd the abovesd sume of forty five pounds, two shillings & 4 d in silver fish or other pay to the content of sd Turner at or within space of five yeares that is to be understood pay nine pounds yearly from the day of the date heare of, then this above written instrument & everything hearein contained is to be voide & of none effect, otherwise to stand in full force & vertue. *Signed*: William Porr [mark]. *Date*: elventh of March in ye year of our Lord one thousand six hundred eighty one. *Witnesses*: John Barton; William Andrew. *Acknowledged*: 18:of August:1682 John Barton & William Andrew took oath they saw William Porr sett his hand ot this instrument. *Recorded*: 18:August:1682.

BRIDGETT OLIVER to DANIEL EPES – (6:352) Bridgett Oliver relict & administratrix of Thomas Oliver of Salem late deceased sold to Daniel Epes of Salem (scoolemaster) for consideration of thirty five shillings in hand paid as alsoe of new board fence of about eight poles in length and five foot high, which sd Epes hath at his own charg caused to be sett up, & is bound to mainetaine betwixt sd Epes & Oliver, so long as shee shall lawfully possess what she now injoyes, which fence viz: boards, posts, railes, & setting up, together with tenn shillings in money & other considerable expense & cost which sd Epes hath beene at for sd Oliver's use, amounting in all to thirty five shillings which added to the former makes up the full & just sum of three pounds ten shillings: I sd Oliver have with consent of Selectment of Salem whoe have underneath subscribed in order to the further payment of debts which estate of Thomas Oliver is liable to pay & alsoe for the pr'sent supply of my owne necessityes as by order of court held at Salem 1680, a smale p'cel of land which husband dyed lawfully possessed containing neere two poles or rods scituate in Salem towne bounded by streete on west by sd Olivers land on south by sd Epes on east & north. *Signed*: Bridgett Oliver [mark]. *Date*: 14 June 1681. *Witnesses*: John Hathorne; William Andrews. *Acknowledged*: 14 June 1681. *Recorded*: 5:August:1682.
Bridgett Oliver having desired advice from the Selectmen of Salem for the selling of a smale p'cell of land about two poles on back side of her house for the relieving of her necessity in order to her pr'sent supply hath advice granted from Selectmen of Salem to Bridgett Oliver for the sale of the land aforesd unto Mr. Daniell Epes scoolemaster 9th May:81.
This ia a true coppy taken out of Salem records, p. John Hathorne, Recorder to the Selectmen.

EDMOND BATTER to DANIELL EPES – (6:355) Edmond Batter of Salem (marchant) sold to Daniell Epes of Salem (scoolemaster) for consideration of ten pounds in hand paid, certaine smale tract of land containing twelve rods scituate in towne of Salem neere scoole house bounded with land of Mr. Zarobabell Endecott on north & east, the house and land of Thomas Oliver on south & streete on west. *Signed*: Edmond Batter. *Date*: 18 Aprill 1679. *Witnesses*: possession given by turfe & twigg in part for whole – Joseph Horne; Benjamin Horne. *Acknowledged*: by Joseph Horne and Benjamin Horne 26:7 mo:1682. *Recorded*: 5:6 mo:1682.

SAMUELL BENNETT to JOHN HATHORNE – (6:357) Samuell Bennett of Rumney marsh sold to John Hathorne of Lynn for valuable consideration in hand received, one p'cell of upland lying in Lynn containing by estimation five acres beinge formerly in possession of Edw'd Burcham of Lynn lying between the frash marsh & Farrington's plaine bounded northerly upon land of John Newhall Jun'r & sotherly upon a lott of land of Robt. Mansfeild butting easterly upon a smale brooke that runeth into aforesd fresh marsh & westerly upon tenn acre lotts. *Signed*: Samuell Bennett. *Date*: 17 February 1670. *Witnesses*: Richard George [mark]; Priscilla Shoane [mark]. *Acknowledged*: 16:1 mo:76:7. *Recorded*: no date.

CHRISTOPHER LATTAMORE to ROBERT HOOPER – (6:359) Christopher Lattamore of Marblehead (vintner) and wife Mary sold to Robert Hooper of Marblehead (planter) for consideration of twenty shillings in hand paid, p'cell of land next adjoining dwelling house of said Robert Hooper at the south end and back side being his wood yard & runing from sd end aboute sixteene foot in length to our owne stone wale & from back side of his house about twelve foot to the hill ward in bredth all along his house & on ward till it come to the stone wale again above as now fenced & inclosed. *Signed*: Christopher Lattamore [mark]. *Date*: 30 December 1680. *Witnesses*: Samuell Cheever; William Hines. *Acknowledged*: 20 March 1681:2. *Recorded*: 5:6 mo:1682.

EDWARD HOLEMAN to ROBERT HOOPER – (6:360) Edward Holeman of Marblehead (cooper) & Richard wife [sic] sold to Robert Hooper of Marblehead (planter) for consideration of twenty shillings in hand paid, p'cell of land where on house of said Robert Hooper stands lying before our doare being about thirty eight foot in length & eighteene foot in bredth at Marblehead. *Signed*: Edward Holemen [mark]; Richard Holeman [mark]. *Date*: 30 December 1680. *Witnesses*: Phillip Brimblecorne [mark]; Walter Addams [mark]. *Acknowledged*: 20 March 1681:2 by Edward and Richard. *Recorded*: 5:6 mo:1682.

ZAROBABELL ENDECOTT and JOHN ENDECOTT to DANIELL EPPS – (6:362) Zarobabell Endecott of Salem with sonn John Endecott of Salem (gent.) sold to Daniell Epps of Salem (scoolemaster) for consideration of fifteene pounds in hand paid, a considerable p'cell of land containing about three or fower score poles or rods in Salem towne as it lyes bounded by the street viz: main streete on west viz: eight foot & a halfe fronting that streete & soe to runn upon a straite line to end of sd Endecott's land & soe bounded on north with land of sd Endecott soe as to make up sd Epes his land of an equall breadeth on both ends viz: fower poles & halfe broad bounded on east by land of Mr. William Brown's once belonging to sd Endecott in bredth about fower poles & a halfe bounded on south with land of John Priest & land of Bridgett Oliver till it comes againe to maine streete. *Signed*: Zerobabell Endecott; John Endecott. *Date*: 20 June 1681. *Witnesses*: John Hathorne; John Croade. *Acknowledged*: 20 June 1681 by Zerobabell Endecott & John Endecott & Elizabeth wife of Zerobabell consented and gave up thirds. *Recorded*: 5 August 1682.

MATHEW DOVE and HANNAH DOVE to RICHARD HARRIS – (6:365) Mathew Dove of Salem (laborer) sold to Mr. Richard Harris of Salem (marrenor) for consideration of a valuable sum of money in hand paid, small quantity of land being thirteene pole lying in towne of Salem upon which dwelling house of Richard Harris standeth which land is in bredth two pole & eighteene inches north & south and east & west six pole six foot and is bounded on south with land of Jonathan Eger & west highwaye or streete on east with Goodman Meachum his land. *Signed*: Mathew Dove; Hannah Dove [mark]. *Date*: 27 April 1680. *Witnesses*: Frances Neale; Richard Ingersoll. *Acknowledged*: Hannah Dove wife to Mathew Dove doe give consent and Mathew Dowe acknowledged and Hannah wife gave up right of dowry 8 August 1682. *Recorded*: 8:6 mo:1682.
It is further agreed & is true intent and Mathew Dove doe grant & sett over unto Richard Harris three foot of ground in bredth added on north side of pr'misses throughout from lane of highwaye to land of Isaac Meachum which was omitted in the first draft of this bill of sale but is intended & included in same. *Signed*: Mathew Dove. Signed sealed & delivered by sd Mathew Dove on this back side for want of roome on other side relating to memorandum in margent. *Witnesses*: Hilliard Veren; Robert Fuller.

JOHN PEASE JUN'R and MARGARETT PEASE to JOHN MARSHALL – (6:368) John Pease Jun'r of Salem (joyner) sold to John Marshall of Salem (marchant) for consideration of fifty two pounds in hand paid, my dwelling house with about halfe acre of ground upon which sd house is standing together with a shop scituate in township of Salem bounded westerly with land formerly William Robinsons late deceased eastward by highwaye and northerly by land of John Pease sen'r alsoe three acres of ground in north feild belonging to Salem bounded easterly and partly northerly upon land formerly Thomas Spooners deceased & by the land of John Pease sen'r north south & westerly. *Signed*: John Pease Jun'r; Margarett Pease [mark]. *Release of Dower*: Margarett wife doe yield dower. *Date*: 22 August 1682. *Witnesses*: Hilliard Veren; John Horne. *Acknowledged*: 22 August 1682 by John and Margarett and Margarett yielded right of dowry. *Recorded*: 22:August:1682.

SAMUELL MORGAINE and ELIZABETH MORGAINE to AMBROSSE GALE – (6:371) Samuell Morgaine of Marblehead (cooper) with consent of wife sold to Ambrosse Gale of Marblehead for consideration of sixty pounds that is to say thirty pounds in silver and thirty in goods at money price in hand, one new house standing in Marblehead adjoyning of one side to John Chin's land & other side joyning close home to sd Morgaine's old dwelling house as alsoe the ground thereto belonging, that is to say, the ground new house stands upon as alsoe back side ground beginning from the corner of lento next to Samuell Morgain's end of his lento of his dwelling house soe to range for the ground of the back side from the sd corner of Morgain's lento of his old dwelling house downe along close to the lower aple tree, where sd Ambrose Gale marked with his knife, upon a line & from the tree straite upon a line to a rock that stands in the lower fence towards the northeast where there is a stake drove downe. *Signed*: Samuell Morgan; Elizabeth Morgan [mark]. *Release of Dower*: Elizabeth wife doe give up dower. *Date*: 22 August 1681. *Witnesses*: Eleazar Ingolls; Edm. Hunphryes. *Acknowledged*: 23 August 1682 by Samuell Morgan and wife. *Recorded*: 23:August:1682.

SAMUELL MORGAN and ELIZABETH MORGAN to AMBROSS GALE – (6:374) Samuell Morgan of Beverly (planter) and Elizabeth wife sold to Ambross Gale of Marblehead (marchant) for consideration of seaventy pounds in hand paid, tract of land in Marblehead containing in the front about forty five foot next the streete & about twenty in bredth on back side next meddow of Nathaniell Walton & in length about four pole bounded with lands of Mathew Clearke on easterne side & lands of Ambross Gale on westerne side & with streete & aforesd meddow on other sides, together with dwelling house standing thereon, as alsoe the frute trees & fences & a cowes commonage appropriated to sd house. *Signed*: Samuell Morgan; Elizabeth Morgan [mark]. *Date*: _ ___ 1682. *Witnesses*: John Atwater; Thomas Hayres. *Acknowledged*: 23 August 1682 by Samuell and Elizabeth. *Recorded*: 23:August:1682.

ROBERT HOOPER and ELIZABETH HOOPER to WILLIAM HEWET – (6:376) Robert Hooper of Marblehead (planter) & Elizabeth wife sold to William Hewet of Marblehead (marrenor) for consideration of thirty pounds sterling fifteene pounds whereof being alredy in hand paid & the remainder secured to be paid by a bill given under sd Hewet's hand, all that dwelling house we live in standing on hill neere Mr. Lattamore, together with ground house stands upon, the ground being lately purchased of Edward Holeman as by deed from him will appeere: & alsoe the wood yard adjoyning to house on back side containing two or three pole & fenced in with stone wale alsoe one cowes comonage appropriated to sd house together with tract of land on other side of the highwaye before the doare being an orchard & garden by estimation quarter of an acre lying betweene and bounded with lands of Roger Russell & Christopher Lattamore's fish yard formerly bought of him from the day of death of sd Robert Hooper & Elizabeth wife & not before. *Signed*: Robert Hooper [mark]; Elizabeth Hooper [mark]. *Date*: 23 September 1681. *Witnesses*: Samuell Cheever; Edward Holeman [mark]. *Acknowledged*: by Robert Hooper 2 September 1682 and Elizabeth Hooper acknowledged and consent 25 August 1682. *Recorded*: 2:September:1682.

SAMUELL SMITH to THOMAS SMITH – (6:379) Samuell Smith of Boston (marenor) sold to brother Thomas Smith of Boston (mariner) for consideration of eighty pounds in currant money in hand paid, all that my part share in and unto a certaine farme or tract of land lying within township of Wenham now in tenure & occupation of Alexander Maxee & was sometime the estate of our grandfather Samuell Smith formerly of Wenham tornner deceased and by him left unto oure father Thomas Smith marrenour long since deceased & now of right belonging unto sd brother Thomas & myselfe however butted and bounded all my estate right & title in & unto all lands both arable pasture & woodland, meadow, marsh: that sd Thomas Smith shall have my whole right whatsoever (be it one third part) in & unto sd farme. *Signed*: Samuell Smith. *Date*: 6 October 1679. *Witnesses*: Joseph Brisco [mark]; Isa Addington. *Acknowledged*: 6 October 1679. *Recorded*: 4:September:1682.

GEORGE KEASER to THOMAS MOULD & MARY MOULD – (6:382) George Keaser of Salem (tanner) have given & granted & doe give grant & confirme to Thomas Mould & Mary his wife & to their heirs of their body lawfully begotten between them for divers good causes especially good will & natural affection unto son in law Thomas Mould & daughter Mary his wife & upon theire mariage together, twelve acres of marsh lying in township of Lynn in first divission of Rumney marsh & is bounded easterly with two acres of marsh belonging to aforesaid George Keaser being part of fourteene acres formerly bought of John Poole & Robert Driver westerly with the marsh of John Gillow butting easterly upon the last division & northerly upon upland of Allen Bread sen'r, alsoe a parcell of upland ground, part of that ground where my dwelling house standeth, to the uper end northward of my land there adjoining to my sd house, the sd p'cell containing thirty rod or pole of ground & is bounded northerly p'tly with land of Mr. William Browne Jun'r & p'tly with land of Joseph Porter easterly with land of Capt. Richard More sotherly with land of sd George Keaser & westerly with lane or highwaye that goes downe to the south river, only upon this condition that sd Thomas Mold or Mary his wife or any of theire heires lawfully begotten as aforesd shall not at any time heareafter sell, alienate, makeover, sett to lease or lett for terme of life the granted pr'misses or any part thereof but same shall alwaies be & firmly remaine to said Thomas & Mary & theire heires lawfully begotten betweene them & their successors forever. *Signed*: George Keaser. *Date*: 16:1677:8. *Witnesses*: Timothy Lindall; Elizur Keaser. *Acknowledged*: 21 August 1682. *Recorded*: 4:September 1682.

RICHARD BRACKENBURY to JOHN BRACKENBURY – (6:385) Richard Brackenbury of Beverly sold to John Brackenbury of Boston (marrenor) for consideration of valuable sume of money alredy in hand paid, a certaine p'cell of upland & meddow ground lying in township of Beverly containing eighteene acres bounded on south west by the land of Paule Thornedike northwest by contry roade northeast towne highwaye leading to Macrell Cove and south easterly by river or sea: alsoe an other p'cell of upland ground in towne of Beverly being bounded on southwest by land of Paule Thornedike southeasterly by towne highwaye northeasterly by red oake tree marked & soe to run on a line unto a walnutt tree marked standing in north corner of sd land & northwest on or by land of Thomas Woodbery. *Signed*: Richard Brackenbury [mark]. *Date*: 1 September 1682. *Witnesses*: John Hale; Samuell Hardie. *Acknowledged*: 9 September 1682. *Recorded*: 9 September 1682.

RICHARD BRACKENBURY to JOHN PATCH SEN'R – (6:388) Richard Brackenbury of Beverly (yeoman) sold to John Patch sen'r of Beverly (yeoman) for consideration of valuable sum of money in hand, a certaine p'cell of upland ground in township of Beverly bounded on southwest by land of John Brackenbury on north west by fence p'taining to Tho. Woodberry on north east by brooke & on south east by land of Jonathan Boyles: alsoe an other p'cell of upland ground in township of Beverly containing five acres being bounded southwesterly by town way leading to Macrel Cove on norwest by highwaye and by land of Paule Thornedike southeasterly by sd John Patch & northeasterly by land of John Lovett sen'r. *Signed*: Richard Brakenbury [mark]. *Date*: 1 September 1682. *Witnesses*: John Hale; Samuell Hardie. *Acknowledged*: 9 September 1682. *Recorded*: 9th:September:1682.

On the margin: In the original record of which this is a copy the parcel of land here last described is the first described & viceversa.

MARY DARLING to THOMAS MAULE – (6:390) Whereas the within named Mary Darling did make within deed of sale to sd Thomas Maule for sd halfe acre of land with her father John Darling's consent since which time sd Mary being marryed to Benjamin Fuller of Salem (bricklayer) I sd Benjamin Fuller now husband of sd Mary with consent of my said wife for divers good & lawfull considerations & having a desire that the sale of sd land may be confirmed & secured from any after claime from me or my heirs or assigns or any other by from or under me doe give up all my right & interest in within bargained pr'misses unto sd Thomas Maule freely consenting to & allowing of sd Mary my wives act & deed therein. *Signed*: Benjamin Fuller. *Date*: 14:September 1682. *Witnesses*: Hilliard Verin; Jeremiah Neale. *Acknowledged*: 14:7 mo:1682. *Recorded*: 14:7 mo:1682.

This above written was an indorsement on back side of Mary Darling's bill of sale & belongs thereto which is recorded in Book 5th:foll:102.

MOSES MAVERICK and EUNICE MAVERICK to AMBROSS GALE – (6:391) Moses Maverick of Marblehead (marchant) with free consent of wife Eunice sold to Ambross Gale of Marblehead (fisherman) for consideration of thirty six pounds in hand paid, all remainder of land formerly unsold being two acres by estimation which was formerly & is now in possession & occupation of sd Gale for fishery & adjoynes to land of John Merriott & abutts upon the harbour excepting that tract of land whereon the fort is build & a highwaye thereto upon any occasion, as alsoe excepting & reserving the pr'vilidge of keeping a catch or other fishing vessell & convenient roome for making sd fish, to be injoyed by myselfe, my heires or assignes forever. *Signed*: Moses Maverick; Eunice Maverick. *Date*: 15 Aprill 1674. *Witnesses*: & possession given Samuell Cheever; Edward Woodman. *Acknowledged*: 16:3 mo:1674 & Eunice yielded thirds. *Recorded*: 19th:7 mo:1682.

JOHN ELETHORPE to RICHARD NEVERS – (6:393) John Elethorpe of Manchester sold to Richard Nevers of Gloster for consideration of forty pounds in hand paid, a certaine tract or p'cell of land in township of Bradford containing fower score and sixteene acres bounded on north by land of Widdow Mighill, John Waston, Robert Heseltine & part against John Heseltines land: being the head of theire Merrimak devission of land, on east butting upon Johnsons pond on south & west by land undivided, the bounds by the pond southeast being a white oake marked JE the south west corner being bounded with a white oake with same marke, runing at the west end by a red oake tree neere about the middle bredth marked on south & north side to the end of John Heseltine's land. *Signed*: John Elethorpe. *Date*: 12 October 1682. *Witnesses*: Sam: Hardie; Mary Hardie. *Acknowledged*: 12 October 1682. *Recorded*: 12: October ____.

MOSES MAVERICK and EUNICE MAVERICK to AMBROSE GALE – (6:395) Mr. Moses Maverick of Marblehead (marchant) with free consent of Eunice wife sold to Ambrose Gale of Marblehead (fisherman) for consideration of tenn pounds ten shillings whereof eight pounds was in silver & other fifty shillings in goods at price currant which money hath beene well & truly paid, one p'cel of land, one acre as now layd out in Marblehead & adjoyning to Samuell Sandy to south west & to sd Ambrose Gales fence towards south east, running down toward the north east toward sd Maverick's island. *Signed*: Moses Maverick; Eunice Maverick. *Release of Dower*: Eunice wife doth yield up right of dowry. *Date*: 15 March 1672:3. *Witnesses*: Samuell Ward; Thaddeus Riddan. *Acknowledged*: 16 3 mo:1674 & Eunice wife yielded thirds. *Recorded*: 19:7 mo:1682.

HARLACKENDINE SYMONDS to DANIELL EPPS – (6:397) Harlackendine Symonds of Ipswich (gent.) sold to Daniell Epps of Salem (scoolemaster) for consideration of valuable sume of money in hand paid, a certaine tract of land lying on both sides of Lamparell river, belonging partly to Dover & p'tly to Exetor in New Hampshire containing about three hundred acres comonly caled Island Falls lying adjacent to & bounded p'tly by the lands of Mr. William Symonds or his heires of Robert Wadley & Jonathan Thing with utensills for a mill according to my fathers will, also all my tract of land in New London in Conetticot colloney which I bought of Mrs. Margarett Lake containing three hundred acres bounded easterly by land of Major Palmer & John Beebe's northerly by the comon about fower miles from the meeting house together with all my other lands & rights at New London; alsoe all my estate at Ipswich. *Signed*: Harlackendine Symonds. *Date*: 25 September 1682. *Witnesses*: Robert Kitchin; Joseph Fowler. *Acknowledged*: 25 September 1682. *Recorded*: 26:September:1682.

HENRY BARTHOLMEW to SARAH BARTHOLMEW – (6:399) Henry Bartholmew Sen'r of Boston have given granted & passed over unto my daughter Sarah Bartholmew, all my right & title of that farme that I bought of Allexander Lillington caled James his farme & is now lett unto & in possession of Nathaniell Cauell to be injoyed & possessed by her at her day of marriage & thence forth forever: alsoe all such sum or sums that are due & paiable to me from sd Cauell for rent or that are due & payable to me from sd Cauill upon my & all acts whatsoever & doe heareby declare & order that at aforesd time all bills of sale or conveyances in any possession be delivered to her unto whome of right they doe belong & alsoe the covenant signed by the said Cauvill & myselfe by which he doth hold the sd farme of me & all such accounts out of my booke by which it may be made appeere what is justly due & paiable unto me and that this deed of guift may be fully ratified & confirmed to sd daughter. *Signed*: Henry Batholmew. *Date*: 7 of 7th month 1681. *Witnesses*: Mammassett Marstone; George Edwards. *Acknowledged*: 7 September 1681. *Recorded*: 26:7 mo:1682.

ELIZABETH MANNING, THOMAS WALTER and MARY GRAYE to LOTT GOURDING – (6:400) Thomas Walter & Mary Graye of Salem sold to Lott Gourding of Bostone (manneror) in consideration of eighty two pounds ten shillings in hand paid have sold all that our house & land lying in Salem which was formerly the house & land of our father Robert Gray late of Salem deceased & since the house & land of Capt. Nicholas Manning of Salem & by him mortgaged to Mr. John Browne & Mr. Henry Bartholmew overseers & feoffees in trust for the children of sd Robert Graye & by them recovered from sd Manning in our right: which house & land is butted & bounded & dementioned according as is exspressed in sd mortgage which bears date fourteenth March 1664 & give up all our right & interest that we or either of us have in that part of a p'cell of upland & medow in Salem next unto land of Mr. John Hathorne caled the broade field: being about five acres & which was ingaged for the securing of our interest.

Also Elizabeth Manning in consideration of twenty five pounds in hand paid relinquish right in or unto the house & land abovementioned or that part of the broade feild aforesaid or any other part of estate of sd husband Nicholas Maning which I may have by right of dower. *Signed*: Elizabeth Manning [mark] Mary Graye [mark]; Thomas Walter. *Date*: 29 September 1681. *Witnesses*: & possession of house & land given & received John Browne; Samuell Gardner sen'r. Witness to signing of Thomas Walter: Hilliard Veren; J. Barton. *Acknowledged*: 1 October 1681 by Elizabeth Maning and Mary Graye; 21:9 mo:1682 by Thomas Walter. *Recorded*: 29:7 mo:1682.

RESOLVED WHITE and ABIGAIL WHITE to WILLIAM LORD JUN'R – (6:403) Resolved White of Salem and Abigail wife & executrix of will of William Lord deceased sold to William Lord Jun'r for divers good causes especially love & naturall affection to William Lord Jun'r kinsman to sd William Lord deceased & sonn of William Lord sen'r now surviving & more especially in order to the fulfiling of will of sd William Lord deceased have given sd William Lord Jun'r that dwelling house sd William Lord sen'r his father lives in with the ground it stands upon adjoining to south end of sd house containing about fower or five rod or more of ground & bounded, to begin a little distance of the northeast corner of the house at the gate post that is Samuell Graies bounds there & from thence to run sotherly to southwest corner of kerb of well upon a strait line

& from thence to runn upon a strait line as the well post stands to within three foot of the back side of the house William Godsoe have a pt of & soe to runn westerly three foot distance of back side of house to ground of Wm. Godsoe & on west side the grounds of sd Godsoe is bounds till it come to dwelling house by these presents given & granted & soe runns east side of sd house to sd gate post the first bounds & soe running is bounded easterly with land of Samuel Gray & sotherly with three foot of ground to be left on back side of housing which is p'tly Wm. Godsoe's: alsoe one acre of bastard marsh pt of that fower acres comonly knowne to be land sd William Lord dyed possest of which sd acre now given & granted is to be the westermost end of it & to take in whole bredth of it at that westerly end next land that was Widdow Spooners until it make up a full acre which is partly bounded viz: westerly & sotherly with land of sd Spooners northerly with the upland of Capt. John Corwin formerly bought of Nicholas Manning, William Lord Jun'r paying yearly unto Resolved White or Abigaile White fifty shillings to be paid quarterly twelve shillings six pence a quarter during terme of Abigaile White's naturall life; also to have sd acre of meddow after the decease of sd Abigail White with liberty to draw water at the well also it is covenanted sd William Lord Jun'r shal suffer Wm. Godsoe to com through his ground from three foot to be left on back side of his house direct to the well to draw water. *Signed*: Resolved White; Abigaile White [mark]. *Date*: 17 February 1670/80. *Witnesses*: Hilliard Veren sen'r; Henry Higgenson. *Acknowledged*: 29:10 mo:1680 by both. *Recorded*: 29:7 mo:1682.

ROBERT GOODELL AND MARGARETT GOODELL to ELIZABETH BENNETT – (6:407) Robert Goodell of Salem (husbandman) sold to Elizabeth now wife of Henry Bennett & to the heires lawfully begotten in wedlock of body of sd daughter Elizabeth for divers good causes alsoe for a valuable sume pd by daughter Elizabeth & her former husband John Smith deceased but more especially in consideration of my former promise & ingagement & that naturall affection unto sd daughter Elizabeth & her children, certaine p'cell of land caled tenn acres yet containing about fifteene acres & is part of that land not far form my dwelling house: the sd p'cell of land is bounded with my meddow easterly & northerly & with a swamp of mine that lyeth betwixt house of sd Elizabeth & house of my sonn Isaacke Goodell also all timber woods underwoods growing & lying upon sd swamp or sd land last above mentioned with free egress & regress to fetch wood & timber off swamp land from time to time for my sd daughter or her heirs lawfully begotten as aforesd notwithstanding any colatteral bargaine with my son Isaack for sd swamp alwaies excepting the wood & timber for the use of sd daughter & heirs: also six acres of land adjoyning to forementioned tenn acres & lying betweene the same & land of sd Robert Goodell & a brooke that runs into the meddow & the land of Thomas Flint; alsoe two acres of meddow lying at great river soe caled & is adjoyning to two acres of meddow now of Zachariah Goodell. *Signed*: Robert Goodell; Margarett Goodell [mark]. *Date*: 14 August 1678. *Witnesses*: Henry Skerry sen'r; Anthony Needham [mark]. *Acknowledged*: 14:6 mo:1678. *Recorded*: 29:7 mo:1682.

LOTT GOURDING and ELIZABETH GOURDING to JOHN BARTON – (6:410) Lott Gourding of Boston (marrenor) sold to John Barton of Salem (cherurgeon) for consideration one hundred ten pounds in hand paid, my dwelling house with a shop & the ground the sd housing stands upon & is adjoyning & belonging to sd house containing yard garden & oarchard, it being that house & land that was formerly Nicolas Manning's in Salem the sd p'cell of land containing by estimation five score & ten rod or pole of ground or neere thereabouts as it now lyes bounded viz: at the front eastward next streete or lane beginning at the post that is the bound betweene bargained pr'misses & Robert Gray's land to run upon a strait line in the front to corner bounds of Wm. Browne Esq. ground which is fower pole & two inches neerest & from that southeasterly bounds next the streete to runn westerly upon a strait line five pole & eight foot neerest & from thence turning with an elboe & running northerly one pole & fower foot & halfe & from thence turning againe & runing westerly upon a strait line thirteene pole & four foot neerest & from thence runing then northerly to the sother side of the land formerly Tho. Olivers deceased being on that northerly line eight pole & nine foot & halfe & from thence to runn easterly nine pole & eight foot & from thence sotherly five pole & six inches & from thence to run easterly upon a straite line to first bounds mentioned betweene Robert Gray's & the pr'misses which last easterly line is nine pole & three foot neerest, the fences as they stand standing as the bounds for the most pt, the sd land as the dementions are thereof as aforesd stands bounded all on the south side p'tly by land or orchard of Wm. Browne Esq. & p'tly by ground & outhousing of Mr. John Gedney & westerly by oarchard of sd John Gedney & then on north as first easterly line runs by land of John Preist & its next turning line sotherly it buts easterly against the end of Samuel Beadle's ground & alsoe Robert Gray's ground & northerly from thence to the streete by same land of Robert Graye & easterly by sd highwaye or streete. *Signed*: Lott Gourding; Elizabeth Gourding. *Release of Dower*: wife Elizabeth yield dower. *Date*: 16 October 1682. *Witnesses*: with seizing & possession of pr'misses given John Browne; Hilliard Veren. *Acknowledged*: 16 October 1682 & wife Elizabeth consented & yielded thirds. *Recorded*: 17:8 mo:1682.

SAMUELL VERRY and NATHANIELL CARRELL (6:414) The testimony of Samuell Verry sen'r aged about sixty fower yeares & Nathaniell Carrell aged about forty fower yeares saith y^t to theire certaine knowledg Thomas James claimed held injoyed & possessed a farm of about one hundred & forty acres of upland besides meddow lying & adjoyning unto the farme of Mr. Frances Johnson's on pt of the one side & Mr. Edmond Batter on other side with the butts, brooke on Brookesbee on the sotherly end or southeast for more then thirty yeares past viz: from June 1652 & before untill this pr'sent time without being dispossessed by any p'son or p'sons by any claime of theirs or pr'tence of claime thereto & is bounded as followeth, beginning with the fence as it now stands by the brooke betweene Mr. Frances Johnson his farme & aforesd farme of Thomas James unto a black cake stump upon the topp of the hill above the now dwelling house upon sd farme of Thomas James & is by the fence of Robert Folletts & from thence to a heape of stones where stood a blacke oak tree formerly which was a bound tree betweene Mr. William Browne John Smale & Thomas James & from that heape of stones to the stump of a white oak tree which the ship carpenters cutt downe & by which is now marked a smale birch tree & soe to a black oake tree that stands a litle within Wm Shaw's fence, from thence to a white oake tree that stands betweene the land that was formerly Mr. Batter's & Thomas James' & soe from thence to a large white oake tree standing betweene the bounds of aforesd farme & from thence to a place y^t belongs to Samuel Verry at aforesd Brookeby which was caled by name of Asses plot & soe upwards as the brook runns to first named bounds.
Samuell Verry & Nathaniell Carrell tooke their oath to the testimony this 2^d October 1682 before Wm Browne Assistant. Recorded: 26:8 mo:1682.

JOHN ALFORD and CHARITY ALFORD to NATHANIELL PICKMAN – (6:416) John Alford of Salem (fisherman) & Charity my wife sold to Nathanielll Pickman of Salem (house carpenter) for divers good considerations especially a valuable sume in hand paid by father in law Nath'll Pickman, all right we have in any pt or p'cell of lands formerly of Anthony Dike father of said Charity deceased. *Signed*: John Alford [mark]; Charity Alford [mark]. *Date*: 31 October 1682. *Witnesses*: Hiliard Veren; Margarett Rich. *Acknowledged*: 1 November 1682 by both. *Recorded*: first November 1682.

ROBERT GLANFEILD and LIDIA GLANFEILD to WILLIAM HIRST – (6:417) Robert Glanfeild of Salem (marenor) with consent of Liddea wife sold to William Hirst of Salem (marchant) for consideration sixty five pounds in hand paid, a certaine house & ground it being the house I now live in with all ground that house stands upon with all ground adjoyning & belonging there unto being in Salem bounded westerly & northerly with the land of John Browne comonly caled Elder Brown sotherly with a p'cell of ground of John Browne Jun'r deceased formerly lying as vacant land & by a lane easterly that runs from the maine streete to south river side and if Robert Glanfeild pay unto William Hirst the full sume of sixty five pounds in money with interest after the rate of eight percent p'annum at or before first day November 1684 then this bargaine & sale to be voyde & of none efect butt if default of paiment shal happen to be made in pt or whole then to stand & remaine in full power. *Signed*: Robert Glanfeild; Lidia Glanfeild. *Date*: 25 October 1682. *Witnesses*: Edward Grove; George Addams. *Acknowledged*: 27 October:1682 by both. *Recorded*: 27:October:1682.

THOMAS GRAVES and HANAH GRAVES to WILLIAM SMITH – (6:420) Thomas Graves of Lynn (husbandman) sold to William Smith of Lynn (husbandman) for consideration of twenty pounds sterling in hand paid, a certain p'cell of land containing fower acres w'ch is pt of his house lott, as alsoe his orchard containing three quarters of one acre adjoyning to aforesd fower acres: the fower acres of land together with the orchard is bounded eastwardly northerly & sotherly upon land of sd Thomas Graves & westwardly with land of Robert Rand & the towne comon together with his dwelling house & corn house standing upon sd land but as for comon liberties & pr'vilidges this is to be understood that sd Thomas hath sold unto sd William a proportionable part thereof only for fower acres reserving the rest unto the remaining part of his house lott aforesd by way of an equall proportion acre for acre with aforesd fower acres which sd Thomas Graves have sold unto sd William Smith. *Signed*: Thomas Graves [mark]; Hanah Graves [mark]. *Release of Dower*: with consent of Hannah wife in refference to the surrendering up her thirds. *Date*: 1 March 1666. *Witnesses*: Robert Rand [mark]; Andrew Mansfeild. *Acknowledged*: 13 November 1682. *Recorded*: 13:9 mo:1682.

JOHN PEASE SEN'R to HUGH PASCO – (6:423) John Pease sen'r late of Salem now of Enfeild in Hampsheere Massachusetts sold to Hugh Pasco of Salem (marrenor) for consideration ninety pounds sterling in hand paid or secured to be paid, one acre & halfe of land with a dwelling house standing thereupon with the barne & all the out housing fences & appurtenances thereto belonging in Salem & is bounded with the lane or highwaye easterly & westerly by land of John Robinson northerly by land of Robert Pease sen'r & sotherly land of John Marshall formerly of John Pease Jr. alsoe about six acres of upland lying on easterly side of aforesd highwaye & is bounded with said waye westerly land of Mr. Samuell Gardner sotherly land of Josiah Sothwick easterly & with land p'tly of

Samuell Eborne sen'r & p'tly land of William Osbourne northerly alsoe the barne standing thereupon alsoe one p'cell more of upland & meddow containing by estimation seaven or eight acres lying in north feild soe caled belonging to Salem bounded by land p'tly of Sam'll Gardner & p'tly land of Samuell Gaskin in sotherly land of John Bullock westerly land of Caleb Buffum northerly & land of John Marshall most part & some land of Robert Stone a small part on easterly side or end. *Signed*: John Pease [mark]. *Date*: 13 November 1682. *Witnesses*: Hilliard Veren; Robert Pease sen'r [mark]. *Acknowledged*: 14 November 1682. *Recorded*: 14:9 mo:1682.

JOHN BACHELOR to JOHN CRESY – (6:426) John Bachelor of Salem (yeoman) sold to John Cresy of Salem (tailer) for consideration of valuable sume of money in hand paid, a certaine p'cell of land containing twelve acres in township of Salem & is bounded easterly by lands of Abraham Warren & John Greene there to run from a stake in the brooke by sd Greene's dwelling house unto a white oake tree which is the head bound of sd Warren's land soe to runn on a line southwesterly from sd white oake unto a walnut bush & heape of stones about it being a corner bounds at that place & soe to runn southeasterly from thence to stake by swamp side being the corner bounds at that place alwaies provided that if said Cresy shall sell or dispose of said land at any time hearafter then sd John Bacheler shall have first proffer or refusal thereof upon reasonable term paying for it as it shall be adjudged to be worth by other men. *Signed*: John Bacheler. *Date*: 16 January 1681. *Witnesses*: John Carrill; Samuell Hardie. *Acknowledged*: 23 August 1682 & wife Mary did release right of dowry. *Recorded*: 15:9 mo:1682.

JOHN GREENE to JOHN CRESY – (6:428) John Greene of Salem (yeoman) sold to John Cresy of Salem (taylor) for consideration sixteene pounds in hand paid, a certaine p'cell of upland & swamp ground containing six acres & three quarters or thereabouts in township of Salem & is bounded eastwardly by lands of Nicholas Hayward & Joseph Bacheller westerly by lands of John Greene & John Cresy northerly by land of Nicholas Hayward sotherly by land of John Greene & Joseph Bacheler. *Signed*: John Greene [mark] *Date*: 13 November 1682. *Witnesses*: Samuell Hardie; Miriam Bacheler. *Acknowledged*: 15 November 1682. John Green's wife Mary gave up thirds 15 November 1682. *Recorded*: 15:9 mo:1682.

DANIELL RUMBOLL to WILLIAM CURTICE and ALCE CURTICE – (6:430) Daniell Rumboll of Salem (blacksmith) have given & granted to William Curtice and wife Alce for naturall love & affection unto son in law William Curtice & his wife Alce whoe is my only daughter as alsoe for other divers good causes, more especially for what sd William Curtice hath ingaged himselfe as by a bond under sd William Curtice's hand bearing date with date of these pr'sents well & sufficiently to maintaine & provide for me both for food, loging & rainment, house roome & firing comfortable & necessary both in sickness & in health as alsoe phissick & due atendance in time of sickness as the Lord may see good to vissitt me with all before I depart this naturall life & afterwards to afford unto me a desent & Christian burial all & singular my goods, chattels, lands, housing, cattell, money, plate, dues, debts, rings, household stuffe, brasse, pewter & all my other substance whatsoever, quick & dead, within doare or without doare, of whatever kind & nature soever, condition or quality soever the same be, either in my owne custody or possession or in custody & use of any other p'son or p'sons whomsoever or wheresover. *Signed*: Daniell Rumboll [mark]. *Date*: 18 March 1681:2. *Witnesses*: John Weston; Richard Croade. *Acknowledged*: 20 March 1681:2. *Recorded*: 22:9 mo:1682.

SAMUELL SHRIMPTON from JOHN SWINERTON & HANNAH SWINERTON – (6:433)   Samuell Shrimpton of Boston (marchant) doe acknowledge to have received of John Swinerton & Hannah his wife, relict & sole administratrix of estate of James Browne formerly of Salem (marchant) one hundred thirty pounds in full paiment of what is owing unto me from estate of Jas. Browne wherefore I doe heareby remise, release, discharge & forever quitt claime unto said John Swinerton & Hannah his wife administratrix & either of them of & from all actions, sutes, cause or causes of action & sute debts, dues, reckonings, accounts, sume or sums of money claimes & demands whatsoever, which I ever had, now have, could or might at any time or times forever hearafter challenge prosecute or demand or from them sd John & Hannah or either of them or of or from estate left by sd deceased James Browne or any part or p'cell thereof for or by reason of any matters, transactions, dealings or causes or things whatsoever.   *Signed*: Samuel Shrimpton. *Date*: 14 November 1682. *Witnesses*: Nehamiah Willoughby; Isaac Addinton. *Acknowledged*: 16 November 1682. *Recorded*: 14:10 mo:1682.

ABRAHAM COLE and SARAH COLE to THOMAS WALTER – (6:434) Abraham Cole of Salem (tailor) sold to Thomas Walter of Salem (marrenour) for valuable consideration in hand paid, a certaine p'cell of land containing about fourteene pole & halfe it being that p'cell of land left to me by my father Thomas Cole deceased in Salem & is bounded on west with streete at which end it is sixty foot & halfe in bredth & runns backward to east bounded to the land of Joshua Buffum & soe from thence by a straite line to land of Priscilla Hunn & soe from thence bounded to land of sd

Abraham Cole south. *Signed*: Abraham Cole; Sarah Cole. *Date*: 4 December 1682. *Witnesses*: Thomas Adams; William King; Anthony Dike. *Acknowledged*: 4 December 1682. *Recorded*: 14:10 mo:1682.

MOSES MAVERICK and EUNICE MAVERICK to EPHRAIM SANDIN – (6:436) Moses Maverick of Marblehead with free consent of Eunice wife sold to Ephraim Sandin of Marblehead for consideration of a certaine sum of money in hand paid, one messuage, tenement or dwelling house with all the land belonging to sd house being one quarter of an acre lying in Marblehead standing upon the hill in the marsh formerly caled the litle neck together with a cowes comonige & covenant to sd Sandin that he shall have a cartwaye to goe to his house between Richard Reith's house & Mr. Riddan's stone wale forever & sd Ephraim Sandin shall have the pr'vilidge of a foot path from the waters side to come to his house in the marsh that is to say to come along by the bank or on the bank to carry one load or two of woode in the winter. *Signed*: Moses Maverick; Eunice Maverick. *Release of Dower*: Eunice wife doth yield dower. *Date*: 25 December 1677. *Witnesses*: Ambros Gale [mark]; Edw. Humphryes. *Acknowledged*: 2 July 1680 by both. *Recorded*: 4:10 mo:1682.

JEREMIAH NEALE and MARY NEALE to ANN NEALE – (6:439) Jeremiah Neale of Salem (carpenter): To Ann Neale: whereas Ann Neale relict & administratrix to my brother John Neale deceased hath a quantity of land lying in Salem neere adjoyning unto me Jeremiah Neale which was formerly John Neale's her deceased husbands land upon which shee doth intend to builde and make best use of shee can for the maintainance of her & hers & whereas the townsmen of Salem have confirmed unto me a small tract of land lying to the westward of my sisters land & soe on front of sd land for naturall affection I have unto my sd sister & her now children & other good considerations have sold said sister & her children & the heirs soe much of that p'cell of land which I have granted me by townsmen of Salem as shee by her building & improvement or her now children shall have occasion to make of heareby emptying myself of & from all claime to the same & to the only use & behoofe of my sd sister & her now children provided that what of sd land that my sd sister & her now children shall not make use of by building or other improvement for their uses: but & if she or her now children shall sell any of her land abovementioned & soe make use of any part of that quantity of land I had given me by the townsmen of Salem what shee or her now children or any of them shall sell I Jeremiah Neale am to have my equall share or proportion according to what quantity of sd land given me by the townsmen she they or any of them shall sell. *Signed*: Jeremiah Neale; Mary Neale [mark]. *Date*: 1 March 1682.

Witnesses: Frances Neale sen'r; Frances Neale Jun'r. *Acknowledged*: 9 December 1682 by Jeremiah & Mary wife. *Recorded*: 16:10 mo:1682.

JOHN RAMDELL and ELIZABETH RAMDELL to ZACHEUS CURTICE JUN'R – (6:441) John Ramdell of Rowley village sold to Zacheus Curtice Jun'r one p'cell of upland in Rowley village containing by estimation one acre & halfe bounded as followeth northwest & northeast with land of John Goold & on east with land of sd Goold & on south with land of sd Curtice, stake & heape of stones at all fower corners. *Signed*: John Ramdell; Elizabeth Ramdell [mark]. *Date*: 18 December 1676. *Witnesses*: with consent of their wives as wee seeing them Calliam Makcallon [mark]; Thomas Wenmar [mark]; John Goold. *Acknowledged*: 28 November 1682. *Recorded*: 16:10 mo:1682.

ROBERT GOODELL to ZACHARIAH GOODELL – (6:442) Robert Goodell of Salem sold to sonn Zachariah Goodell of Salem for a valuable sume in hand paid, sixty acres of land in township of Salem being part of eleven hundred acres of land granted by the towne of Salem for small lotts lying neere my house having the land of Job Swinerton sen'r on northeasterly side of it land of Job Swinerton Jun'r on north west end & the land of Lott Killum, Isaac Goodell & Jonathan Walcutt on southwest side & land of sd Swinerton's on southeast the corner bound is an oak with stones about it on northeast corner the bound is a white oake by a swamp side bounded on norwest corner with a stake by Wigwam rock, & with a stake on west & with a great white oake on south next to Isaac Goodell's land. *Signed*: Robert Goodell. *Date*: 26 October 1665. That concerning sixty acres abovesd it is to be understood y^t fifty acres more were given by sd Robert Goodell as a legacy for his portion & other ten acres were sold to him for a valuable sume & this is intended before the inscription of the witnesses. *Witnesses*: Nathaniell Felton; John Bacheler. *Acknowledged*: 14:6 mo:1678. *Recorded*: 19:10 mo:1682.

ROBERT GOODELL to ZACHARIAH GOODELL – (6:445) Robert Goodell of Salem sold to sonn Zachariah Goodell of Salem for divers causes especially fower pounds in hand paid, two acres of fresh meddow in township of Salem neere the river comonly caled great river lying betweene sd river & brooke comonly caled Mr. Norrice's brook having meddow of John Smith on one side of it & the sd brooke on the other side runing all the length of it by it, one end of it is bounded with a smale brooke or gully, the other end at the pine swamp neere Bald Hill. *Signed*: Robert Goodell. *Date*: 1 February 1667. *Witnesses*: Lott Killum; Mary Foster [mark]. *Acknowledged*: 14:6 mo:1678. *Recorded*: 19:10 mo:1682.

MALLACHY PEALE to CAPT. JOHN PRICE, MR. HILLIARD VEREN and MR. JOHN RUCK – (6:446) This bill bindeth me Mallachy Peale of Stafford county in Virginia, marchant to pay or cause to be paid unto Capt. John Price Mr. Hilliard Veren Mr. John Ruck & company of Salem in New England the full & just quantity of twenty thousand pounds of tobacco to be paid in good clean marchantable wheate & good sound marchantable porke on demand it being due on ballance of all accounts to this day, to be paid one halfe in wheate and one halfe in porke or neere thereabouts. *Signed*: Mallachy Peale. *Date*: 26 October 1682. *Witnesses*: Daniell King; Richard King; John Croade. *Acknowledged*: Mr. Daniell King & John Croade took oathes they saw Malachy sett his hand & seal to this instrument 23:10 mo:1682. *Recorded*: 23:10:1682. Whereas I was concerned in company with Capt. John Price Mr. Hilliard Veren Mr. John Ruck &c. I doe heareby acknowledge y^t contence of this bill is due to Capt. John Price & company my owne part being deducted out before. *Signed*: Mallachy Peale. *Witness*: John Croade. Taken upon oath by John Croade 23:10 mo:1682.

MALACHY PEALE to DELIVERANCE PARKMAN – (6:448) I doe hearby oblige myselfe to pay or cause to be paid unto Mr. Deliverance Parkman or order, on demand at or neere my habitation in Virginia, the full & just quantity of fifteene hundred pounds of good sound tobacco to be paid one halfe in wheat & one halfe in porke or neere that proportion. *Signed*: Malachy Peale. *Date*: 27 October 1682. *Witnesses*: Hilliard Veren; Samuell Williams. *Acknowledged*: 23 December 1682 Hilliard Veren & Sam'l Williams made oath that they were pr'sent as witnesses when sd Peale did signe. *Recorded*: 23:10 mo:82.

1681:2:March:16
Deliverance Parkman master of catch Fraternity of Salem in New England

	lb s p
To entry bond p'mit dispatc-	02:00:00
To twenty tun port dues 15 d p	01:05:00
To Governors duties	01:00:00
	04:05:00

p. contra cred^t

By Malichy Peale account
Discharged with payment of   04:05:00
Errors excepted by N. Spencer Collector
This is a true coppy of Corcnall Spencer's act.

                                                    Malachy Peale

Gent.

Pay to the proportionable parts of this accocunt to Mr. Hilliard Veren or order in which you will oblige S'r yo'r servant

                 Malachy Peale

To Capt. John Price & company in Salem
    This is a true coppy of the original account atteste
                 John Croade

PAULE MANSFEILD and DAMARIS MANSFEILD to EBENEZER GARDNER – (6:449) Paule Mansfeild of Salem (fisherman) sold to Mr. Ebenezer Gardner of Salem (marrenor) for consideration five pounds in hand paid, a certaine p'cell of marsh ground containing halfe an acre lying in Salem neere clay brooke & is bounded by towne comon land by clay brooke westerly, on north & south by marsh of sd Ebenezer Gardner's & by castle hill land easterly. ***Signed***: Paule Mansfeild [mark]; Damaris Mansfeild [mark]. ***Date***: 25 December 1682. ***Witnesses***: John Roapes; Benjamin Bly. ***Acknowledged***: Paul Mansfield acknowledged & Damarice wife did release right of dower 25:10 mo:1682. ***Recorded***: 26:December:1682.

ELEAZER LINSEY and JOHN COATES – (6:451) The testimony of Eleazer Linsey aged about 36 yeares & John Coates aged about 21 yeares, these two p'sons above written testifieth that when Thomas Male's new house was raised that theire was sufficient rome left betweene the fence next Richard Croad's house to clabord the whole side of Thomas Male's new house without removing any part or p'cell of abovesd fence, for we claborded part of sd new house on that side next Richard Croad's & had roome enough to doe our work betweene new house & the fence from one end of said house to other end thereof for fence as neere as well could be ranged from one end of Thomas Male's land to other end on a straite line; & to the truth hearof we abovesd John Coates & Ebenezer Linsey witness sworne 28:June:1681.

JOHN REEVES aged about 72 yeares testifieth to his knowledge the house of Tho. Male bought of George Deane doth stand wholy on the town's ground & the fence y^t fenced the heads of the lotts left the said house without about two foot & the front of Thomas Male's new house standeth about 14 foot on the town's ground being sett upon a sellar that John Kitching had made in townes comon sworne 22:June:1681.

THOMAS ROBBINS testifieth that fences that fenced in the lotts that were Barber's & Barnes which land was since John Kitchins ranged behind the house that Thomas Mall bought of George Deane leaving the sd house wholy out the sd fences ranged to Rich'd Croads house or where it stands leaving som vacant land betweene the house of Richard Croade & Thomas Male which he bought of George Deane & was at least the whole bredth of sd house. Sworne 23:June:1631.

ROBERT HODG to WILLIAM BROWNE – (6:453) Robert Hodg of Salem (marrenor) sold to William Browne of Salem for consideration of full & just sume of one hundred & sixty pounds I owe & stand justly indebted to William Browne Esq. for severall goods &c. received of sd Browne, my dwelling house with the ground it stands upon & is adjoyning & belonging thereunto containing twenty eight or thirty rod of ground or thereabouts lying in Salem & bounded with the land of Capt. William Browne Esq. easterly, the land of Mrs. Hannah Veren as her fence stands, northerly the lane that goes downe to burying place westerly & a lane that goes to Capt. More's oarchard sotherly provided that if Robert Hodg pay or cause to be paid unto William Browne the full sume of one hundred sixty pounds in marchantable & refuse fish & graine at price currant as indian corne, wheate or peare or ry at or before first day of January 1684:5 then this sale shall be voyde & of none effect but if default of payment shall happen then to stand in full power. *Signed*: Robert Hodg [mark]. *Date*: 3 January 1682:3. *Witnesses*: Benj[a] Browne; John Atwater. *Acknowledged*: 3 January 1682:3. *Recorded*: 3 January 1682:3.

ELIZABETH TURNER to DANIEL WEBB – (6:456) Elizabeth Turner relict & administratrix of estate of John Turner of Salem sold to Daniel Webb of Salem (marrenor) for consideration fifty pounds sterling in hand paid, the dwelling house & ground adjoyning lying in Salem which was for som yeares since bought by sd husband of Samuell Pickworth of Salem house carpenter sd ground belonging to house containing about six pole & is bounded on east with ground of sd Daniel Webb on west & south with land of William West & north abutting upon street or highwaye. The sale of pr'misses unto sd Daniell Webb being made by my husband John Turner for some years since by my knowledge & consent & purchase paid him. *Signed*: Elizabeth Turner. *Date*: 1 January 1682:3. *Witnesses*: Martha Wooland; William Andrews. *Acknowledged*: 8 January 1682:3. *Recorded*: 10 January 1682.

HANNA SIMMONS to MATHEW BARTON – (6:459) Hanna Simmons the administratrix of Richard Simonds late deceased sold to Mathew Barton of Salem (weaver) for consideration thirty five pounds in hand paid or secured to be paid, a certain p'cell of land containing one sixth pt of an acre with a frame of a house with a sellar under it standing thereupon lying in towne of Salem being that p'cell of land that was lately bought by sd husband Richard Simons deceased & is in length east & west nearest five pole & six foot & in bredth north and south five pole wanting thirteen inches or thereabouts soe much as to make up the full of one sixth part of an acre & is bounded easterly with land of William West sotherly & northerly with land of Edward Woollen & westerly with a lane or highwaye left for the use of the proprietors provided sd Mathew Barton is to leave out towards the lane or highwaye seaven foot in bredth through the front of sd p'cell of land which is to be in part of sd lane or highwaye unto which sd Edward Woollen is ingaged to leave out soe much to add to it as to make a convenient way as appeers by his deed to sd Richard Simmonds. *Signed*: Hannah Simmons [mark]. *Date*: 15 January 1682:3. *Witnesses*: Hilliard Veren; John Ropps. *Acknowledged*: 16 January 1682:3. *Recorded*: 16 January 1682:3.

RICHARD STARR to PHILLIP ENGLISH – (6:462) Richard Starr of county of Essex (cooper) sold to Phillip English of Salem (marrenor) for consideration thirty pounds in hand paid, my moietie or one halfe pt of house & land in Salem which was hearetofore possessed by my father Robert Starr deceased the whole house & all ground thereunto adjoyning & belonging being about an acre which sd house & land was by my father by deed of guift made over unto my sister Susanna Starr & myselfe to be equally divided between us & was accordingly confirmed by an act of Court at Salem the 30th of 9th mo. 1680 bounded upon land of Joseph Swasye westward upon land of Francis Collins eastward upon land of Ellinor Hollingworth southward & upon streete or highwaye northerly together with one halfe part of aple trees or other trees upon sd land. *Signed*: Richard Starr. *Date*: 3 January 1682:3. *Witnesses*: Daniell Webb; Richard Croad. *Acknowledged*: 15 January:1682. *Recorded*: 16 January:1682.

JOHN CORWIN to THOMAS KELAND – (6:465) John Corwin of Salem (marchant) am firmly bound unto Thomas Keland of Bostone (marchant) in whole sume of seaven hundred fifty one pounds & two shillings fower pence to be paid unto Thomas Kelland which paiment well & truly to be made I bynd myselfe for the whole & in the whole firmly by these p'sents dated this thirty first day of March 1682.
The condition of this obligation is such that if above bound John Corwin doe well & truly pay or cause to be paid unto above named Thomas Kelland full & whole sume of three hundred seaventy five pounds eleven shillings two pence in merchantable dry cod fish at money price at Salem at or before or upon the tenth day of July next ensuing then this obligation to be voyde & of none effect or elce to stand in full power & for better security I doe bind & make over to Thomas Kelland my farme house & land lying at head of frost fish river being by estimation one hundred fifty acres of upland & twenty acres of meddow bounded upon land of Benjamin Porter Joshua Rea

Thomas Raiment & Peeter Cloyce in township of Salem which I had by my wife from her father John Winthrop Esq. last deceased. *Signed*: John Corwin. *Date*: 31 March 1682. *Witnesses*: John Cally; Charles Sharpp. John Kally & Charles Sharp testifie they were pr'sent & saw John Corwin signe seale and deliver this instrument. Taken upon oathe Boston 1 Febrary 1682. *Recorded*: 5:12 mo:1682:3.

JOHN HOW and JOHN ROBINSON to JOHN HOW and JOHN ROBINSON – (6:467) John How & John Robinson of Topsfield to prevent great charges & the impossibility of fencing our land as it lay before we made this exchange & doe agree that our bounds are as followeth: the swamp that said John How has of John Robinson doe begin on south side of swamp at an ash tree marked with a heape of stones at it from thence runing up the swamp side to an elm tree marked with a heape of stones at it from thence to a red oake marked & stones at it & from thence up the swamp side till it doe meete with Daniell Clearke's line this is the bounds of the land that sd John How has of sd John Robinson upon exchange. The bounds of the land John Robinson has of John How is as followeth: being at a walnut tree marked with a heape of stones at it downe the swamp side to an ash tree marked with a heape of stones at it from thence to a stake with a heape of stones at it & from thence by the swamp side to a stake with a heape of stone as it which is a corner bounds between Deacon Thomas Perkins & sd John How: this last p'cell of swamp y^t John How has exchanged with John Robinson lyes on north side of swamp. *Signed*: John How; John Robinson [mark]. *Date*: 13 Aprill 1682. *Witnesses*: John Gold sen'r; Joseph Byrbe Jun'r. *Acknowledged*: 28 June 1682 by both. *Recorded*: 5:12 mo:1682.

JOHN CORWIN from JOHN WEST and THOMAS WEST – (6:468) John Corwin of Salem doe acknowledge myselfe to have received of John West & Thomas West his son the full sume of one hundred & twenty pounds due by bill or bond which is in full paiment for farme they are possest of 25 January 1682. *Signed*: John Corwin. *Witnesses*: Nathaniel Felton; Edmond Bridges. *Acknowledged*: by Capt. John Corwin 1 November 1682. *Recorded*: 15:February:1682.

EDMOND BATTER to HILLIARD VEREN and DORCAS VEREN and SARA VEREN – (6:469) Edmond Batter of Salem (marchant) sold to Hilliard Veren of Salem & daughters Dorcas & Sara for divers goods causes especially naturall affection unto Hilliard Veren sen'r my brother in law & Dorcas & Sara his daughters my two cozens, a certaine p'cell of land containing about fifty rod or pole of ground lying in Salem at the west end of that land of mine adjoyning to now dwelling house & is six pole on the front to the streete or highwaye on south & six pole & three foot in bredth behind adjoyning to the land of Mr. Edward Norrice on north & bounded on east with land of sd Edmond Batter & west with lane or highwaye that goes downe to the north river & on east & west sides the land is about eight rod & halfe or neere nine rod to have unto sd Hilliard Veren for & during his naturall life & after his decease to sd Dorcas & Sara his daughters or the longest liver of them, in case either of them depart this life before they come to be possest of pr'misses & to their heires & assignes. *Signed*: Edmond Batter. *Date*: 18 January 1669. *Witnesses*: with seizing & possession of pr'misses given Benjamin Felton; William Dounton. *Acknowledged*: by Benj. Felton & Wm. Dounton 8:9:81. *Recorded*: 5:12 mo:1682.

ELIZABETH WALTON to NATHANIELL WALTON and MARTHA MUNJOY – (6:471) Elizabeth Walton of Marblehead relict of Mr. William Walton deceased & sole adminstratrix of estate of sd Walton being with consent of my children & order of county court possessed of the whole estate & impowered & injoyned to pay debts which sd estate did owe & being myselfe disabled & incapacitated without sale of som pt of the land to discharge the same by virtue & authority of sd order in consideration of sum of forty pounds equally paid to creditors towards discharge of aforesd debts by my two children Nathaniell Walton & Martha Munjoy widdow, sold Nathaniell Walton & Martha Munjoy one halfe or moitie of lott lying betixt Mr. Mavericks tenement & Richard Rowlands land together with the old barne upon it the sd halfe or moitie being that pt which lyeth next to the lands of Rich'd Rowland & is bounded on northeast with his & Nicholas Andrews & John Waldrons lands, alsoe & being twenty fower pole in the front & abutting on highwaye and about twenty nine pole on water side & about fower score pole in length to run from highwaye back to the harbour through whole lott. *Signed*: no signature. *Date*: 18:Aprill 1677. *Witnesses*: James Dennes; John Norman. *Acknowledged*: 9 March 1681:2. *Recorded*: 7:12 mo:1682:3.

JOHN PUTNAM SEN'R to NATHANIELL PUTNAM SEN'R – (6:472) John Putnam sen'r of Salem (yeoman) sold to Nathaniell Putnam sen'r of Salem (yeoman) for divers causes especially a valuable consideration in lands to me made over by waye of exchange by Nathaniell Putnam sen'r as by deed of sale bearing date with these pr'sents, severall p'cels of land as followeth: one p'cell of land of about twenty acres bounded with land of Capt. John Corwin on south & east the land of John Leach on north & brooke which is the bounds between Daniell Andrew & it on west: alsoe fifteene accres of land, seaven & halfe acres of it being formerly reserved out of my father John Putnam deceased his deed to sd Nathaniell Putnam & the other seaven acres & halfe of it reserved out of sd Nathaniell's father in law Hutchinson's deed sold to sd John Putnam; alsoe a certain strip of land lying upon easterne side of Davenport's farme beginning at the conckernut tree which is the southeast corner bounds of Davenport's farme & from thence upon a straite line to the red oake & from thence to the old stump with a heape of stones which is one of the bounds of Davenports farme & Kenestones bounds which is now in possesion of Daniell Andrew all abovesd lands lying in Salem. *Signed*: John Putnam sen'r. **Date**: 19 February 1682:3. *Witnesses*: John Browne; Jonathan Corwin; John Hathorne; Hilliard Veren. *Acknowledged*: 19 February 1682:3. **Recorded**: 22:February:1682:3.

The disposition of John Browne Jonathan Corwin John Hathorne & Hilliard Veren these deponents being pr'sent when Nathaniell Putnam and John Putnam signed, sealed & delivered deeds of sale each to other for lands to say, severall p'cells sold to each other by way of exchange & there being some scruples about twenty acres conveyed to Nathaniell by John Putnam which was a grant formerly to theire father John Putnam deceased the sd Nathaniell for satisfaction to his brother John's scruple did afirme avouch & declare that he never had noe other land ever laid out for his father's former grant but this twenty acres mentioned on sd deed dated 19:February:1682:3. *Signed*: John Browne; Jonathan Corwin; John Hathorne; Hilliard Veren. The above subscribed fower p'sons to the above written testimony gave oath to truth thereof & that they were witnesses to sd agreement & subscribed as witnesses thereto, alsoe the p'ties viz: Nathaniell & John Putnam then acknowledged the same to be theire true meaning & agreement. 19:February:1682 3 before me Bartholmew Gedney Assistant.

NATHANIELL PUTNAM to JOHN PUTNAM SEN'R – (6:477) Nathaniell Putnam of Salem (yeoman) sold to John Putnam sen'r of Salem (yeomen) for divers causes especially a valuable consideration in lands to me made over by waye of exchange by John Putnam sen'r as by deed of sale bearing date with these pr'sents, severall p'cells of land as followeth: one p'cell of land containing about twenty acres bounded northerly with Cheevers land easterly with land of Daniell Andrewes sotherly with land of sd Nathaniell Putnam westerly land of Thomas Putnam: also all my right in one halfe part of about forty acres of land of Leift. Davenports soe caled that was formerly granted to Richard Waterman; alsoe five acres of land where John Sheppard's house stands bounded by the highwaye sotherly to a stake neerest the corner of James Hadlock's fence having the land of sd Nathaniell Putnam easterly to a stake where a heape of stones lyes neere Mrs. Bailes line, having Mrs. Bailies land northerly to a spring neere the head of spring having Mrs. Bailies land westerly the said spring being the bounds betwixt them downe to the highwaye to a little tree marked & soe to the first stake mentioned all the above said p'cells of land lying in Salem. *Signed*: Nathaniell Putnam. *Date*: 19 February 1682:3. *Witnesses*: John Browne; Jonathan Corwin; John Hathorne; Hillliard Veren. *Acknowledged*: 19:12 mo:1682. *Recorded*: 22:February:1682:3.

John Browne Jonathan Corwin John Hathorne & Hilliard Veren testifieth & saith that they being pr'sent when Nathaniell Putnam assigned his deed to his brother John Putnam bearing date 19:12 mo:1682:3 there being obscurity or mistake in exspressing easterly bounds of the 20 acres of land in sixth line of sd deed the sd John & Nathaniell did both declare that for (easterly with land of Daniell) insteed thereof is to be understood (easterly with a strip of land of Nathaniell Putnam's) which they would be understood both to agree upon & consent unto & that to be the right bounds there. *Signed*: John Browne; Jonathan Corwin; John Hathorne; Hilliard Veren. The above subscribed fower p'sons to the above written testimony gave oath to the truth thereof & that they were witnesses to the sd agreement & subscribed as witnesses thereto 19:12 mo:1682:3 and the p'ties viz: Nathaniell & John Putnam then acknowledged the same to be theire true meaning & agreement before Bartholmew Gedney Assistant.

RALPH FOGG and SUSANA FOGG to JOHN PUTNAM – (6:481) Ralph Fogg of Salem sold to John Putnam for consideration sd John hath well & truly contented & paid according to the articles herewithall signed before date of these pr'sents sume of twelve pounds in full paiment of sd sale, the farme of fower score acres which the towne of Salem gave him lying betweene old father Putnam's farme & Daniel Raies & more eight acres of meddow lying neere the house that John Hathorne lived in which meddow was alsoe from towne of Salem. *Signed*: Ralph Fogg; Susana Fogg. *Date*: 14th of 2d mo:1652. *Witnesses*: signed & delivered 28:2 mo:52 Phillip Cromwell; Elias Stileman Jun'r. *Acknowledged*: 20:10:1653 by both. *Recorded*: 22:February:1682:3.

WILLIAM KING to ROBERT STONE – (6:482) William King of Salem (carpenter) sold to Robert Stone of Salem (marrenor) for valuable sume in hand paid, one halfe of my part of tract or p'cell which sd Robert Stone & sd William King formerly bought of Issac Burnap deceased as by his deed of sale to us appeereth w'ch was formerly a part of Mr. Edmond Batter's farme the one halfe of my part which is the one fourth part of the whole p'cell bought as aforesd of said Isaac as it lyes bounded according to & as is exprest in sd deed. *Signed*: William King. *Release of Dower*: Katheren wife doe yield up dower. *Date*: 20 May 1676. *Witnesses*: William Hathorne Jun'r; Thomas Robbins [mark]. *Acknowledged*: 3:4:76. *Recorded*: 22:February:1682:3.

FRANCES SKERRY to WILLIAM KING and ROBERT STONE – (6:484) Frances Skerry of Salem (husbandman) with consent of wife sold to William King and Robert Stone of Salem for valuable consideration in hand paid, twelve acres upland within township of Salem by Mr. Downing's farme having meddow of sd Mr. Downing on northwest of it & land of John Hill wheelwright on other side easterly. *Signed*: Frances Skerry. *Date*: 26 December 1662. *Witnesses*: Edw. Norrice; Joseph Prince. *Acknowledged*: 14:11 mo:62 & wife yielded thirds. *Recorded*: 22:February:1682:3.

ISAACK BURNAP and ELIZABETH BURNAP to ROBERT STONE and WILLIAM KING – (6:486) Isaack Burnap of Salem (husbandman) with consent of wife sold tc Robert Stone & William King both of Salem for consideration of thirty seaven pounds in hand paid, a p'cell of upland lying in Salem that is within township thereof which was formerly given to Mr. Batter by towne of Salem after that his farme was laid out & caled Mr. Batter's plaine being bounded southward with sd farme & eastward with land of Thomas Golthwite which he bought formerly of sd Mr. Batter also westerly with a swamp belonging to William Lord sen'r northwest with land of Ellen Robbinson. *Signed*: Isaack Burnap; Elizabeth Burnap [mark]. *Date*: 30 March 1664. *Witnesses*: John Kitchin; Edw. Norrice; Michaell Shaflin [mark]. *Acknowledged*: 7:9 mo:64 & Elizabeth wife yielded thirds. *Recorded*: 22:12 mo:1682:3

ISAACK BACON to ROBERT STONE and WILLIAM KING – (6:487) Isaack Bacon of Salem (marrenor) sold to Robert Stone & William King of Salem for consideration ninety fower pounds sterling in hand paid, dwelling house with out houses, orchards, yards, fences together with all land adjoyning thereto containing twenty two acres of land alsoe twenty seaven acres of upland and meddow lying disjoined from aforesd house & two & twenty acres of land all which are being in north neck in Salem neere the old mill & bounded that is to say the houses & two & twenty acres adjoyning with land of Capt. Trask on south with land of Rich'd Bishop on north & land of Mr. Thomas Gardner elder on west & land of Daniell Sothwick on east: alsoe said twenty seaven acres of upland lying together seaven acres thereof being meddow & is bounded with land of Edward Beachum on north & land of Edward Gaskin on south & partly east & land of Mr. Thomas Gardner aforesd on west being all the land that the father of sd Isaac Bacon did formerly possess & injoy in that place & now possessed by sd Isaack as right heire & owner. *Signed*: Isaac Bacon. *Date*: 19 June 1665. *Witnesses*: Sarah Mason [mark]; Hilliard Veren sen'r. *Acknowledged*: 19:4 mo:1665. *Recorded*: 23:February:1682:3.

JOHN MASSEY to FRANCES SKERRY – (6:491)   John Massey of Salem (yeoman) sold to Frances Skerry of Salem (yeoman) for divers good causes & especially for two acres & halfe of upland & marsh now lately bought of Frances Skerry as by bill of sale appeeres bearing date with these pr'sents, certaine p'cell of ground being p'tly a yard & p'tly oarchard & garden & p'tly earable land all containing about two acres it being land where I had late a dwelling house & did formerly dwell being in Salem & is bounded northwesterly by the waie that lyes betweene it & north river northeasterly by land of Mr. Phillip Cromwell southeasterly by lane or highwaye that goes to the ferry & southwesterly by land of Frances Skerry. **Signed**: John Massey. **Release of Dower**: Sarah wife doe yield up dower. **Date**: 31 January 1682:3. **Witnesses**: Hilliard Veren; Samuell Gardner Jun'r. **Acknowledged**: 5 February 1682. **Recorded**: 23:February:1682:3.

FRANCES SKERRY to JOHN MASSEY – (6:493)   Frances Skerry of Salem (yeoman) sold to John Massey of Salem for divers good causes especially of a certaine p'cell of land now late bought of John Massey containing about two acres according to a bill of sale bearing date with these pr'sents, certaine p'cell of upland and marsh containing about two acres and halfe lying in Salem neere the north ferry bounded northerly with waye that goes betweene sd land & north river easterly by land of Capt. George Corwin sotherly by a cove or creeke that comes in of salt water & westerly by the land of sd Frances Skerry provided & agreed upon as true intent & meaning that this sd p'cell of land by these pr'sents sold shall be security for making good his sd John Massey's sale to me of two acres of land as by deed bearing date with these pr'sents appeereth untill the children of sd John Massey shall have paid them theire severall legacies given them by will of theire grandfather Jeffery Massey deceased & soe discharges from them to quitt thiere claime to any interest in said land. **Signed**: Frances Skerry. **Release of Dower**: Bridgett wife doe yield dower. **Date**: 31 January 1682:3. **Witnesses**: Hilliard Veren; Samuell Gardner Jun'r. **Acknowledged**: 5 February 1682:3. **Recorded**: 23 February:1682:3.

WILLIAM PEARCE to JOHN CROMWELL – (6:496)   William Pearce son of Richard Pearce late deceased with consent of Elizabeth his mother hath put himselfe apprentice to John Cromwell of Salem slautherer the science or trade of a slautherer which he now useth, to be taught & with him after the manner of an apprentice to dwell & serve from twenty fifth day of December last past unto the full end & term of eight yeares from thence next following & fully to be compleat & ended by all which terme of eight yeares the sd apprentice sd John Cromwell & Hannah his wife well & truly shall serve, theire secrets shall keepe close, theire comandments lawfull & honest every where he shall gladly doe, hurt to his said master or Mrs. he shall not doe nor suffer to be don, but shall lett if he may or imeadiately admonish his sd master or Mrs. thereof, taverns he shall not frequent, from the service of his master & mistress day or night he shall not absent or prolong himselfe, but in all things as good & faithfull apprentice shall beare & behave himselfe toward his sd master & Mrs. & all his during the terme aforesd: & sd John Cromwell to his sd apprentice the science or art of a slautherer, which he now useth, shall teach & informe or cause to be taught & informed the best way that he may or cann, & alsoe shall teach his sd apprentice or cause him to be taught to read & wright & alsoe shall find to his sd apprentice apparel, meate, drink, washing & lodging & all other necessaryes meete & convenient for an apprentice as well in sickness as in health for & during terme aforesd & at end thereof to dismiss his sd apprentice with doble apparell throughout both linen & wollen, one sute for Lord's days & one sute for working days. *Signed*: William Pearce [mark]. *Date*: 19 February 1676. *Witnesses*: Hilliard Veren sen'r; Edmond Bridges; Elizabeth Pearce [mark]. *Acknowledged*: none. *Recorded*: 26:12 mo:1682:3.

JOHN PEASE SEN'R – (6:498) The testimony of John Pease sen'r aged about 53 yeares. Saith that in his knowledge the land that my father in law Goodell sold to his son in law John Smith was laid out by my father Goodell's order & appoyntment several years before the land that my father gave to his son Isaac Goodell & when sd John Smith's land was laid oute & bounded on the northeasterly side it was bounded by a swamp & some meddow only reserving a highwaye for my father Goodell to fetch his hay out of meddow, soe that as the sd swamp & meddow bounded sd Smith's land was rounding or elbowing there & not straite from corner bounds to corner bounds & afterwards when sd Isaack Goodell's land was laid out it bounded upon John Smith's northeasterly side bounds as his bounds did run as aforesd & because John Smith's land lying elbowing & not straite upon square measure would cutt of some quantie of sd Isaack's land therefore there was soe much added on other side to make up his full upon a square measure & further saith not. Sworne before me 7:9 mo:1682. William Browne Assistant. *Recorded*: 26:12:1682:3.

JOSEPH NORMAN to SAMUELL LEACH – (6:499) Joseph Norman now being of New England county of Essex sold to Samuell Leach brother in law for valuable consideration of moneys in hand paid, all right in & to any part or p'cels of lands or meddow or any other estate which was formerly my father John Norman's now deceased & being now in custody or possession of brother John Norman as executor or administrator to my sd father's estate left by my mother Arabella Norman deceased. *Signed*:

Joseph Norman. *Date*: 18 October 1681. *Witnesses*: Thomas West; Frances Coy. *Acknowledged*: 17 October ____. *Recorded*: 9:March:1682:3.

JOHN NORMAN to SAMUELL LEACH – (6:500) I within named John Norman for & in consideration of Joseph Norman's right in his father's estate (John Norman deceased) which Samuell Leach had made over to him from sd Joseph, as by a writing dated the 18:8 mo 1681 appeareth: I say, in sd Joseph's right, I, John Norman as administrator, doe assigne to Samuell Leach, sd Joseph's assignee, halfe an acre of marsh, lying in the pond, & adjoining to within named one acre & halfe of marsh. *Signed*: John Norman. *Date*: 13:March:1682:3. *Witnesses*: Manasseth Marston; Hilliard Veren. *Acknowledged*: 13:March:1682:3. *Recorded*: 13:March:1682:3.
This above writing belongs to another writing, which it reffers to, which other writing is recorded in book ye 5th:foll 28:this being written on the back side pr. me Hilliard Veren Recorder.

JOHN RUCK to HANNAH GEERISH – (6:501) John Ruck of Salem (marchant) legall executor to the last will & testement of Widdow Spooner deceased, have & doe according to her will & my owne discretion sold to Hannah Geerish of Salem wife to Benjamin Geerish, three p'cells of land, (besides what household stuff & other moveables which he hath alreddy received) the p'cels of land are as followeth viz: the one halfe of the former acre lott which was comonly caled Cotles lott, to be divided cross from Revis's lott to John Pickering's lott, fronting norward to the main streete, bounded to the land of Robert Kitchen on the one side, & on the other side with the land of Olde Reeve's: as alsoe about three quarters of an acre of salt marsh, lying by som marsh of Samuel Gardner Jun'r on the one side, & by a p'cel of marsh of Widdow Roapes on other side now Castell hill in south feild: as alsoe a five acre lott of upland bordering on the land of Goodman Beachum & Goodman Tompkins on one side & on other side bordering, or joyning to the land of John Pease formerly, but now in possession of Caleb Buffum, & one end of said lott bordering upon som land of Robert Stone's, & the other end bordering upon a ten acre lott which was Thomas Spooner's but now in possession of Thomas Ruck. *Signed*: John Ruck. *Date*: thirtieth day of November one thousand, six hundred, eighty two. *Witnesses*: John Croade; Thomas Ruck. *Acknowledged*: 1:of December, 1682 Mr. John Ruck Sen'r. *Recorded*: 13:March:1682:3.

RICHARD HAVEN, JUN'R – (6:503) Richard Haven, Jun'r of Lynn the purchaser of land sold me by this deed & contained therein, in consideration of two thousand acres of land in the Colloney of Conetticott, belonging to my father, Richard Haven, Sr. of Lynn which my said father hath sold unto me, I do heareby assigne & pass over all the land contained in this deed,

that was mine, that I purchased of my father in law Daniell Hutchins with all its pr'vilidges & imunyties or w'soever & every part thereof, as firmly as this instrument doth declare to be mine. *Signed*: Richard Haven Jun'r [mark]. *Date*: Aprill the 4th, 1682. *Witnesses*: Oliver Purchas; Daniell Hutchins. *Acknowledged*: 5th day of Aprill 1682. Recorded: 3 Aprill:83.
This refers to the first deed made from Daniell Hutchins to Richard Haven Junr & is recorded in foll 6th, in this book.

JOHN CROMWELL to JOHN PUDNEY – (6:504) John Cromwell of Salem (slautherer) sold to John Pudney of Salem (husbandman) for consideration twenty pounds hand paid or secured to be paid, a certaine p'cell of land, containing ten acres, as it was laid out & granted to Thomas Greene by the towne of Salem, within bounds of sd towne neere unto a farme caled Mr. John Humphery's farme & was lately sold to me by Remember Salmon & is bounded northward with the land of said John Pudney, being at a walnut tree which is John Pudney's corner bounds, at northwest, from thence to an oake at the northeast corner standing by a great rock from thence to a black oake marked on the fower sides, at the southeast corner joining to the comon from thence bounded to the comon on the southwest side, to a wallnut tree that is marked with fower markes & from thence to the first bounds. *Signed*: John Cromwell. *Date*: nineteenth day of March, one thousand six hundred eighty two 1682:3. Witnesses: Benjamin Marston; Hilliard Veren. *Acknowledged*: 20:March:1682:3. Recorded: 20:March:1682:3.

JOHN NORTHY SEN'R to RICHARD KNOTT – (6:506) John Northy sen'r of Marblehead (fisherman) sold to Richard Knott of Marblehead (cherurgeon) for consideration a certaine sume of money well & truly pd., a certaine p'cell of land lying in Marblehead, containing about one acre, & is bounded on the north side & on west on land of sd Knott's, on the south joyning to the land of William Nickes, & on east it joyneth to the land of abovesd John Northy's. *Signed*: John Northey. *Date*: six & twentieth day of November, one thousand, six hundred & eighty. *Witnesses*: Richard Walker; Daniell King. *Acknowledged*: 24 of March, 1682:3. *Recorded*: 26 March:1683.

HILLIARD VEREN to DELIVERANCE PARKMAN – (6:508) Hilliard Veren sold to Deliverance Parkman of Salem (marrinor) for consideration thirteen pounds in currant money in hand pd or secured to be paid, all my right title & interest in the within bargaine & sale of sd p'cell of land according as is therein mentioned & bounded. *Signed*: Hilliard Veren. *Date*: this twenty fifth day of March one thousand six hundred eighty &

three. *Witnesses*: John Pickering Jun'r; Richard Flinder. *Acknowledged*: 4:Aprill:1683. Recorded: 4:Aprill:1683.
This refers to the deed recorded in foll. 76 in this book.

THOMAS TUCK, JOANE TUCK and JOSEPH HARRIS to JOHN SMALE – (6:509)   Thomas Tuck of Beverly (blacksmith) & Joane, my wife and Joseph Harris of Beverly (husbandman) sold to John Smale of Salem (yeoman) for consideration sume of tenn pounds & five shillings to me Thomas Tuck & Joane my wife pd, a certaine p'cell of land, containing three acres, scituate, lying & being in Salem, at the greate cove in the north neck soe caled, bounded pa'tly with the marsh of sd John Smale & partly with the marsh of Thomas Brackett sotherly & easterly, & som land that was formerly Thomas Reed's deceased pt'ly westerly & northerly & som land of sd John Smale pt'ly westerly. *Signed*: Thomas Tuck [mark]; Joane Tuck [mark]; Joseph Harris. *Date*: twenty third day of June, one thousand six hundred & seventy nine. *Witnesses*: John Burton sen'r [mark]; Edward Grove. *Acknowledged*: Thomas Tuck & Joane, his wife 18 June:1681 before me; Joseph Harris acknowledged 22 Aug:1682. *Recorded*: 3:April:1683.

TIMOTHY HICKES to DELIVERANCE PARKMAN – (6:512) Timothy Hickes of Salem (shipwright) sold to Deliverance Parkman of Salem (shipwright) for a valuable consideration in hand paid, a dweling house with the land adjoyning, containing twenty five rod or pole of ground, it is bounded with the streete or highway to south & west & with the land of Mr. Norriss to the north & the land of Mr.Veren sen'r to the east, which land is lying & being situate in Salem. *Signed*: Timothy Hicks. *Date*: sixth day of August, one thousand, six hundred, seaventy & three. *Witnesses*: Henry West; Hilliard Veren, Jun'r; Hilliard Veren Sen'r. *Acknowledged*: 22^d February:1682:3 by Hilliard Veren Sen'r & Henry West. *Recorded*: 4:Aprill:1683.
I Hilliard Veren of Salem doe by these pr'sents yield up all my right, title, interest in within bargained p'cel of land alowing of the within sale thereof to sd. Deliverance Parkman.   *Signed*: Hilliard Veren. *Date*: 3^d day of Aprill:1683. *Witnesses*: Richard Flinders; John Pickering, Jun'r. *Acknowledged*: Hilliard Veren acknowledged ye above written to be his act & deed, this 11:of April:1683.

ROBERT DRIVER SEN'R and PHEBE DRIVER to ROBERT DRIVER JUN'R – (6:514)   Robert Driver Sen'r of Lynn (tailor) sold to Robert Driver Jun'r of Lynn & he being naturall son of sd Robert Driver sen'r for consideration of his natural affection to Robert, his son, together with other good considerations moving him thereunto: hath with the consent of his now wife, in refference to her surrending up her thirds, according to law of dower, a certaine p'cell of land situate, lying & being in towne of Lin, containing fower acres, it being part of the house lott of the sd Robert Driver, Sen'r & is bounded easterly, with land of John Davis, & of Widow Rooten, northerly with town comon, & southwardly with the meeting house path, in that corner next land of Widdow Rooten, & soe as sd path lyeth unto the gutter or run of water, & then the sd run of water to be the bound, & westerly with land of or in the possession of William Crofts, together with comons, liberties or pr'vilidges whatsoever, belonging unto ye aforesd fower acres. If sd Robert, his son shall sell, his brother Robert Potter shall have it, paying as much & as good pay as another. *Signed*: Robert Driver, sen'r; Phebe Driver [mark]. *Date*: twenty fifth day of January:1684. *Witnesses*: Joseph Armitage; Robert Potter. *Acknowledged*: 21:2 mo:1677 & Phebe his wife yielded up her thirds. *Recorded*: 4:Aprill:1683.

THOMAS GOLTHWITE and RACHELL GOLTHWAITE to SAMUELL GOLTHWITE – (6:519) Thomas Golthwite of Salem (cooper) sold to Samuell Golthwite for good, cause & considerations but especially naturall affectionate & parentall love unto my sonn Samuel Golthwite, that peece of swampy & meddow ground, which for many yeares since I bought of Edmond Giles, deceased & was before app'taining to Leift. Davenport, sometime an inhabitant heare in towne of Salem, scituate & lying in the pr'cincts & bounds of towne of Salem bounded at or neere from the place caled the "Ash Swamp" sotherly, & soe lyes along from the sd swamp northerly by the brook side toward rock caled the butt rock, part on one side of sd brooke & part on other, which hath beene long since caled Golthwites meddow, by estimation six or seaven acres, being sold & confirmed unto me for soe much meddow theire in that place as was meddow mowable or would make meddow from the land bordering upon it, according then Leift Davenport's right in the pr'misses. *Signed*: Thomas Golthwaite [mark]; Rachell Golthwite [mark]. *Date*: the day & yeare above written [no date]. *Witnesses*: Joseph Neale; Richard Croade. *Acknowledged*: May 1682 by Richard Croade & Joseph Neale. *Recorded*: 4:Aprill:1683.

ROB^T. COLLENS and HESTER COLLENS to JOSEPH BELKNAPP – (6:519) Robt Collens of Haverhill (yeoman) & Hester his wife sold to Joseph Belknapp of Boston (glover) for consideration ye sume of seaventeen pounds of current money in New England well & truly pd., all that their messuage or tenement, scittuate, lying & being in Haverhill, with all the land belonging to the same, containing fifteene acres, being butted & bounded sotherly by the highwaye, westerly & northerly by land of John Williams esterly by land of Ezra Rolfe, or otherwise however, the sd messuage is bounded or reported to be bounded & alsoe a peece or p'cell of meddow land adjoining to the upland of the pr'misses caled Duch meddow, containing by estimation fower acres, together with all houses edifices, buildings, fences, profitts, pr'vilidges, comodyties, rights, hereditaments & appurtenances whatsoever to the same belonging or in any wise appertaining, or therewith now used occupied & enjoyed provided that if above sd Robert Collens, or assignes, shall or doe well & truly pay or cause to be paid, unto above named Joseph Belknap sen'r the full & just sume of seaventeen pounds of currant money of New England, on or before the first day of November next, ensuing the day of the date of these pr'sents then this pr'sent indenture, sale & grant & every clause & article therein contained shall seaze, determine, be voyde & of none effect this indenture or anything therein contained to the contrary thereof, in anywise not withstanding. *Signed*: Robert Collens. *Date*: twenty fourth day of June. Anno:Dom: one thousand, six hundred eighty two. *Witnesses*: William Gilber; Eliezur Moody sen'r; John Hayward, sen'r. *Acknowledged*: 24th of June, 1682. *Recorded*: 28:June:1682.

JOHN LAMBERT SENR to JOHN LAMBERT JUN'R – (6:523) John Lambert senr of Beverly (fisherman) gifted to John Lambert Jun'r of Salem (marrenor) for consideration of divers good & reasonable causes & out of my own free good will, paternall love & harty afection unto my very loving grandson, John Lambert junr, my now dwelling house, standing in towne of Beverly neere the meeting house, & all the land thereunto adjoining, which p'taineth to me, said John Lambert senr containing two acres, according as it is bounded in Nathaniell Master's his deed given unto me, bearing date eight day of May, in one thousand, six hundred, sixty & seaven, and alsoe about two acres of land, scituate & lying in towne of Beverly on west side of the contry roade as it is bounded & described in the fore mentioned deed of Nathaniell Masters his: & alsoe another pr'cell of ground, scituate & lying in township of Beverly, containing five acres adjoining unto two acres last mentioned, which p'cell of land the sd John Lambert sen'r bought of William Hoare of sd towne of Beverly as appears by a deed of sale under his hand & seale, bearing date tenth day of August, one thousand, six hundred and seventy: all the sd p'cells of land with the dwelling house, oarchard, timber, wood, trees, fences & all other things w^{t}soever do p'taine or anywise belong unto pr'emisses to be to said John Lambert, Junr. *Signed*: John Lambert sen'r [mark]. *Date*: the third day of November Anno:Dom: one thousand, six hundred eighty & two. *Witnesses*: Roger Haskins; Samuel Hardie; John Lovett secundus [mark]. *Acknowledged*: 2^d December 1682. *Recorded*: 1:May:1683.

SAMUELL EDMONDS to HENRY ROADES – (6:526) Samuell Edmonds of Lynn (joyner) sold to Henry Roades of Lynn (yeoman) for consideration fifty shillings in hand pd, one acre of fresh meddow land, lying & being in Lynn, in a certain fresh marsh soe caled, that was in possession of William Merriam of Lynn, whose dwelling is neere the sd marsh, which said acre of marsh is bounded northerly by the meddow now Josiah Roades meddow, sold to him by sd Samuell Edmonds, westerly by the bridge or cause waye that goes through the sd meddow southerly by now land of Samuell Edmonds aforesd, easterly by land of Joseph Edmonds of Lynn aforesaid. *Signed*: Samuell Edmonds. *Date*: twentieth day of November one thousand six hundred eighty & two. *Witnesses*: Hilliard Veren; Israell Thorne [mark]. ***Acknowledged***: 20:9 mo:1686. *Recorded*: 3^d of May:1683.

RICHARD HAVEN SEN'R to HENRY ROADES – (6:528) Richard Haven Sen'r of Linn doe bind myself to pay or cause to be paid unto Henry Roades sum of six pounds and tenn shillings in current money of New England as having borrowed soe much in money of sd Henry Roades & for true p'formance bynd over one acre & a quarter of salt marsh, lying in Rumney Marsh lying west unto John Burrells on east, and Richard More on west: the sd. Henry Roads being to have the benefitt of sd acre & a quarter of meddow, untill sd Richard Haven sen'r doe return sd Henry Roades or his heirs or assigns sd six pounds & ten shillings in money again. *Signed*: Richard Haven. *Date*: 17th day of March 1681:1682. *Witnesses*: Daniell Gott; Richard Haven Jun'r [mark]. ***Acknowledged***: 27th day of June 1682. *Recorded*: 3:May:1683.

SIMON BRADSTREETE and ANN GARDNER – (6:529) Articles of agreement made & concluded at Salem second day of March 1676 betwixt Mr. Simon Bradstreete of Boston & Mrs. Ann Gardner of Salem aforesaid:
1. Whereas by the all wise providence of God there is a marriage intended & in convenient time to be consumated betwixt the sd Symon & sd Ann & that by law & custom, the whole estate of sd Ann upon marriage would become the sd Simonds, & after his death the thirds of all his houses, lands, reall estate would belong to sd Ann duering her natural life, in consideration whereof it is mutualy agreed & concluded by free & voluntary consent of the p'ties abovesd, that sd Simond shall enjoy & possess the estate of sd Ann both reall and personal, with the profitts and incomes thereof, only duering his natural life, & then to leave it wholly & intire to sd Ann her heirs & assignes, forever, excepting only such pt thereof as may be consumed by fire or enemies, or other acsedents or unavoidable casualties, without the neglect or neglect or defalt of the said Simond. The sd. Simon, doe hereby provise & obleige himselfe, to take care at his own proper cost

& charges, to keep the houses in Salem wherein sd Ann now lliveth together with ye fences belonging thereunto, in good & tenant like repair as now it is.

2. The sd Simon doe hereby promise & obleige himselfe, to take clame at his own propor cost & charges, to keep the houses in Salem wherein in ye sd Ann now liveth together with y^e __ and fences belonging thereunto in good & tenant like repaire as now it is.

3. And what money or other estate of any kind sd Simond shall receive at any time of sd Anns, a p'ticular account thereof being kept shal be returned to her againe imeadiately after death of Symond in the same specie it was accrued or that w'ch is equivolent thereunto (excepting before excepted) and that the whole estate of sd Simond shall & is hereby ingaged in the first place to the pr'formance heareof.

4. Lastly, it is freely left to the liberty of each p'ty before mentioned, at his or her death, which by the providence and good pleasure of God shall happen first, to give unto the other surviving, besides what is pr'ticularly heare agreed, as a testimony of love & good will, what at theire departure out of this world, shall seem good unto them, which shall be in leiw & sattisfaction of all other rights or demands whatsoever. In witness whereof the pr'ties aforesd have hereunto to sett theire hands & seals. *Signed*: Simon Bradstreete; Ann Gardner. ***Recorded***: 17:May:1682.

This instrument was signed, sealed & delivered in my pr'sence the 6th day of June 1676 by both p'ties. Daniell Denison Assist.

ROBERT BRIMSDON and REBECKA BRIMSDON to PHILLIP GREELY – (6:531) Robert Brimsdon of Boston (marchant) with the full & free consent of my now wife Rebecka Brimsdon sold to Phillip Greely of Salsbury in New England for consideration one halfe pt. of the catch Phillip & Mary, whereof Phillip Greely was late owner & all the appurtenances to ye catch belonging, all my house & land of twenty six foot long & eighteen foott wide or thereabouts, scituate & being in Salem in New England aforesaid & all the land thereto belonging, containing twenty fower pole of land & all the fencing & other, the liberties, pr'vilidges & appurtenances thereto belonging, the which land is butting & bounded as followeth viz: on east with land of Jacob Pudeater, on west with land of John Williams, cooper, on the north with land sometimes in hand of Thomas Wattson, & on the south with the comon or comon land &c & all the estate, right, title, interest, propriety, possession, claime & demand of said Robert Brimsdon, thereunto or to any part thereof mentioned till the fourth of May next & Mr. Greely is to have the rent from the day of the date hereof. *Signed*: Robert Brimsdon; Rebecka Brimsdon [mark]. ***Release of Dower***: Rebecka wife of sd Robert Brimsdon doth freely surrender & yield up all her rights of dower & title of thirds. ***Date***: the one & twentieth day of February one thousand, six hundred & eighty 1680:81. *Witnesses*: John Viall Jun'r; Thomas Kemble. *Acknowledged*: Robert Brimsdon and Rebecka Brimsdon February 23:1681. *Recorded*: 1:June:1683.

JOHN PATCH to CAPT. GEORGE CORWIN – (6:535) John Patch of Beverly (husbandman) with consent of wife sold to Capt. George Corwin of Salem (marchant) for consideration the sum of eight pounds in hand alreddy paid, three acres of meddow ground, lying & being scituate in Beverly, & being bounded as followeth viz: on northwest with the upland belonging to Nathaniell Stone, on northeast with meddow ground of Capt. Thomas Lothrop, & on south with upland of Samuell Corning Jun'r. *Signed*: John Patch [mark]. *Date*: this eight day of May, one thousand, six hundred, seventy five. 1675. *Witnesses*: Edward Norrice; William Andrew; John Whiting Jun'r. *Acknowledged*: 8:3 mo:75. *Recorded*: 8:June:1683.

GEORGE CORWIN and ELIZABETH CORWIN to ISAACK WOODBERY – (6:536) George Corwin of Salem (marchant) sold to Isaack Woodbery of Beverly (marrenor) for consideration the sume of seaven pounds, tenn shillings current money of New England in hand paid, three acres of medow ground, lying & being scituate in Beverly & being bounded on northwest with upland belonging to Nathaniell Stone, on northeast with the meddow ground of Capt.Thomas Lothrop & on south with upland of Samuell Corning Junr. *Signed*: George Corwin; Eliza: Corwin. *Date*: seaventh day of June in one thousand, six hundred eighty. *Witnesses*: Philip Cromwell; Richard Mabee. *Acknowledged*: Capt. George Corwin & Ms. Elizabeth Corwin 7th of June 1683. *Recorded*: 9:June:1683.

SIMON BRADSTREETE – (6:539) Whereas Simon Bradstreete of Boston Esqr. did in the lifetime of Samuell Bradstreete, my eldest sonn, & Mercy his wife in consideration of my naturall love & affection to them & care to make provission for theire issue & posterity & for divers other good causes & considerations (but under sundry limitations) promise & ingage to convey & confirme to my sd son Samuell & Mercy his wife & heires of theire bodyes forever all that my mansion or dwelling house at Lynn, wherein Capt. Thomas Marshall dwelleth, with the whole farme consisting of upland, marsh & medow thereto belonging together with all barns, stables, outhouses, hortyards, gardens, fences, mounds & comons, with all other profitts, pr'vilidges, waies, easements & appurtenances thereto belonging or any waies appertaining and whereas by ocasion of my sons, removeall & death of his sd wife & himselfe the premisses have not hetherto been setled & confirmed, according to my ingagement & intention, & for as much as now there is not any other issue of my sd sonn by his sd wife Mercy surviving, save only Mercy theire daughter: therefore I sd

Simon Bradstreete have given & granted, & by these pr'sents doe, give, grant, assigne, enfeofe, make over & confirme unto said Mercy Bradstreete, my grandchild all that my sd mansion house at Lynn, with the whole farme, both of uplands, marsh, meddow, now in tenure & occupation of Capt. Thomas Marshall, together with all barns, stables, outhouses, hortyards, gardens, fences, mounds & comons, together with all other profitts, pr'vilidges, waies easements & appurtenances from & imediately after the departure of me sd Simond Bradstreet out of this life reserving only the rent or sum of ten pounds p' annum in money to be paid to Ann Bradstreete my beloved wife out of the rents, issues & profitts of sd houses & farme during the term of her naturall life: provided never the less & my true intent & meaning is that if my said grandchild Mercy Bradstreet shal marry with & leave a husband surviving that such husband shall during his natural life possess & injoy the premises & profitts thereof, yielding & paying the sd annuity of ten pounds to my said wife during her natural life but if after the death of said Mercy my grandchild & such husband or husbands as she shall be married to noe issue lawfully begotten betweene them shall survive, or if afterwards such issue should fail & be wholy extinct, then I doe hereby give & grant sd house, farme & pr'misses to the heires of my sd sonn Samuell & to theire heires & assignes forever, still reserving annuity of ten pounds pr' annum out of the rents & profits thereof, to my sd wife, Ann Bradstreete during her naturall life as aforesd. *Signed*: S. Bradstreet. *Date*: first day of June one thousand, six hundred eighty & three. *Witnesses*: Samuell Morrell; Richerd Wharton. *Acknowledged*: 1 June 1683 by Hon'ble Simon Bradstreet, Esq. *Recorded*: 11:June:1683.

JOSEPH REDNAP to THO. LAIGHTON JUN'R – (6:542) Joseph Rednap of Lyn (cooper) freely give grant & confirme to Tho. Laighton Jun'r of Lyn (husbandman) whoe married my daughter Sarah, for divers considerations moving me thereunto unto Thomas Laighton one smale p'cell of upland & therewith the pr'vilidge of the comons of a halfe house lott, formerly caled old Cromwells lott, which is now in my possesion: which smale p'cell of upland containeth half an acre, one part of which land the dwelling house & barne & lentos of sd Thomas Laighton his standeth upon the said land being bounded with land of sd Joseph Rednap on north, & with land of sd Tho. Laighton on south; butting upon land of Widdow Rooten's on west, & on the towne comon on east, with all & singuler pr'vilidges & appurtenances thereunto belonging. Indenture made 16th of May 1681. *Signed*: Joseph Rednap [mark]. *Date*: 8th daye of June 1681. *Witnesses*: Crispus Brewer; Samuell Tarbox. *Acknowledged*: 8 June 1681. *Recorded*: 7:July:1683.

BETTERICE BERRY and RICHARD CROAD – (6:544) These are to certifie unto whomsoever it may concerne that Betterice Berry, aged about eighty three yeares, rational & conpus mentes, came pr'sonelly before me this second day of July in year of our Lord one thousand six hundred, eighty & three & testified upon her corporall oath, y^t Richerd Croad now living in Salem, in New England, & heare present in health before me: she knows to be the reputed sonn of Richerd Croad of Frampton in ye county of Dorcett, in old England, sen'r & ~~Anstice, his wife, & that she was pr'sent at the birth, of this Richard Croad Jun'r, now before me~~ [sic]. She this deponent declaring that shee very well knew sd Richard Croad sen'r & Anstice his wife, & that she was pr'sent at the birth of this Richard Croad Jun'r, now before me, when borne of Anstice wife of sd Richard Croad sen'r being on a Sabbath day in morning, which time (it being before the marriage of this deponent with any man) she ownes before me that shee was known & caled by the name of Betterice Burt & she caled the midwife whose name was Goodwife Hathailie to the travell of aforesd Anstice, there being no other woman pre'sent but sd midwife & one goodwife Dammer & this deponent whoe affirms that she received from the hands of the midwife, this Richard Croad now living in Salem, imeadiately after he came into the world. Ateste. Bartholomew Gedney Assist. In the Government of his Majesties Colony of Massachusetts in New England.

WILLIAM STERLING and ANN NEALE – (6:546) Whereas there is an intended marriage betweene William Sterling of Haverhill, & Ann Neale, widdow of Salem, and in order to the consumation thereof, in order to the setling of things between them relating to their outward estate.

First They have mutuelly agred as followeth: viz: that what estate in house & land the sd Ann is possest of, for her use & her children's as administratrix to the estate of her former husband John Neale, deceased, shell be & remaine to her & her sd children & assignes, & that said Wm. Sterling shall have noe right, title or interest therein or any part thereof, only the rent & improvement of said houses & land to be to use of sd William & Ann after theire marriage, & soe long as they shall live together as man & wife.

2ly That for what houseold goods & moveables the sd Ann have & shall bring with her in marriage, shall be to theire use & mutuall comfort together, while they both survive together, & if sd William decease before said Ann & leave her a widdow, that then the sd moveables to return to sd Ann, but if please God to give them a child or children together in marriage, that shall be then surviving at her decease shall be & remaine to those children otherwise to be & belong to her & her children by her first husband, what shall be remaining of sd estate.

3ly It is mutualy agreed by & betweene them sd. William & Ann, that if it shall please God that he sd William depart this life, & leave the sd Ann a widdow that she shall have & hold & injoy to her use, the third part of all estate of sd William, in house & lands according as the law directs, soe long as the sd Ann shall live a widdow, but in case of her marriage with another man y^n that thirds to returne to the heires of sd William.

4ly. It is alsoe agreed mutualy, that in case the sd Ann should depart this life before sd William & shall leave children or child by sd William, that what moveables as abovesd brought by her shall be & remaine to her children, but in case shee have noe childredn by sd William, that shall be then surviving, then what of those goods or estate that shal be then remaining, to be to the use & delivered up into possesion of her children by her former husband: memorandum, it is to be understood, & it is agreed upon as the intent & meaning, as in first article, that when any of the sd Ann her children by her former husband, shall come to age & demand their interest in lands or housing aforesd, that they are to have it delivered them, & soe the proportion or rent or improvement thereof no longer to be exspected by sd William.

5ly And lastly it is mutualy agreed upon, by & betweene parties abovesd, that whatever debts or legacies is due from the estate to any p'son or p'sons whatsoever, or whatsoever is owing to the estate from any p'son, to say, the estate of sd Ann as administratrix, the sd William Starling is not at all to be concerned with or liable to make any paiments in that kind out of his owne estate, or what as aforesd the said Ann shall bring with her to him, nor shall receive any debts due to her or her estate before marriage to his use, but shall be wholy free & disengaged from any ingagements in that kind. And it is further agreed upon the consumation of marriage as abovesd, that the sd Ann may bring with her her two youngest children, whom sd William is free to take with her his said wife, & maintain upon his own cost & charge, upon & in consideration of, in & by these articles before exspressed. ***Signed***: William Sterling; Ann Neale [mark]. ***Date***: 22 March 1682:3. ***Witnesses***: Hilliard Veren; John Norman; Jeremiah Neale. ***Acknowledged***: William Sterling & Ann Neale acknowl. 24 Apr 1683. ***Recorded***: 7:July:1683.

JONATHAN PICKERING to ENSIGNE THOMAS BANCROFT – (6:549) Jonathan Pickering of Salem sold to Ensigne Thomas Bancroft of Linn (yeoman) for consideration sume of twelve pounds in money in hand paid, a certaine p'cell of meddow and fresh marsh ground, more or less, scituate lying & being in bounds of Lynn in a meddow caled Reedy meddow bounded eastward by some meddow of Andrew Mansfeild, westerly by som medow formerly of Henry Collens, now in possession of Andrew Mansfield, northerly by som upland of sd Thomas Bancroft, &

sotherly by the swamp caled the darke Swamp. the sd pr'cell of meddow, containing three acres. *Signed*: Jonathan Pickering [mark]. **Release of Dower:** Jane wife yield dower. *Date*: twelfth day of October one thousand six hundred eighty & two. *Witnesses*: Thomas Parkes [mark]; Hilliard Veren. *Acknowledged*: 27 June:1683. *Recorded*: 7:July:1683.

EDWARD BERRY JUN'R to EDWARD BERRY SEN'R – (6:552)
Whereas Edward Berry sen'r of Salem (weaver) did by deed of guift bearing date the sixteenth day of May one thousand six hundred seaventy & seaven for the considerations therein mentioned, which were that I his sonn Edward Berry Junr of Painton in county of Devon in Kingdom of England should provid for my sd father Edward Berry sen'r meat, drink, washing, lodging, apparell & all other things necessary for him during terme of his naturall life as by sd deed of guift more at large it doth & may appeere, freely, cleerely & absolutely give & grant, assigne, convey & confirme unto me sd sonn Edward Berry Jun'r, all that his dwelling house in Salem with his ground adjoining thereunto & all that his land in Beverly, caled Draper's Poynt & all the liberties & pr'vilidges thereunto belonging: all which I was to have & to hould, together, with all his goods & chattels, implements, debts, bills, bonds, specialtyes, necessaryes, sums of money & all manner of other things, as well immoveables as moveables, of what kind, quality & condition soever they may be, to me sd Edward Berry, my heires, executors, administrators & assignes forever, nevertheless I sd Edward Berry Jun'r for valuable considerations me thereunto moving, but more especially at the request of my sd father & in obedience unto him have & hereby fully, clerly & absolutely remis, release & acquitt, & discharge my sd father Edward Berry Sen'r from sd deed of guift & from all & everything therein contained, upon any account w'soever & from every pt thereof & from any benefitts that I might have received thereby & doe hereby renounce & disclaim, both for myselfe, my heires, executors & administrators to have any right thereto or interest therein & doe hearby declare the same to be null & voyde to all intents & purposes & that my sd father his heires, executors, administrators & assignes shall & may as freely & peaceably have, hould, possess & enjoye same & every pt thereof as he might or could have done, if he had not signed sd deed of guift to me in manner aforesd. *Signed*: Edward Berry Jun'r. *Date*: tenth day of July: one thousand six hundred & eighty three. *Wtinesses*: Signed, sealed & delivered & six pence in money delivered by sd Edward Berry Jun'r to his sd father as an ernest of his father's quiett repossession of all pr'misses aforementioned & whatever else was given in said deed of guift in pr'sence of us Richard Waye; Thomas Blackford; John Goffe; Thomas Kemble. *Acknowledged*: July 11th 1683 Edward Berry Jun'r. *Recorded*: 11:July:1683.

WILLIAM CASH to PHILLIP CROMWELL – (6:554) William Cash of Salem (marrenor) sold to Mr. Phillip Cromwell of Salem for consideration a valuable sume in hand received, my dwelling house & ground in Salem with all the pr'vilidges & appurtenances thereunto belonging. *Signed*: William Cash. *Date*: 12 October 1677. *Witnesses*: John Cromwell; Richard Croade. *Acknowledged*: by John Cromwell & Richard Croade 9:10 mo:1679. *Recorded*: 11:July:1683.

JEREMIAH SHEPPARD and MARGARET BISHOP – (6:556) The deposition of Jeremiah Sheppard aged 33 yeares or thereabout, whoe testifieth the debt due by bond dated February 5th 1673 from Margaret Bishop the widdow relict & executrix of Thomas Bishop deceased & Thomas & Samuell Bishop her sonns was originally the debt of sd Thomas Bishop unto Worshipfull Richard Saltonstall Esq'r & by vertue of an assignment made by sd Mr. Saltonstall, the administrators of the estate of the Reverend Mr. Jonathan Michell, late of Cambridge, deceased, obtained a judgment of Cambridge County Court October 2:1677 & moneys not being tendered accordin to obligation given, as well by sd Thomas Bishop deceased, as alsoe renued by his executors to administrators of sd Jonathan Michell as will appeere by theire bond dated February 5th 1673: the lands whereof the said Bishop deceased dyed seized, the said land after legall demand of money by the marshall, viz: the farme in Ipswich whereof Samuell Ingalls was tenant, was taken in execution & possession given to the parties concerned, the administrators of sd Jonathan Michell deceased, the scituation, quantity, bounds & apprisement whereof the returne of the Marshall on the Register more p'ticulerly declare: sworn in Court at Salem by Mr. Jeremiah Sheppard 26:4 mo:1683. Atteste Hilliard Veren Cler. *Recorded*: 11:July:1683.

THOMAS ROOTES SEN'R TO THOMAS ROOTES – (6:557) Thomas Rootes Sen'r of Salem gifted to Thomas Rootes: whereas the Selectmen of towne of Salem did in yeare 1636 give unto my mother the Widdow Mason twenty acres of land & to my brother Richard twenty acres of land & to myselfe twenty acres of land, in all sixty acres of land, all being in the township of Salem as refference to records in Salem being had more largely will appeere, now I Thomas Rootes sen'r as well for & in consideration of love & naturall affection which I have & doe beare unto my kinsman Thomas Rootes, my brother Josiah his sonn, & other good causes have given unto my aforesd kinsman all right, title & interest I have, might have or ought to have to aforementioned sixty acres of land or any part thereof. *Signed*: Thomas Rootes. *Date*: 20 June 1655. *Witnesses*: Jeremiah Neale; Zebulon Hill; John Hill. *Acknowledged*: 27 June 1683. *Recorded*: 27:June:1683.

THOMAS LAUGHTON SEN'R to THOMAS LAUGHTON – (6:558) Thomas Laughton sen'r of Lyn gave to sonn Thomas Laughton of Lin from meer motion & free will this instrument or indenture upon serious consideration y^t sd son Thomas Laughton shall carefully, conscionably and dilligently take care of & maintaine mee & my deare wife, wee both of us being aged & stricken in years & thereby much disinable to bodyly labour & for divers considerations grant this instrument or indenture. *Signed*: Thomas Laughton sen'r. *Date*: 22:July:1685. *Witnesses*: Samuell Tarbox; Benjamin Redknap. *Acknowledged*: by Mr. Oliver Purchase as atturney to Mr. Thomas Laughton sen'r of Lyn at Boston 22 July 1685 this refers to folio:9: in this book. *Recorded*: no date.

JOHN NEWMAN to JOHN GREENE – (6:560) John Newman of Salem (marchant) sold to John Greene of Salem (yeoman) for consideration thirty pounds in currant sterling money in hand paid, a certaine p'cell of land containing ten acres or thereabouts lying in bounds of Salem in a place knowne by name of Ryal's side neck, being bounded easterly by the marsh ground p'taining unto Capt. Wm. Dixy & by the land hired by sd Green & his copartners of the towne of Salem northerly runing up from said Dixie's marsh unto a pine tree marked with N.G. westerly bounded by a great hemlock tree standing at the corner of Rine Cove comonly soe caled, being the westerly corner bounds betweene land of sd John Newman & foresd p'cell of land, sotherly & southeast by the river. *Signed*: John Newman. *Date*: 9 August 1683. *Witnesses*: Samuell Hardie; Free Balch. *Acknowledged*: 11 August 1683. *Recorded*: 11:6 mo:1683.

JOHN FURBUSH to JOHN ROADES JUN'R – (6:562) John Furbush of Marblehead (husbandman) sold to John Roades Jun'r of Marblehead (fisherman) for consideration forty nine pd's sterling in hand paid, all that dwelling house land & oarchard & yard about it with the well & all other pr'vilidges & appurtenances: w'ch sd house & land I lately bought of John Williams as p' deed from him appeereth & is scituate & lying in Marblehead & is bounded toward south & southeast by land of William Wood & towards northeast with a common highwaye & towards north & north westerly by land of William Poate. *Signed*: John Furbush [mark]. *Date*: 14 August 1683. *Witnesses*: Hilliard Veren; John Legg. *Acknowledged*: 14 August 1683. *Recorded*: 14:August 1683.

RICH'D GLASSE and ELIZABETH GLASSE to JOHN LEGG – (6:565) Rich'd Glasse of Marblehead (marrenor) & Elizabeth wife sometime administrator to estate of her former husband Nicholas Fox deceased mortgaged to John Legg of Marblehead (marchant) for consideration forty seaven pounds, all that oure tenement lying in Marblehead containing by estimation one quarter part of an acre wheron we now dwell being bounded on east & south sides with lands of John Stacy, on west with streete, on north with land of Thomas Sowden together with dwelling house thereon, fences, cow comonage, pr'vilidges and all appurtenances to sd tenement belonging provided if sd Richard Glasse doe pay or cause to be paid to John Legg the full sume of forty seaven pounds in marchantable & refuse fish & macrell in manner following at price currant (that is to say) eleven pounds fifteene shillings p' annum at two severall paiments in June & October at end of voyages in the specie abovesd viz: the first quarter pt of the debt in the months abovesd in year 1684 & second eleven pounds & fifteene shillings in same months 1685 & eleven pounds fifteene shilings in the same months 1686 & eleven pounds fifteene shillings more thereof in same month 1687 being the full remainder of sume that then this grant & sale shall be voyde & of none efect but if defalt happens in the payment of any of the summs that then sd John Legg shall by virtue of these pr'sents enter same absolutely as his owne & injoy it forever, being accountable only for what of sd sume shall appeer to be pd by Richard Glass. *Signed*: Richard Glasse [mark]; Elizabeth Glasse [mark]. *Date*: 13 August 1683. *Witnesses*: Samuell Cheever; William Browne. *Acknowledged*: 14 August 1683 by Richard Glasse & Elizabeth wife. *Recorded*: 14 August 1683.

NATHANIELL PICKMAN SEN'R to BETHIA SILSBY – (6:568)
Nathaniell Pickman sen'r of Salem (carpenter) give & confirme to Bethia Silsby & to her heires & assignes, for divers good causes especially for love & naturall affection to daughter Bethia Silsby widdow a certaine p'cell of ground p'tly upon which her dwelling house standeth, being pt of that ground of mine adjoyning my dwelling house & lyes betwixt the burying point in Salem & the water, the dementions & bounds are as followeth viz: the sd p'cell of land to begin next my oarchard fence & soe to run sotherly to that peece I gave to my son Sanders, which is five pole or neere five pole & the other way in bredth from the burying poynt down westward by my orchard fence, it runns fower pole or neere fower pole & at the side next adjoining to my sonn John Sanders from the burying point downe westerly to the water it is to neere four poles or somewhat lesse & is soe lying bounded sotherly with land of John Sanders easterly by burying poynt northerly by my oarchard fence & westerly partly by my ground & partly by the water. *Signed*: Nathaniell Pickman sen'r. *Date*: 2 February 1679:80. *Witnesses*: Hilliard Veren sen'r; John Sander. *Acknowledged*: 16 June 1680. *Recorded*: 14 August 1683.

I Nathaniell Pickman have as an adition to within granted premisses for convenencye of a wharfe & pr'vilidg of the water give, grant & confirme to sd daughter Silsby (then widdow) now wife of Alexander Cole. I give grant & confirme to sd Alexander Cole & to Bethia his wife soe much ground to the west of within granted pr'misses for the convenience of a wharfe, to say thirty foot in bredth from line or bound of John Sanders by his wharehouse to extend northerly as line of within pr'misses doe runn on westerly side & soe to runn that bredth of thirty foot westerly into water soe farr as he may without prejudicing any others before granted pr'vilidg. *Signed*: Nathaniell Pickman sen'r. *Date*: 17 September 1683. *Witnesses*: Hilliard Veren; Robert Bronsdon Jun'r.

RICHARD HALLEY and JOANNA HALLEY to JOHN FURBUSH – (6:572) Richard Halley of Marblehead (fisherman) with consent of wife sold to John Furbush of Marblehead for consideration twenty fower pounds silver, one new dwelling house which I doe now dwell in, in Marblehead, together with seaven pole of ground in length & in bredth as it is fenced & unfenced lying in Marblehead between Robert Knight's house & William Bartoll's of one side & John Abbetts house & William Wattells of other side. *Signed*: Richard Halley; Joanna Halley [mark]. *Date*: 22 May 1683. *Witnesses*: William Waters; Edw Humphrys. *Acknowledged*: 2 June 1683. *Recorded*: 14:August:1683.

EDWARD HOEMAN and ANN HOEMAN to JOHN FURBUSH – (6:574) Edward Hoeman of Marblehead (fisherman) with consent of wife sold to John Furbush of Marblehead for consideration twenty pounds money in hand received, my now dwelling house lying in Marblehead adjoining neere to the house of Richard Haley with ground the said house stands upon, together with all ground, appurtenances & pr'vilidges thereunto belonging, as it is recorded in the towne book of Marblehead. *Signed*: Edward Hoeman [mark]; Ann Hoeman [mark]. *Date*: 22 May 1683. *Witnesses*: William Waters; Edw Humphries. *Acknowledged*: 2 June 1683. *Recorded*: 14:August:1683.

MANNASSETH MARSTON to JOHN HIGGENSON JUN'R – (6:576) Mannasseth Marston of Salem sold to John Higgenson Jun'r of Salem for consideration tenn pounds in hand paid, all that p'cell of land which I bought of towne of Salem containing forty acres lying within township of Salem on north side of Ipswich river & is bounded as doth appeere by town record viz: upon John Phelps' bound upon Ipswich river northerly to a young white oake neere sd Phelps oarchard & soe easterly from sd white oake to a pine tree upon the brow of a hill neere Redding bounds & from thence about forty poale east sotherly to a rock & from the rock sotherly to a young white oake upon the edge of the swamp belonging to Samuell Gardner sen'r & from thence westerly to a pine tree ye corner bounds of sd Gardner's land & soe ranging with sd Gardner's line downe to Ipswich river & from thence to aforesaid Phelps' bound on said river. *Signed*: Manasseth Marstone. *Date*: 8 March 1678:9. *Witnesses*: Joseph Grafton; John Hathorne. *Acknowledged*: 13 December 1680 and Marcy manefested consent yielding up thirds. *Recorded*: 14:August:1683.

THOMAS SAVAGE, EPHRAIM SAVAGE, PEREZ SAVAGE and EBENEZER SAVAGE – (6:579) Thomas Savage, Ephraim Savage, Perez Savage & Ebenezer Savage sonns & executors of will of Thomas Savage Esq'r late of Boston deceased, whereas Thomas Savage Esq. in and by his will did give & bequeath unto his daughter Sarah Higgenson: all his land scituate in towne of Salem or two hundred pounds which shee should accept of: & whereas Mr. John Higgenson of Salem marchant, husband of sd Sarah, together with her have made theire election of the land, now for the due satisfaction & discharge of sd legacy aforenamed executors have granted, assigned, enfeofed, released & confirmed unto sd John Higgenson his heires & assignes all that piece or p'cell of land which our said father dyed seazed of by purchast from the executors of will of Capt. Walter Price scituat & lying on Winter Island within pr'cincts or limitts of towne of Salem containing by estimation fower acres of upland and meddow, being fenced in to the sea or Winter harbour with a stone wale & bounded east southerly & south westerly with comon land & northerly & easterly with the sea & Winter harbour, together with dwelling house & all other houses, edefices, buildings & fences erected & standing upon sd land. *Signed*: Thomas Savage; Ephraim Savage; Thomas Savage for Perez Savage as his aturney; Ebenezer Savage. *Date*: 18 August 1683. *Witnesses*: John Wiswall sen'r; George Tomson. *Acknowledged*: Capt. Thomas Savage for himselfe & Perez Savage: Mr. Ephraim Savage & Ebenezer Savage all acknowledged in Boston 18:6 mo:1683. *Recorded*: 14:August:1683.

ELIZABETH GRAVES and EDWARD FARRINGTON to MATHEW FARRING JUN'R – (6:582) Elizabeth wife of Mark Graves being at a place caled Jeffery's Creeke in county of Essex administratrix of estate of John Farrington her former husband deceased with Edward Farrington eldest sonn of aforesd John Farrington deceased sometime of Marblehead (cooper) sold to Mathew Farrington Jun'r of Lynn (yeoman) for divers good causes especially sume of one hundred pounds in hand paid which said Elizabeth Graves & Edward Farrington her son acknowledge, all that p'cells of land in Lynn formerly belonging to former husband John Farrington deceased viz: one halfe pt of a corne mill it being a tide mill with halfe the barne with one parcel of upland & meddow thereunto adjoining, bounded as followeth: with land of Job Knights easterly & upon land of Daniell Needham sotherly & westerly upon sd Mathew Farrington's owne land & northerly upon land of John Fuller sen'r: three acres of salte marsh lying in towne marsh, bounded westerly with the lands of Mr. Samuell Cobbitt & southerly with lands of ~~Mr.~~ Benjamin Jenson northerly with lands of Joseph Halls and easterly with lands of Mathew Farrington sen'r. *Signed*: Elizabeth Graves [mark]; Edward Farrington. *Date*: 18 August 1683. *Witnesses*: John Fuller sen'r; Mathew Farrington. *Acknowledged*: 17 August 1683 by Elizabeth Graves & Edward Farrington. *Recorded*: 28:August:1683.

GRIFFIN EDWARDS, JOHN MILES and ANN MILES to BENJAMIN FARR – (6:585) Griffin Edwards now inhabiting in Bostone gent. & aturney & administrator on behalfe of his mother in law Mrs. Ann Miles who is the reputed only heire surviving of Colonel John Humphries Esq'r deceased & shee is the now wife of Mr. John Miles minister at Swansey, a plantation in coloney of Plimouth sold to Benjamin Farr of Lynn for consideration one and twenty pounds & five shillings currant money in hand paid, a certaine p'cell of meddow land lying in a certain meddow caled Rumley marsh belonging to towne of Lynn containing four acres & a halfe by estimation accounted, the one halfe part of nine acres soe accounted that did formerly belong & appertaine to Col. John Humphris Esq. deceased bounded by the marsh of Richard Hudd ~~Esq'r~~ on eastward & by marsh of John Burrell sen'r which he purchased on westward & was other halfe of nine acres aforesd & by Bennett's creeke on northward & by the maine river that vessells pass to & froe in that parteth betweene Lynn & Boston on southward. *Signed*: Griffin Edwards; John Miles; Ann Miles. *Date*: 8 October 1681. *Witnesses*: William Bassett; Daniell Johnson. *Acknowledged*: 29 October 1681 by Griffin Edwards, John Miles & Mrs. Ann Miles his wife. *Recorded* 18:Sept:1683.

JOHN ELWELL to WILLIAM PINSON – (6:588) John Elwell of Salem (fisherman) sold to William Pinson of Salem (fisherman) for consideration sixty eight pounds in hand paid or secured to be paid, all that my dwelling house with ground it stands upon & all ground adjoining thereunto scituate in Salem as now bounded viz: sotherly with the wharfe or water side against south harbour, the land & housing of Mr. Hollingsworth easterly, of Jacob Allen northwesterly & house and land of John Clifford westerly sd land containing eleven or twelve rod of ground. *Signed*: John Elwell [mark]. *Date*: 14 March 1677:8. *Witnesses*: Edward Moule; Hilliard Veren sen'r. *Acknowledged*: 14:1 mo:77:8. *Recorded*: 19:Sept:1683.

Jane Elwell acknowledged her consent & gave up thirds 4 april 1682.

JOHN GATCHELL and WIBRO GATCHELL to HENRY MAINE – (6:591) John Gatchell of Marblehead with consent of Wibra wife sold to Henry Maine of Marblehead for consideration tenn pounds money, one peece of ground or land containing halfe an acre as it is now staked out being in Marblehead bounded with land of Christopher Codner's towards the northward & towards eastward the highwaye of lane & John Roades sen'r his garden & towards south joining to land of John Roades sen'r & westward joining close to John Gatchell's land together with trees standing in land. *Signed*: John Gatchell; Wibro Gatchell. *Release of Dower*: Wibra wife doth yield up dower. *Date*: 30 April 1683. *Witnesses*: Samuell Gatchell; Edw. Humphryes. *Acknowledged*: 29 September 1683. *Recorded*: 29:Sept:1683.

JOHN PETHERICK to JOHN SEARLE – (6:593) John Petherick of Marblehead neck (fisherman) sold to John Searle of Marblehead for divers good causes especially fifty pounds sterling in hand paid, a certaine p'cell of land containing by estimation halfe an acre or thereabouts with the dwelling house standing thereupon lying on sd neck belonging to Marblehead & is part of that acre of land I late bought of William Browne of Salem Esq'r & was by him bought of Christopher Lattamore: which sd p'cell of ground now bargained & sold is that part of sd acre that lyes next to the harbour which bounds it northerly & soe taking whole bredth of about fower rod & extends or goes soe farr up from sd harbour & running sotherly square one rod in length beyond the well & is bounded sotherly with other pt of sd acre of mine and westerly with land of mine & by the land of Andrew Tucker easterly. *Signed*: John Petherick [mark]. *Release of Dower*: Miriam wife yields up dower. *Date*: 5 October 1683. *Witnesses*: Hilliard Veren; Henry Skerry sen'r. *Acknowledged*: 5:8mo:1683. *Recorded*: 4 October 1683.

WILLIAM BROWNE to THO. CROMWELL – (6:596) William Browne of Salem (marchant) and Sarah wife sold to Tho. Cromwell of Salem (tayler) for consideration thirty two pounds in hand paid, one dwelling house together with plott of land whereon sd house standeth formerly in occupation of sd William Browne & is scituate betweene the house and land of Phillip Cromwell on west & the lane that goes to the water side and wharfe whereon the warehouse of sd William Browne standeth on east butting to the maine streete whereon the meeting house standeth on north & thence back southward to nine foot of sd Brownes stable as it now standeth, the p'tition fence betweene sd Browne & said Cromwell to be divided in equall halves & sd Cromwell to keepe & maintain the halfe eastward & sd Browne to keepe & maintaine the halfe westward home to Phillip Cromwells fence. It is to be understood that the dividing fence is to runn upon a strait line nine foott from the stable abovesd home to Phillip Cromwell's fence abovesd. *Signed*: William Browne. *Date*: 20:2 mo:1664. *Witnesses*: with seazon & possession given according to law. Elias Stileman; Thomas Robinson. *Acknowledged*: by Capt. Elias Stileman 15:October:1683. *Recorded*: 16:October:1683.

SAMUELL APLETON JUN'R to SAMUELL HAYMAN and NATHAN HAYMAN – (6:598) Samuell Apleton Jun'r of Lynn mortgaged to Samuell Hayman and Nathan Hayman of Charlestown (marrenor) for consideration one hundred pounds lawfull money in hand paid, my farme & mantion house comonly knowne by name of the Ironworkes farme, excepting only soe much of sd farme as is alreddy mortgaged unto the Hon'ble Simon Bradstreete Esq'r Governor of collony which containeth lesse than one quarter part of sd farme, as by my deed unto him dated in February last doth appeere containing six hundred acres lying within the limitts of towne of Lynn bounded northerly by John Hawks sen'r easterly by Lynn comon sotherly by Henry Roades wheeler & Dyamond westerly by Daniell Hitchins,, provided that Samuell Apleton shall pay or cause to be paid unto Samuell Hayman and Nathan Hayman one hundred pounds of lawfull money in Charlestown at or before the 11 October 1689 & eight pounds in like lawfull money for forebearance on or before 11 October yearely untill the principle be paid: in such case payment being made without fraude or further delay then above sale & grant shall be voyde & of none effect. *Signed*: Samuell Apleton. *Date*: 11 October 1683. *Witnesses*: Laurance Hammond; Jos. Wolcott. *Acknowledged*: by Mr. Samuell Apleton 11 October 1683. *Recorded*: 23:October:1683.
The release of this mortgage from Haymans, Samuell & Nathan is recorded in 9th booke of Salem records for lands in folio 4 & 5.

EPHRAIM JOANES and MARY JOANES to JOHN WENBORNE – (6:602) Ephraim Joanes of Marblehead (fisherman) sold to John Wenborne of Manchester for consideration valuable sum of money, house and orchard & 3 acres of upland lying in plaine above the saw mill bounded with a cartwaye on the northeast on the southwest & northwest with rocky hills & on the southeast with Samuell Leach's land; and 3 acres of upland in the neck lying betweene land of widow Pickworth and Leach's land & three qr'ters of an acre or thereabouts of meddows lying upon the sawmill pond and next unto Aron Bennetts meddow situate, lying and being within bounds & limits of abovenamed towne of Manchester. *Signed*: Epharaim Joanes [mark]; Mary Joanes [mark]. *Date*: 14 July 1683. *Witnesses*: Abigaile Browne; Mary Pray. *Acknowledged*: 14 July 1683 by both. *Recorded*: 2:9 mo:1683.

EZEKIELL NEEDHAM to THOMAS NEWHALL – (6:604) For consideration of a valuable sum of money, Ezekiell Needham of Lynn having for myselfe, my heires, executors, administrators & assignes sold a certaine tract of land containing 60 acres situate in bounds of Lynn neere upon or unto Dogg Pond so called w'ch sd land is more largely specified in deed signed and sealed & delivered by me Ezekiell Needham unto Thomas Newhall sen'r of Lynn as proper right & interest forever; now that said land &c sold by me may be & remaine firme & sure according to law unto Thomas Newall from any future molestations from heires of me sd Ezekiell Needham & Sarah my now wife that either now or maye be for the future Bee it knowne that we Ezekiell Needham & Sarah my now wife for ourselves our heires &c & every of y^m for security of aforesaid Thomas Newall of possession of aforesaid bargained sixty acres doe by these presents grant make & bind & deliver our homestead soe called viz: the land given to us by Mr. Daniel King sen'r, our hon'rd father, now deceased containing thirty three acres by estimation & is more fully expressed & bounded in deed of guift made & confirmed by our aforesaid father as in the records at Salem in book, the third, page 173 with the housing that is build thereupon of every sort and moreover Ezekiel Needham & Sarah his wife doe covenant & promise to & with said Thomas Newall that at the day of the date hereof that they the sd Ezekiell & Sarah doe stand possessed of leagall right & good inheritance in fee simple of oure homestead aforesaid boath of land and housing thereupon & is absolute & free from all or any ingagement p'son or p'sons whatsoever & that they have full good right & lawfull authority in theire names to grant, make over, bind & deliver unto same & deliver sd homestead unto sd Thomas. The condition of this obligation is such that if Mrs. Sarah Needham & heires both of Ezekiell Needham & Sarah his now wife for the time future hereafter accept of this aforesd homestead both land & houses thereupon that is by these presents bound as aforsd & alsoe of land called Smith's Hill with all building thereupon which is not contained in this bond or obligation, if they aforesd shall accept of pr'mises aforesaid &c mentioned in this condition as full sattisfaction for their right & interest in sixty acres sold as abovesd & secured by this instrument & not molest sd Thomas Newall of peaceable & quiet injoyment of purchass of sd sixty acres: the homesteed aforesd with Smith's hill soe caled with all buildings thereon is by these pr'sents by said Ezekiell Needham made over & bound unto them as aforesd & upon theire acceptance & performance, to be & remaine to her & them from this time & forever & this obligation or bond to be voyde but in case sd Mrs. Sarah Needham or the heires of sd Ezekiell Needham or Sarah his now wife doe not accept of conditiion as sattisfaction but shall molest & trouble sd Thomas Newall then obligation to stand & to be in full force & the homestead hearby bounded granted & delivered by these pr'sents to be &

remaine to sd Thomas Newhall. *Signed*: Ezekiel Needham [mark]; Sarah Needham [mark]. *Date*: 30 Nov 1679; *Witnesses*: Oliver Purchis; Ralph King. *Acknowledged*: 17 Nov 1683 by both. *Recorded*: 27:9 mo:1683.

EZEKIELL NEEDHAM and SARAH NEEDHAM to THOMAS NEWALL SEN'R – (6:608) Ezekiell Needham of Lynn & Sarah his wife sold to Thomas Newall Sen'r of Lynn for consideration ninety pounds, a certain p'cell or tract of land, scituate lying & being in bounds aforesaid of Lyn containing three score acres and being bounded easterly with the line y^t divideth betweene Salem & Lynn as it is now stated & laid by late running thereof by men apoynted by each towne & soe p'formed & agreed upon westerly by the comons appertaining to the towne of Lynn, northward by a certaine farme comonly called Mr. Humphries, but now Major Rainsbery's farme, southwardly by the comons alsoe appertaining to towne of Lynn: all that tract of land being by estimation soe much as is aforesaid & bounded after the manner as is aforesaid or verry neere & being upland, woodland, meddow lands and swamps therein and thereunto belonging of what nature soever which Ezekiel Needham either purchased or obtained of Mr. Daniell King sen'r of Lynn, deceased with all estate right title interest & demand of sd Ezekiell Needham & Sarah his now wife in & to p'mises. *Signed*: Ezekiell Needham [mark]; Sarah Needham [mark]. *Date*: 30 November 1679. *Witnesses*: Oliver Purchis; Ralfe King. *Acknowledged*: 17 November 1683 by both. *Recorded*: 27:9 mo:1683.

JOSEPH HARDY to NIKLIS FULGIM – (6:611) Shipped in good order & well conditioned by Joseph Hardy for acc't of Mr. Niklis Fulgim upon good ship called the Returne whereof is master for this present voyage Abraham Lewis & now riding at anchor in Barbados & bound for James River to saye one barrell of rum, one piece of browne ozenberge, one piece of blew lining, one sugarloafe, being marked & numbered as in margin & are to be delivered in like order & well conditioned att port of James river, ye danger of seas only excepted unto sd Fulgim or his assignes he or they paying freight for sd goods, the freight already paid with primage & avarage. The master or purser of sd ship hath affirmed unto three bills of lading all of this tenor & date one of w'ch three bills being accomplished other two to stand voyde. *Signed*: Abraham Lewis. *Date*: at Barbadoes 14 Nov 1683. *Recorded*: 10 Sept 1684.

JOSEPH HARDY to JNO. WALTIN – (6:612) Shipped in good order & well conditioned by Joseph Hardy for account of Mr. Jno. Waltin in & upon good ship called the Returne whereof the master for this pr'sent voiage Mr. Abraham Lois & now riding at anchor in ye roade at Barbados & bound for James river in Virginia; to saye one barrell of rum, one suger loafe being marked and numbered as in margin & are to be delivered in like good order & well conditioned att ye port of James river the danger of ye seas only excepted unto John Walltin or to his assigns, he or they paying freight for sd goods; already paid, with primage & average acustomed. The master or purser have affirmed to three bills of ladinge all of this tenure & date of which 3 bills being acomplished & the other two to stand voide. *Signed*: Abraham Lois. *Date*: at Barbodos 14 November 1683. *Recorded*: 10 Sept 1684.

SAMUEL BELNAP and JOSEPH BELNAP to THOMAS LAUGHTON SENR – (6:613) Samuel Belnap of Mauldon (joyner) and Joseph Belnap of Boston (glover) with the concent of their own wives in reference to theire surrendering thirds sold to Thomas Laughton senr of Lynn for consideration 10 pounds sterling, a certain p'cell of land one acre & three quarters of an acre of land scituate & being in the towne of Lynn aforsd which is part of an house lott which was formerly Abraham Rednap's house lott father unto sd Samuel & Joseph Rednap & bounded eastwardly with a lane comonly caled Rooton's lane westerly with land of Joseph Rednap, eastwardly of Eliezer Linsey & Widdow Rooten & northerly with lane or street w'ch lyeth betwixt sd land & the house lott of Mr. Thomas Laughton senr with all liberties and privilidges whatsoever belonging unto sd one acre & three quarters of one acre of land. *Signed*: Joseph Belnap; Samuel Belnap; Hanah Belnap. *Date*: 14 Apr 1671. *Witnesses*: Benj Rednap; Peter Brackett. *Acknowledged*: 15 April: 72 by Joseph Belnap & 19 Sept 1683 by Samuel Belnap. *Recorded*: no date.

ANDREW WOODBERRY, FRANCES COLLENS and SUSANNA CLAP to EDWARD BUSH – (6:615) Andrew Woodberry and Frances Collens of Salem both Administrators to estate of Elizabeth Cockerell widdow deceased & Susanna the late wife of Edward Clapp of Dorchester in the county of Suffolk, deceased, joynt administrator with the aforsd Andrew and Frances sold to Edward Bush of Salem (seaman) for a valuable sume to us in hand paid, a dwelling house with outhouse together with about one quarter of an acre of ground adjoining thereunto. The sd house & ground being scituate & is lying in Salem aforesd & is bounded on the west with house & ground of Elias Mason both sd houses adjoining & on the north with the highwaye or comon & on east with a strip of land the sd Bush lately bought of Paule Mansfield. *Signed*: Frances Collens; Hanna Colens [mark]; Andrew Woodberry; Susanna Clap [mark]; Mary Woodberry [mark]. *Date*: seaventh day of Jan 1669. *Witnesses*: Richard Hide; Jonathan Ager. *Acknowledged*: 11 July 1674 by Susanna Clapp; 11 Dec 1683 by Andrew Woodbery & Mary Woodberry. *Recorded*: 12 Dec 1683.

WILLIAM BUCKLY to JOHN FOWLE and PETER FOWLE – (6:617) William Buckley of Salem in consideration of 20 pounds which I do here by acknowledge myself to stand indebted unto Peter Fowle of Charlestowne alsoe 14 pounds more I acknowledge myself to be indebted to John Fowle brother to sd Peter Fowle of Charlestowne, mortgaged one p'cell that is scituate lieing & being in township of Salem containing two acres or thereabouts bounded on the northfeild side upon line of Nathaniel Ingersoll's land the road being at the northwest end of the land it being forty pole in length & eight pole in breadth the length of land is to be extended upon line of sd Nathaniel Ingersoll beginning at road & according as will appear by a deed given to sd Wm Buckley by Joseph Huchinson whoe sould sd Buckley this land as alsoe my dwelling house which stands upon sd land, the condition of this mortgage is y^t sd John Fowle & Peter Fowle is for the paiment of sd 20 pounds & said 14 pounds to give unto Buckly four yeares time to pay sd sums begining first of November next insueing that is to have fouer years day of pay according as it shall be by agreement made between them for the paiment of sd monies yearly & provided that sd William Buckley shall pay every paiment till debts be cleared then this bargained pr'misses to be voyde & for non paiment y^t sd William Buckley shall faile sd John Fowle & Peter Fowle then sd house & ground to be divided betweene them. *Signed*: William Buckley. *Date*: 5 October 1681. *Witnesses*: William Pitt; Edward Humphrey. *Acknowledged*: no date – by Wm Buckley & his wife Sarah concented. *Recorded*: 15 Jan 1683:4.

SAMUELL APPLETON and ELIZABETH APPLETON to HENRY ROADS SEN'R – (6:620) Samuell Appleton of Lin (gent.) sold to Henry Roades sen'r of Lin for consideration sum of forty one pounds, a certaine p'cell of marsh comonly knowne by name Blouds lot marsh containing eight acres & a quarter, scituate & lieing in the township of Lin it being a neck of marsh which is bounded east south & west by great river which runneth under great bridge & north upon the upland now in possession of the Hawthornes alsoe two islands or spots of creek thatch or sedg lieing in the river against sd marsh. *Signed*: Samuell Appleton; Elizabeth Appleton. *Date*: 21 November 1683. *Witnesses*: Ruth Marshall; Mary Marshall. *Acknowledged*: 26 November 1683. *Recorded*: 16 Jan 1683:4.

JONATHAN NEALE to DANIELL LAMBERT – (6:623) Jonathan Neale of Salem (cordwinder) sold to Daniell Lambert of Salem (shipwrite) for consideration sum of ten pounds fifteen shillings currant mony, a certaine p'cell of land containing twenty one rod & halfe or thereabouts scituate lieing and being in Salem & is bounded with lane or highwaye Westerly with land partly of Samuell Wakefield & partly the land of Samuell Shadock Junr w'ch they lately bought of me Jonathan Neale northerly with land of John Mason easterly & land of sd Jonathan Neale southerly; alsoe to have the privilige of sd highwaye of about twenty eight foot: viz which is to be a waye in comon with the rest of the proprietors I have or shall sel land to in that field. To have & to hould sd twenty one pole & halfe of land, according to the dementions thereof in bredth fronting upon sd lane thre pole & to run back to Goodman Mason's land seaven pole & thre or fower foot. *Signed*: Jonathan Neale. *Date*: 17 June 1682. *Witnesses*: Hilliard Verin; Daniell Bacon. *Acknowledged*: 16 January 1683:4. *Recorded*: 16 January 1683:4.

JNO PRICE and ELIZABETH PRICE to BENJAMIN GERISH – (6:626) Jno Price of Salem (marchant) and Elizabeth Price widow legall executor & executrix to will of Captain Walter Price, deceased sold to Benjamin Gerish of Salem for consideration full & just sume of fivety pounds to us in hand allredy paid, one dwelling house wherein Nicholas Bartlett formerly dwelt together with one quarter of an acre of land thereunto adjoining lieing & being situate in towne of Salem having now dewlling house of William Cash on east side thereof bounded with a cove to the north with streete or highwaye to south with a lane or highwaye down to the cove on west & John Price & Elizabeth his mother promise to grant possession to sd Benjamin Gerish. *Signed*: John Price; Elizabeth Price. *Date*: 1682. *Witnesses*: Edmond Batter; John Hathorne. *Acknowledged*: 1 Dec 1683 by Capt. John Price & Elizabeth Price & Sarah wife of John Price relinquished right. *Recorded*: 19 January 1683:4.

FRANCIS NICOLE to WILLIAM GODSOE – (6:628) Francis Nicole of Salem (joyner) sold to William Godsoe of Salem for considerable valew to me in hand alreddy paid, a certain parcel of land containing by estimation two acres, lying & being scituate in towne of Salem by north river side being bounded on southwest with the cove y^t runns up to end of Jno Williams his feild on northwest with the river & on northeast with a cove that runs to the lanes end & to Marchall Skerry's orchard & with lane to southeast with Jeremiah Neale's land & John Smiths. *Signed*: Francis Nicole. *Date*: 31 July 1683. *Witnesses*: Jonathan Gardner; John Guppe. *Acknowledged*: 14 August 1683. *Recorded*: 21 January 1683:4.

HILLIARD VEREN SENR to ROBERT HODGE – (6:629) Hilliard Veren sen'r of Salem sold to Robert Hodge of Salem (mariner) for consideration sume of twenty-six pounds five shillings mony in hand paide or secured to be paide, a certaine p'cell of land containing betweene twenty nine or thirty pole or rod, & is that percell of land I bought of Hilliard Veren Jun'r late deceased & was parte of that land belonged to his dwelling house & is that perc'l lieing without his garden fence southward & is bounded by sd garden fence of sd Hiliard Veren deceased northerly with the land of Capt William Browne easterly with the lane that goes to the burying poynt westerly & with a strip of land Capt Browne bought to leave for a highwaye to goe to Capt More's sotherly. *Signed*: Hilliard Veren. *Date*: 15 May 1680. *Witnesses*: John Pickman; Joseph Tayler. *Acknowledged*: 16 Sep 1681. *Recorded*: 23 January 1683:4.

MARGARET LORD to WILLIAM GODSOE – (6:631) Margaret Lord of Salem, daughter of William Lord sen'r sold to William Godsoe of Salem for valuable consideration to me in hand already paid by brother in law William Godsoe, part of a dwelling house together with the ground on which it stands & adjoining thereunto containing by estimation five or six pole lying & being scituate in towne of Salem neare unto the meeting house & being bounded as followeth viz: on north with land of my brother Samuell Gray on west with other end of ye sd house of William Godsoe on east with some lands of Capt Elias Stileman on the south with south river or highwaye this being that portion of house & land that was allotted unto me by the last will & testament of my aunt Mrs. Abigaile White, executrix to the last will and testament of her former husband William Lord sen'r, deceased & by his order and apoyntment. *Signed*: Margaret Lord [mark]. *Date*: 1 July 1682. *Witnesses*: Joseph Mayo; Edmond Norrice. *Acknowledged*: 2 July 1682. *Recorded*: 23 January 1683:4.

JOHN GRAFTON and SAMUELL GARDNER for JOHN GARDNER to JOSHUA GRAFTON – (6:631) John Grafton of Salem (marrenor) administrator of estate of Mr. Joseph Grafton, deceased & Samuell Gardner, aturney of John Gardner of Nantuckett the other administrator of sd Joseph Grafton, deceased sold to Joshua Grafton for consideration one hundred & twenty pounds, the greater part of said sume being due to Joshua Grafton grandchild of sd Joseph Grafton deceased out of estate of sd Joseph deceased & the other part being more than twenty pounds pd by sd Joshua Grafton unto his brother Joseph Grafton of town of Salem, tailer as part of his portion or interest in the said estate, dwelling house kitchin & outhouses with all ye ground housing stands upon & is thereto adjoining & belonging containing one acre being house & ground sd Joseph Grafton, deceased lived in in his lifetime scituate lying & being in Salem & is bounded by the south harbour southesterly by house & land of Mrs. Turners relect widdow of Mr. John Turner deceased northeasterly the land of Mr. Joseph Hardy northwesterly & southwesterly the land of sd John Grafton. *Signed*: Jno Grafton; Samuell Gardner. *Date*: 12 December 1683. *Witnesses*: Hilliard Veren; Benjamin Marstone. *Acknowledged*: 13 December 1683 by John Grafton & Samuell Gardner Jun'r. *Recorded*: 23 January 1683:4.

JOHN GRAFTON and JOSHUA GRAFTON – (6:636) Whereas John Grafton & Joshua Grafton both of Salem (mariner) have land lying adjoining from south harbour northerly about halfe wais to a highwaye or the streete that goes from meeting house down to the neck so caled & land of sd John Grafton lyes further throughout to sd street & next adjoining on the easterly side is land that was his father's Mr. Joseph Grafton, deceased whoe was agreed in his lifetime with sd John Grafton to leave a highwaye of twenty foot bredth to allow out of either parties land ten foot for a highway & according by Mr. Joseph Grafton began at the northerly end so far as the house lotts are laid out of his land to allow ten foot of his part & sd John Grafton out of his part alsoe allowed out of his land ten foot bredth intended in like maner to leave out the same breadth throughout to the south harbour that soe there might be a way of that bredth left from south harbour to sd streete against Christopher Babadge I John Grafton administrator of Mr. Joseph Grafton deceased & I Joshua Grafton nephue being now posest of that part of sd Joseph Grafton's land next the south harbour covenant & engage each to the other that we will leave out of our land, either of us ten foot in breth to make a highwaye of twenty foot wide & soe to run that bredth from water side throughout to streete aforesd against sd Babadge's & sd John Grafton doe hearby ingage that sd highwaye that is now lying by agreement of himself & father shall soe be continued to answer to that w'ch is now agreed upon to be laide down for a way to the water that soe the way of twenty foot wide may be continued throughout from sd harbour to sd streete & that forever. *Signed*: John Grafton; Joshua Grafton. *Date*: 14 December 1683. *Witnesses*: Hilliard Veren; Benjamine Marstone. *Acknowledged*: 13 December 1683 by both. *Recorded*: 24 January 1683:4.

BENJAMIN GERISH and HANNAH GERISH to THO MAULE – (6:638) Benjamin Gerish of Salem sold to Tho Maule for consideration ninetee pounds, a certaine parcell of land containing about two acres & halfe of land being the halfe of that lott formerly caled by name of Cotters lott now in possession of sd Benjamin Gerris & is scituate lying & being in Salem bounded to land of Robt Kitchen on one side & on other with land y^t was old Reveses fronting northward to the maine street & southward to other half of sd Cotter's lott. *Signed*: Benjamin Gerrish; Hannah Gerish. *Release of Dower*: Hannah wife yield up dower. *Date*: 22 January 1683. *Witnesses*: Elizabeth Gray [mark]; Elizabeth Cranifure [mark]. *Acknowledged*: 23 January 1683:4. *Recorded*: 25 January 1683:4.

MATHEW PRISE and ELIZABETH PRISE to WILLIAM JAMISON – (6:640) Mathew Prise of Salem (taylor) sold to William Jamison of Charlestowne (taylor) for naturall love & affection I beare unto William Jamison my son in law & other good causes more especiallie y^t William

Jamison hath released me from a mortgage made by me to Mr. George Mahew about or in 1672 of my house & a small parcel of land lying behind it in Salem which mortgage hath since been redeemed by my son in law Jamison hath forever acquitted mee & mine as abovesd from any claime he William Jamison might have a certaine p'cell of land containing twenty eight poles or rod of land sc tuate lying & being in Salem & being part of that land of mine belonging to my dwelling house & is in bredth or front abutting against streete or lane three poles & a halfe & soe runns the same bredth to the land of Joseph Miles easterly with land of sd William Jamison southerly with streete or lane, westerly & with land of Mathew Price northerlie. I Mathew Price have formerly given sd sonn in law William Jamison and Sarah his wife parcel of land by deed bearing date 28 December 1677 in which deed he & his are engaged to allow out of the fronte of theire land a highwaye to come to my now dwelling house: I discharge him sd William Jamison from that engagement. *Signed*: Mathew Price; Elizabeth Price [mark]. *Date*: 31 day of January 1683. *Witnesses*: Francis Neals senr; John Edwards [mark]. *Acknowledged*: 1 February 1683:4 by Mathew Price and Elizabeth wife concented and relinquished dowry and William Jamison acknowledged within is in full satisfaction of all debts of claimes he had or might have made of father in law to 1 February 1683:4. *Recorded*: February 1683:4.

MATHEW PRICE to JOHN EDWARDS – (6:643) Whereas I Mathew Price of Salem & Elizabeth wife are growne antient & itt hath pleased Lord to visit me with a long & tedious sickness so thereby I am disinabled to provide for myselfe & wife and for confidence I have in my son in law John Edwards & his wife Elizabeth of their dutie love & care of me & theire mother my wife Elizabeth & that sd John Edwards doth well, trulie & sufficiently provide for me & my wife during our naturall lifes both in sicknes & helth sufficient drinke, meat, apparell, tendance, lodging, physick & all necessaries meet & convenient for us our comfortable being for soe long tme as it shall please the Lord to continue us on earth, have given granted and sold my housing lands, goods & household stuff & all my estate both reall & personall & I have put sd John Edwards in full possession of all above mentioned pr'misses by delivering unto him one pewter dish in name of all aforementioned. *Signed*: Mathew Price. *Date*: 30 day of January 1683:4. *Witnesses*: William Jamison; Francis Neale sen'r. *Acknowledged*: 1 February 1683:4 & Elizabeth wife relinquished right of dowry. *Recorded*: 2 February 1683:4.

ROGER SHAW to THOMAS CHADWELL, RICHARD ROOTEN, and JOHN HIDE – (6:645) Roger Shaw of Hampton in the county of Norfolk & Pattint of ye Massachusetts sold to Thomas Chadwell, Richard

Rooten and John Hide all of Linn for consideration thirty pounds, all sd house & housing as heareafter exprest which was lately in occupation of late deceased William Tilton & his by way of purchase from John Wing & by him left to Susana his wife as whole executrix & now in hands of Roger Shaw aforesd, by way of contraction of marriage of sd executrix & I sd Roger Shaw sell all aforesaid house & housing with every part & p'cell of ground thereunto belonging scituate in Linn viz: two acres more or less the house now standeth upon, adjoining upon towne common on east & west upon lands of Richard Rooten south up sea & north upon lands of Francis Ingolls; alsoe three acres lying neere Sagamore hill adjoining upon lands of Mr. Edward Holyock on south & east, west & north upon lands of Mr. Daniell King; alsoe fower acres of salt marsh in the town's marsh adjoining upon great river caled Saugus river on the southeast upon land of Mr. Knowls & north upon some upland & west by severall other lotts & alsoe twelve acres of planting ground neere to planting feild of Henry Collins & adjoining east upon rocks on the east side of the towne below the lotts of Robert Rand & the late Henry Ingolls. *Signed*: Roger Shaw. *Date*: 8th of 12th mo 1653. *Witnesses*: Garrard Spencer; Edward Burchum. *Acknowledged*: 16:12:53 & alsoe Susannah wife did agree & was willing to give up her interest. *Recorded*: 5 February 1683:4.

Written on the back side: Charlestowne 19 March 1682 this deed of sale delivered by me Thomas Chadwell of Charlestowne unto Henry Collins of Linn on condition that sd Henry Collins shall in no waies trouble Mr. Thomas Chadwell. *Signed*: Henry Collins [mark]. *Witnesses*: Lewis Butler; John Betts.

HENRY SEWALL to JOHN SEWALL – (6:649)   Henry Sewall of Newbury guifted to John Sewall of Newbery for divers reasons him thereunto moving especially for the entire love & good affection he beareth his second son, his little farm or tenement scituate in Newbury upland & marsh being bounded northerly by Newbury river westerly & southerly with land of Dummer easterly with land of Boynton or however otherwise bounded containing by computation sixty five acres of upland & forty acres of marsh ground & of whomsoever purchased being now in tenure and occupation of Joseph Goodridge. To have & to hold sd little farm or tenement with dwelling house out housing & all privilidges & apurtenances to the same belonging in any wise unto the sd John Sewall & unto Hanah his wife during theire naturall lives & then to be to heires of theire bodies lawfully begotten beetweene them & for want of such issue to the heirs lawfully begotten of body of sd John Sewall & for want of such issue to my youngest sonn Stephen Sewall his heirs & assigns forever provided & it is always to be understood that all the rents & profits of said tenement are to be to the only use & benefitt him sd Henry Sewall & Jane his wife or the survivor of them during their natural lives & by no other thing in this present deed of guift to the contrary not with standing. *Signed*: Henry Sewall. *Date*: 2 February 1683. *Witnesses*: Samuel Sewall; John Alcocke. *Acknowledged*: 2 February 1683. *Recorded*: 6 February 1683:4.

JOHN GOULD to JOHN ROBINSON – (6:651)   John Gould of Topsfield (yeoman) sold to John Robinson of Topsfield (husbandman) for consideration eight pounds, a certaine parcell of meddow containing fower acres scituate lying & being within the bounds of Topsfield & pt of & lyes within bounds of my farme & is bounded & is to goe as the trees are marked by the side of meddow the river on the south & a marked tree at the upland to an ash at river on west & the marked trees are on northeast soe to Mathew Stanllys meddow almost to a poynt to the river alsoe the privilidge of a way for sd Robinson his heirs & assigns forever to pass through my land to & from sd meddow to cart his hay & to make use of his meddow from time to time at all times as he or they may have ocasion. *Signed*: John Gould; Sarah was to sign by no signature listed. *Release of Dower*: Sarah wife doe by these presents freely yield up all dower & interest. *Date*: 28 November 1683. *Witnesses*: Richard Croade; John Prichet. *Acknowledged*: 29 November 1683 by Leiutenant John Gould. *Recorded*: 20 February 1683:4.

DORCAS VEREN, HILLIARD VEREN to WILLIAM LORD, SEN'R – (6:654)   Dorcas Veren, widow & Hilliard Veren son of Phillip Veren deceased of Salem sold to William Lord, sen'r of Salem for consideration ten yew sheep to be chosen out of twenty & a ram lamb & twenty pounds of wool to be paid at or upon the first of ninth month knowne by the name November 1655, one dwelling house & outhouse, one acre of land lying in Salem towne next to land of Francis Lawes on west together with one acre of land in feild neare Henry Reinolds together with two acres of meddow lying in farme that was lately belonging to Phillip Veren sen'r deceased together with certaine goods agreed upon & mentioned in a schedule now in sd house.   *Signed*: Dorcas Veren [mark]; Hilliard Veren. *Date*: 29:1 mo:1655. *Witnesses*: Edmond Batter; Benjamin Felton. *Acknowledged*: 25 June 1656 by Hilliard Veren. *Recorded*: 21 February 1683:4.

I William Lord sen'r doe hearby assigne & make over freely to my kinsman William Lord all my right & title of the within mentioned purchase of house & land as expressed in this bill of sale unto William Lord Jun'r & his heirs forever. *Signed*: William Lord. Date: 14th 3^{d} month 1658. *Witnesses*: Benjamin Felton; Hilliard Veren.

I Hilliard Veren doe acknowledge myself to have received the tenn ewes & ram & 20 lbs of wool as is within mentioned. *Signed*: Hilliard Veren. *Date*: 25:4:1656. *Witness*: Robert Lord.

THOMAS MAULE and NAOMY MAULE to JOHN COOKE – (6:655) Thomas Maule of Salem (tailor) sold to John Cooke (blacksmith) for valueable consideration, a certaine p'cell of land conteigning about fowerteene or fifteene pole of ground it being that p'cell of land I bought lately of William Lord jun'r as p' bill of sale dated 17 August 1671 appeereth lying in Salem & is bounded on north with the streete att which end it is thirty five foot in bredth & runs backward to south end of the dwelling house of sd William Lord & soe from thence by a straite line to land of John Neale which bounds it on the west & so runs to a parcell of ground sold to Thomas Flint & a parcell sold to John Porter senr which bounds that part of pr'misses on north & sd Thomas Flint his p'cell alsoe pt'ly bounding the said bargained pr'misses to west & on east bounded with land of John Mason. *Signed*: Thomas Maule; Naomy Maule [mark]. *Date*: 7 March 1671. *Witnesses*: Hilliard Veren sen'r; Dorcas Hicks. *Acknowledged*: none. *Recorded*: 21 February 1683:4.
There was possession given of the above mentioned pr'misses by turfe & twigge by Thomas Maule to John Cooke in presence of us: William Lord; Thomas Flint.

WALTER PRISE and ELIZABETH PRISE to PETER HARVI – (6:657) Walter Prise of Salem (marchant) sold to Peter Harvi of Salem (shipwright) for valuable consideration, a quarter acre of an acre of land scituate & lying in south feild soe called neere the milne in Salem the sd parcell of land lyes in length on south side neere about nine pole & on north side seaven pole & on the east end five pole broad & is bounded on those two sides & east end by land of sd Walter Price & is bounded or abutts against south river to west at which end it is alsoe five pole broad. *Signed*: Walter Price; Elizabeth Price. *Release of Dower*: Elizabeth, wife, yield up all her dower, & interest. *Date*: 26 February six hundred & seaventy one. *Witnesses*: Hilliard Veren, sen'r; John Price. *Acknowledged*: none. *Recorded*: 22 February 1683:4.

JOHN RUCK and SARAH RUCK to JOHN LAMBERT JUN'R – (6:659) John Ruck of Salem (vinter) sold to John Lambert Jun'r of Salem (fisherman) for consideration six quintals of marchantable dry cod fish, aboute thirty rod of ground, being a part of Ruck's land on back side of dwelling house westward in Salem as now it is bounded and fenced in & is bounded on east, south & west with land of sd Ruck & on north with lane or highwaye. It is to be understood the sd Lambert is to sett up & maintaine what fence that is to be set up & maintained between ye said land & ye land of one ye sd Ruck next adjoining & further sd Ruck doe by these pr'sents covenant & promise for myselfe my heirs, executors & administrators to warrant acquit defend & maintain all & singular pr'misses unto ye sd Lambert his heirs assigns forever against all men laing claime therein to, by, from or under me or any other from me. *Signed*: John Ruck; Sarah Ruck. *Date*: seaventh day of October 1664. *Witnesses*: Edward Hilyard; Gilbert Taply. *Acknowledged*: 7:9 mo 1664 & wife yielded thirds. *Recorded*: 25 February 1683:4.

EDMUND BATTER to HENRY WEST – (6:661) Edmund Batter of Salem (marchant) sold to Henry West of Salem (sadler) for a valuable consideration in hand paid, a certaine parcell of ground containing about twenty rod or pole of ground situate & lieing in Salem & is part of that land adjoining to my dwelling house & is bounded on the west with a p'cell of land lately given & granted to Hilliard Verin & on east with land of sd Edmund Batter on the south with the street or highwaye on which end of sd p'cel of ground abutting against sd streete it is forty foot broad & soe to run toward ground same bredth to the land of Mr. Norrice whose land bounds it to the north. *Signed*: Edmund Batter. *Date*: seaventh day of June 1670. *Witnesses*: Hilliard Verin; Benjamin Felton. *Acknowledged*: 23rd day of February 1683:4. *Recorded*: 26 February 1683:4.

Edmund Batter for a valuable consideration in hand paid sold Henry West a strip of land about the bredth of a length of railes or eleven foot, runing that bredth from street to land of Mr. Weld & is lieing on east side of land within mentioned formerly sould to said West & comes to the end of John Maskoll's house as it now stands. *Signed*: Edmund Batter. *Date*: 10 Day of October 1682. *Witnesses*: Hilliard Verin; Benjamin Marstone. *Acknowledged*: 23 day of February 1683:4.

EDWARD WOOLLEN, SEN'R and MARGERY WOOLEN to HUGH PASCO – (6:663) Edward Woolen, sen'r of Salem sold to Hugh Pasco of Salem (fisherman) for consideration sume of twelve pounds in mony in hand paid or secured to be paid, a certaine p'cell of ground scituate lieing & being in Salem & is that p'cell of land on which dwelling house of sd Hugh Pasco standeth containing thirty pole or thereabouts, & being in length north & south seaven pole & thirteene foot and in breadth east & west fower pole & six foot bounded with land of sd Edw'd Woolen north & south & alsoe on east where is to be a perticular highwaye & on west land of Mr. Joseph Grafton. *Signed*: Edward Woolen [mark]; Margery Woolen [mark]. *Date*: eighteenth day of July 1679. *Witnesses*: Phillip Cromwell;

Hilliard Verin, sen'r. *Acknowledged*: no date. *Recorded*: 27th of February 1683:4.

HILLIARD VEREN JUN'R and HANA VERIN – (6:666) Whereas Hilliard Veren jun'r of Salem deceased before going away his last voyage out of the country left a writing with his father Hilliard Verin as his last will & testament wherein is exprest he gave his wife Hana Veren his house & ground adjoining with the furniture & the rest of estate given in sd will to his father & mother such a part & to his wife such a part as is expressed in sd will or writing and may therein more fully appeare & sd Hilliard Veren the father & Hanah Veren the relict & widdow of ye sd Hilliard Veren deceased for severall good causes & considerations them thereunto moving especially that mutuall love & friendship may be maintained betweene them did come to an agreement in order to a devission of the estate & presented the same to the Court at Salem together with sd will which by sd Court was alowed of & confirmed in conjunction with the will & for further security of sd Hana Veren in peacable injoyment of said house & ground adjoining furniture & alsoe what other part of estate she is to have as by sd will in conjunction in sd writing & sd Hilliard Veren being satisfied it was the mind & will of deceased son that his wife should injoy the said house & ground with the furniture forever doe promise sd Hana Veren widdow to secure & save sd Hana harmless & undamnified in quiet possession of sd house & ground adjoining with furniture & rest of estate as by sd will agreement is her part provided sd Hana secure & save harmless sd Hilliard Veren from being liable to pay Walter Price at his wives decease any more of his legacies than according to what part of proportion sd Hilliard Veren shall receive of sd estate. *Signed*: Hiliard Veren; Hana Veren. *Date*: 23 july 1680. *Witnesses*: Sarah Hathorne; Sarah Babbadge. *Acknowledged*: 29 December 1683 by Hilliard Veren & Hana Veren. *Recorded*: 1 March 1683:4.

JONATHAN NEALE to SAMUELL WAKEFIELD – (6:668) Jonathan Neale of Salem (cordwainer) son of John Neale, deceased & heir to the estate of Francis Lawes deceased with consent of mother Mary, the now wife of Andrew Mansfield & executor of the last will & testament of Frances Lawes, deceased sold to Sauell Wakefield of Salem (taylor) for consideration a valuable sum of mony to me in hand paid before the signing and sealing of these presents by Samuell Wakefield of ye towne of Salem, taylor ye receipt whereof I doe acknowledge & myself therewith fully sattisfied paid & contented, a small quantity of land lieing together videlisett twenty six pole of ground lieing & being in Salem towne being part of land belonging to dwelling house aforesd Francis Lawes lived in in his life time the dementions whereof are as followeth: fower poles northward fronting the maine streete on the west side six poles deep on east side seaven poles deep & on south fower pole & is bounded as followeth, northerly with the maine streete, easterly, westerly & southerly with the land which after my honoured mothers deceas belongeth & apperteineth to me Jonathan Neale. It is agreed upon that sd Samuel Wakefield is to leave out nine foot in breadth on west side, the whole six pole in length towards a highwaye which is there to be left to goe up through my ground of twenty eight foot wide as by agreement & sd Jonathan being obliged to leave out ten foot in bredth & Benjamin Marstone nine foot in bredth.

Samuell Wakefield will maintaine a good sufficient fence on the south side of ye above mentioned bargained pr'misses for so long time as sd Jonathan Neale shall keep the land adjoining to the bargained pr'misses. *Signed*: Jonathan Neale; Mary Mansfield was to sign but no signature listed. *Date*: 12 February 1679:80. *Witnesses*: Richard Harris senr; Frances Neale senr. *Acknowledged*: 19:12 mo79. *Recorded*: 3 March 1683:4.

JONATHAN NEALE to SAMUELL WAKEFIELD – (6:671) Jonathan Neale sold to Samuell Wakefeld in exchange for a strip of land wanting of above mentioned land as there conveyed in front thereof, a parcel of land adjoining unto the above mentioned before sould unto sd Wakefield & lieth at south end of the sd p'cell of land being twelve foot deep throughout the whole breadth of the land above mentioned being alredy in the possession of sd Wakefield laid out with rest & within sd Wakefields fence. *Signed*: Jonathan Neale. *Date*: 29 Feb 1683:4. *Acknowledged*: none. *Recorded*: 3 March 1683:4.

SAMUELL WAKEFIELD to JOHN BULLOCK – (6:672) Samuell Wakefield of Boston (taylor) sold to John Bullock of Salem (ordinary keeper) for consideration one hundred & tenn pounds of good silver currant money in hand pd secured to be paid, a certaine p'cell of land lieing & being in towne of Salem being by estimation aboute twenty eight or thirty poles of land with a dwelling house standing thereupon which land is fower poles in front toward main streete & is bounded as followeth: northerly with main streete easterly with land of Mr. Samuell Shadduck, southerly with land of Daniell Lambert westerly with lane betwixt Mr. Benjamin Marstone & sd house, w'ch land is upon eastward or easterly eight poles & westward or westerly seaven poles videliset all that land I bought of Jonathan Neale with dwelling house standing thereupon all wayes provided that the highwaye or soe much of it as I covenanted with Jonathan Neale for & is since by me laid out by sd John Bullock be made good. *Signed*: Samuell Wakefield. *Date*: 28 February 1683:4. *Witnesses*: Francis Neale senr; Peter

Cheevers. *Acknowledged*: 29 February 1683:4. *Recorded*: 4th of March 1683:4.

ROBERT PEASE and ABIGAIL PEASE to JOHN BULLOCK – (6:676) Robert Pease son of John Pease late of Salem sold to John Bullock of Salem (in holder) for consideration sume of forty pounds currant money, one acre of land with a dwelling house standing thereupon scituate & lying in northfield belonging to Salem bounded by the roade or highwaye westerly the land of William Osburne southerly the land of Samuell Eborne easterly & land of Isaak Cooke northerly alsoe three acres of land lying in sd north field bounded by land of John Burton westerly Job Swinerton northerly Caleb Bufam easterly & land of Samuell Gaskin southerly. *Signed*: Robert Pease [mark]; Abigail Pease [mark]. *Release of Dower*: Abigail wife yield all her right title & dower. *Date*: 24 August 1682. *Witnesses*: Hilliard Veren; George Adams. *Acknowledged*: 24 August 1682 by both. *Recorded*: 5th March 1683:4.

JONATHAN PRINCE and MARY PRINCE to PHILLIP CROMWELL – (6:679) Jonathan Prince of Salem (cordwinder) sold to Phillip Cromwell of Salem (slautherer) for consideration thirty pounds, a certaine p'cel of land, containing about forty pole or rod of land it being pt of that land my father Richard Prince formerly bought of Capt Joseph Gardner deceased scituate lying & being in Salem & is bounded northerly with lane that goes to the towne pound & westerly with streete yt goes to north river southerly partly with land of Samuell Prince & pt'ly with land of Capt. William Browne which he lately bought of Richard Prince Jun'r and easterly with land of sd Capt William Browne which he formerly bought of sd Capt Gardner. *Signed*: Jonathan Prince; Mary Prince [mark]. *Release of Dower*: Mary my wife doe freely yield up all her dower. *Date*: 15 August 1683. *Witnesses*: Hilliard Veren; Thomas Maule. *Acknowledged*: 3 March 1683:4 by Jonathan Prince; Mary Prince. *Recorded*: 5th of March 1683:4.

HENRY PHELPS, NICHOLAS PHELPS and EDWARD PHELPS to WILLIAM FLINT – (6:682) Henry Phelps, Nicholas Phelps, Edward Phelps executors & heirs of Thomas Trusler, deceased sold to William Flint for a valuable consideration in hand paid, all that upland meadow that was Thomas Trusler late deceased scituate & lying at the brick kill & so to the land of John Alderman & Lawrance Southwick in that field containing vivtte acres or thereabout. *Signed*: Henry Phelps; Nicholas Phelps. *Date*: 4:9 mo 1656. *Witnesses*: John Reives; Thomas Cutler [mark]. *Acknowledged*: 6:9 mo 1657 by Henry Phelps, Nicholas Phelps. *Recorded*: 19th of March 1683:4.

PHILLIP CROMWELL and MARY CROMWELL to JONATHAN PRINCE – (6:683)   Phillip Cromwell of Salem (slautherer) sold to Jonathan Prince of Salem (cordwinder) for consideration sum of thirty five pounds, a certain parcel of land containing about forty rods or pole of land together with a dwelling house standing thereupon the sd p'cell of land, & is that house & land that was formerly William Cashes & by him sold to sd Phillip Cromwell & is scituate & lying & being in Salem aforesaid bounded southerly by the streete westerly by the house & land of Mr. Benjamin Gerrish, easterly by the house & land of Thomas Roots formerly the land & house of George Hodges & northerly by a small creeke next the comon land, with all fences garden yard pr'viledges & appertenances belonging thereunto. *Signed*: Phillip Cromwell; Mary Cromwell [mark]. *Release of Dower*: Mary, wife doe yield up all dower. *Date*: 15 day August 1683:4. *Witnesses*: Hilliard Veren; Thomas Maule. *Acknowledged*: 3 March 1683:4. *Recorded*: 5 March 1683:4.

JOHN DIVIN, SENR and HESTOR DIVIN to JOHN DIVIN, JUNR – (6:685)   John Divin, senr of Linn (potter) gifted to John Divin junr of Linn sonn of sd John Divin sen'r for consideration of naturall affection unto his sonn John Divin aforesd together with diverse good cause & considerations with consent of Hestor his now wife, the naturall mother of sd John Divin, Jun'r, a certaine p'cell of upland ground & salt marsh ground lying together in township of Linn & on westwardly side of Linn river which land was formerly Capt Robert Bridges & purchased of Capt Tho Marshall by John Divin, sen'r aforesd the said land containing in estimation ten acres & is bounded eastwardly with the land that was given by sd John Divin, sen'r unto his daughter Mary, lately deceased according to a streight line from the creeke northward by three rocks unto the country highwaye southward the bigest of sd rockes being on top of the hill in pasture northward of cornefeild and the other two rockes in cornefeild at each end of the broke upland westerly with land of John Divin, jun'r which he bought of Joseph Wilson the way that lyeth below the hills which leadeth toward house of sd John Divin sen'r & a small parcel of land yt was land of sd Mary the daughter of sd John Divin sen'r southwardly with the country highwaye & land of sd John Divin Jun'r & northwardly with the salt creeke, as it lyeth unto the fence at the spring caled Strawbery spring except nere an acre of land in corner which was the land of the aforesaid Mary, deceased, on which house standeth. *Signed*: John Divin [mark]; Hestor Divin [mark]. *Date*: 13 day of November 1674 (Indenture made 13 day of November 1674). *Witnesses*: Joseph Armitage; Andrew Mansfield. *Acknowledged*: 25:4 mo 77 by John Divin Sen'r & Hestor Divin yielded thirds. *Recorded*: 10 March 1683:4.

HENRY SEWELL to STEPHEN SEWALL (6:688)   Henry Sewell of Newbury (gent.) sold to Stephen Sewall for divers good causes & especially for the intire affection he beareth to his youngest son Stephen Sewall, all that parcell of land lying and being in towne of Newbury, bounded on north with land of Tristnam Coffin on west with land of Richard Brown on the south with land of Henry Sewall aforesd on the east with the highwaye, containing by estimation about two acres with all privilidges & appertanances thereto belonging as alsoe a hold on comonage which sd Henry Sewall had of his father Henry Sewall deceased. *Signed*: Henry Sewall. *Date*: seaventh of March 1683:4. *Witnesses*: Moses Gerrish; Richard Brown. *Acknowledged*: 8 March 1683:4. *Recorded*: 12 March 1683:4.

LEIFT. JOHN PUTNAM and REBECCAH PUTNAM to THOMAS CHEVER – (6:689)   Leift. John Putnam of Salem (yeoman) & Rebeccah wife sold to Thomas Chever of Malden for a valuable consideration, a certaine tract of land containing fifty acres scituate lying & being within ye township of Salem aforsd the bounds of the sd land to run from a heape of stones at the easterly corner of the field of Ezekiel Cheever of Salem aforesd about northwest joyning to ye land of sd Putnam to a heape of stones at Mr. Ruck's line being the bound betweene Mr. Ruck & Capt Lawthrop formerly of Beverly his land sould to him ye sd Lawthrop by ye sd Putnam as pr deed of sale bearing date ye twenty second of June sixty & nine appeeres & from thence joyning to Mr. Ruck's land to his easterly corner bound being a walnut tree with stones about it & from the walnutt tree to Old Nicholls corner bound being a white oake tree with a heap of stones about it from thence joyning to sd Nicholls land upon a straight line to a heape of stones in Nicolls line being the bound between Leift John Putnam & Ezekiell Chever aforesd & from that heap of stones to a bee tree to be with a heape of stones the said bee tree to be in a straight line from the heape of stones upon Nicholls line up to the first heape of stones at the corner of the field all which sd tract of land as thus it lies bounded. *Signed*: John Putnam; Rebecca Putnam. *Date*: 29 November 1682. Witnesses: Thomas Putnam; Thomas Fuller. *Acknowledged*: 26 June 1683. *Recorded*: 13 March 1683:4.

CAPT JOHN PRICE, SAMUELL WILLIAMS, BENJAMIN MARSTONE and MARY VEREN to THOMAS CHEVER – (6:692) Capt John Price of Salem, administrator to the estate of Mr. Hilliard Veren, Jun'r of Salem deceased, Mr. Samuell Williams Benjamin Marstone & Mary Veren all of Salem admiistrators to estate of Hilliard Veren sen'r late of Salem deceased sold to Thomas Chever of Malden for consideration eighty pounds currant money of New England, a certaine dwelling house &

land with the outhousing thereupon which house & land was formerly Mr. Hilliard Veren Jun'r aforesd mentioned & by sd Veren sould to Ezekiell Cheever of Salem & by sd Ezekiell Cheever was mortgaged to Mr. Veren Jun'r aforesd for a certaine sume of money which mortgage was sued by the adminstrators of Mr. Hilliard Veren Jun'r aforesd at the last county court in Salem in November last past & judgment obteined against sd Cheever & since that quiet & peaceable possession of the aforementioned house and land given by sd Cheever to administrators which sd dwelling & land is in towne of Salem. *Signed*: John Price; Samuell Williams. *Date*: 13 day of March 1684. *Witnesses*: William Greene; William Gedney. *Acknowledged*: 12:March 1683:4 by Capt. John Price & Samuell Williams. *Recorded*: 15 March 1683:4.

HILLIARD VEREN and CAPT. JOHN PRICE to EZEKIELL CHEVER – (6:696) Whereas Mr. Hilliard Veren senr of Salem & Capt John Price administrators to Mr. Hilliard Veren jun'r late of Salem deceased sued a mortgage made to sd Veren by Ezekiell Cheever of Salem & obtained judgment against sd Chever last November court at Salem, above named Ezekiel Chever for preventing charges have freely & voluntarily surrendered up the quiet & peaceable possession of the pr'misses contained in the above mentioned mortgage without execution being levied by the plaintifes for the reason before named unto Capt John Price & Samuell Williams in behalfe of himself Benjamin Marstone & Mary Veren joynt administrators to Mr. Hilliard Veren sen'r late of Salem deceased. *Signed*: Ezekiell Cheever. *Date*: 13 March 1684. *Witnesses*: William Greene; William Gedney. *Acknowledged*: 12th of March 83:4. *Recorded*: no date.

GILES COREY to EDWARD FLINT – (6:696) Giles Corey of Salem (yeoman) sold to Edward Flint of Salem (yeoman) for consideration eight pounds & five shillings, a peice of land containing by estimation one acre scituate & lying in Salem upon the westerne side of the street going towards the mill bridge bounded upon land of Thomas Robbins north westerly upon land of sd Edward Flint & Thomas Flint southwesterly & south easterly & upon the streete northeasterly. *Signed*: Giles Coree [mark]. *Date*: 8 February 1681:2. *Witnesses*: John Putnam sen'r; Thomas Fuller, sen'r. *Acknowledged*: 19 March 1683:4, Mary his wife concented thereunto & freely relinquished her right of dowry. *Recorded*: 20 March 1683:4.

WILLIAM RAIMENT – (6:699) This is to certifie unto whome it may concerne that I William Raiment sen'r doe ingage myselfe hereby never to trouble or molest my father or mother Bishop or any of theirs concerning that they now possess & for my fidelete & truth in this respect, I have hereunto sett my hand this 16th day of March 1669. *Signed*: William

Rayment. ***Date***: 16 March 1669. ***Witnesses***: Roger Conant; William Doge; Exercise Conant. ***Acknowledged***: none. ***Recorded***: 28 March:84.

EDWARD WOOLAND, SENR to JOSEPH HARDY, JUNR – (6:699) Edward Wooland senr of Salem (fisherman) sold to Joseph Hardy, Junr of Salem (marriner) for consideration twelve pounds, five shillings, a certaine p'cell of land scituate & lieng in Salem being a part of yt land of mine belonging to my dwelling house, the sd p'cel of land now sould is containing about twenty one pole or rod of ground & a halfe acccording to bounds & dementions hereafter exprest viz: bounded by the land of sd Joseph Hardy westerly & a perticuler highwaye left by said Wooland easterly betweene w'ch sd highwaye & land of ye sd Hardy, it is in breadth fower Pole five foot & six inches & bounded southerly by land of Mrs. Turner widdow & northerly by land of said Wooland betweene which it is to extend five pole & three foot: also the privilidge of the highwaye to use of sd Hardy, his heirs and assigns in comon with the other persons to whom I have sold land unto in that place of feild. ***Signed***: Edward Wooland [mark]. ***Date***: fifth day of May 1683. ***Witnesses***: Phillip Cromwell; John Cromwell. ***Acknowledged***: 4 May 1683. ***Recorded***: 22 March 1683:4.

WILLIAM DIXE to EDMUND GALE – (6:703) William Dixe of Beverly (yeoman) for good causes & consideration have given to my loving son in law Edmund Gale of Beverly, a certaine point or parcell of ground containing two acres scituate lying & being in Beverly being bounded easterly by land of Andrew Elliot northwesterly by land of Josiah Rootes southwest to run one pole into the swamp from the upland by the sd Capt Dixe his ground southeast by sd Dixe's ground. ***Signed***: William Dixe [mark]. ***Date***: 28 December 1681. ***Witnesses***: Samuell Hardie; Phillip Cox [mark]. ***Acknowledged***: 28th day of March 1683 by Capt William Dixe. ***Recorded***: 24 March 1683:4.

RUTH KNIGHT to PHILLIP KNIGHT – (6:704) Ruth Knight of Salem Village Relict & Administratrix to estate of Jonathan Knight, deceased sold to Phillip Knight of Topsfield for consideration tenn pounds paid to Stephen Johnson of Andever being part of pay for the meadow which my husband Jonathan Knight bought of Stephen Johson, a certain parcel of meddow & swamp as is heareafter exprest by the bounds thereof lying & being in the meddow commonly called Johnsons meddow nere to Andever line bounded on northeast corner with the hed bound of Thomas Fuller, senr to a pine tree marked from there to run southerly to a ponn or the line of the farme which was Governor Billinghams farme from thence to run westerly to a black oak tree marked standing on north side of an island in medow aforesd from thence to run northerly & by west to a rock with a sharp top like the ridge of a house being on the upland on the north side of above said meddow from thence to run southwest to a white oake marked standing on northeast corner of a greate island in meadow abovesd from thence to run west to another white oake marked being upon the aforesd island from thence to run north & by west to a great stone being on upland with a white oake marked by it being on west end of abovesd medow bounded on north side with upland. *Signed*: Ruth Knight [mark]. *Date*: 19 March 1684. *Witnesses*: Thomas Putnam, Jun'r; Benjamin Stacy [mark]. *Acknowledged*: 20 March 1683:4. *Recorded*: 20 March 1683:4.

PHILLIP KNIGHT and MARGARET KNIGHT to RUTH KNIGHT – (6:707) Phillip Knight of Topsfield (husbandman) and Margaret, my wife sold to Ruth Knight of Salem Village (Relique) Administratrix to the estate of Jonathan Knight Deceased for consideration six pounds alredy in hand paid, a certaine parcell of upland & swamp containing eleaven acres & a halfe which I have in township of Salem being bounded on easterly corner with a heape of stones & holes dugg round them from thence to run northerly over a swamp comonly called the great Ashin swamp to a heape of stones & a stake in the middle of them being on north side of above sd swamp from thence to run westerly aboute eighteene rods to a stake with stones round it which is alsoe on the south side of the above saide swamp with the fence of Thomas Cave now lyin upon the bounds from thence to run southerly over the abovesd swamp to a stake & a heape of stones round it & from thence to run west northwest to a stake with a heape of stones on south side of above sd swamp hard by abovesaid Caves fence: the former last mentioned bounds being asoe the bounds of above sd Thomas Cave's land from thence to run southerly to a white oake marked by Peter Prescott fence which is alsoe Peter Prescotts bounds from thence to runn easterly to abovesd heape of stones with holes dugg round them which is alsoe Peter Prescotts bounds. *Signed*: Phillip Knight [mark]; Margaret Knight [mark]. *Date*: 19 March 1684. *Witnesses*: Thomas Putnam, Jun'r; Ann Putnam. *Acknowledged*: 20:March 1683:4. *Recorded*: 26 March 1683:4.

STEPHEN JOHNSON and ELIZABETH JOHNSON to JONATHAN KNIGHT – (6:709) Stephen Johnson of Andever (carpenter) and Elizabeth, my wife sold to Jonathan Knight of Salem Village for consideration twenty pounds alredy in hand paid or security given, all that parcell of meddow which I have in township of Andever aforesd lying nere a medow comonly caled Falls medow containing by estimation about three acres & being bounded on east with a ponn & on the north & west with the upland & on the south with a swamp. *Signed*: Stephen Johnson, senr; Elizabeth Johnson. *Date*: Fifteenth day of November 1681. *Witnesses*:

Christopher Osgood; John Abbut. *Acknowledged*: 15th day of 9 mo:1681 (Stephen); 16th of ye 9 mo:1683 (Elizabeth). *Recorded*: 27 March 1683:4.

THOMAS CAVE to JONATHAN KNIGHTS – (6:711) Thomas Cave of or nere unto Salem (husbandman) sold to Jonathan Knights of Salem (husbandman) for consideration valuable sum in hand paid, a certaine p'cell of land containing fifteene acres being part of that land or farme sd Thomas Cave & Phillip Knights lately bought of Mr. John Ruck & is bounded with Hathornes medow southerly the land of Leift. Thomas Putnam westerly & land of sd Thomas Cave northerly & easterly. *Signed*: Thomas Cave. *Date*: 3 December 1673. *Witnesses*: none. *Acknowledged*: 20 March 1677:8. *Recorded*: 27 March:1683:4.

JOHN LOVEJOY to JONATHAN KNIGHT – (6:713) John Lovejoy of Andevor sold to Jonathan Knight of Salem for divers good reasons especially in consideration of eight pounds to be paid at Capt. George Cuwin's at Salem within a twelve month after date hereof, two acres & a halfe of medow as it lies by the outside of Andever line joyning to land comonly caled Gov'r Belingham's farm & bounded with the upland on south & west & north & on the east with a swamp. I abovesd Lovjoy the proper right heire of abovesd medow: doe confirme it upon above mentioned time to abovesd Knight. *Signed*: John Lovjoy [mark]. *Date*: 16 November 1681. *Witnesses*: William Chandler; Thomas Osgood. *Acknowledged*: 16:9 mo:1681. *Recorded*: 27 March:1684.

EDWARD BISHOP to EDWARD BISHOP – (6:715) Edward Bishop of Beverly (husbandman) for some causes & considerations best knowne unto myself give & bequeath to son Edward Bishop of Salem (husbandman), all my land in New England which containes by estimation fifty seaven acres or thereabout, forty acres of sd land lyeth in Salem & is now in possession of sd Edward Bishop Jun'r & is bounded westerly with the land of Osmond Trask northerly with land of Joshua Ray easterly with land of Peter Woodbery & land of Cornelius Baker & southerly with Salem comon & five acres of medow ground lying in Topsfeild bounded easterly with land of John Blake & southerly with the river & westerly with land of Nicholas Woodbery northerly with land of Thomas Perkins: other twelve acres lying in Beverly is in possession of the aforesaid Edward Bishop sen'r six acres of it lying nere Beaver ponn being bounded easterly with land of Edward Dodge & land of Joseph Dodge southerly with land of Josiah Rootes westerly with land of Henry Herrick & land of William Dodge & northerly with land of Robert Hibbert, the other six acres lying in the raile field being bounded on west with common road or highwaye & northerly with land of Benjamin Balch & easterly with land of Lott Conant & land of Benjamin

Balch & southerly with land of Lott Conant provided & excepted that I sd Edward Bishop sen'r am to keep in my owne possession said twelve acres of land in Beverly as proper right during natural life then to fal unto said Edward Bishop Jun'r. *Signed*: Edward Bishop [mark]. *Date*: 8 October 1673. *Witnesses*: Benjamin Gerish; Edward Norrice. *Acknowledged*: 7:8 mo:73. *Recorded*: 28:March:1684.

WILLIAM NICOLLS to ISAACK BURTON – (6:717) William Nicolls of Topsfeild (husbandman) sold to Isaack Burton for divers good causes & considerations especially for love & afection unto adopted son Isaack Burton, a certaine quantity of land of thirty acres being bounded northerly with Benjamin Porter's land twenty five poles from the bounds of John Robinson & Benjamin Porter up brooke easterly with owne land westerly he is to go thirty six poles butting upon land of John Putnam & southerly with land of John Putnam & on northwest with land of John Robinson provided it be understood I [sic] said Isaack Burton dy without heire lawfully of his body that then this land shall returne to sonn John Nicholls provided alsoe that soe much of the thirty acres that shall be within my feild I reserve to my own & wife's use during our naturall life. *Signed*: William Nicols [mark]. *Date*: 4 January 1678. *Witnesses*: John Putnam sen'r; Jonathan Putnam. *Acknowledged*: 15:11 mo:78. *Recorded*: 29:March:1684.

BENJAMIN GERISH to WILLIAM OSBURN – (6:719) Benjamin Gerish of Salem (march't) sold to William Osburn of Salem (husbandman) for consideration twenty pounds in hand paid and secured to be paid, a certaine p'cell of land containing five acres lying in northfeild in township of Salem & is on one side p'tly with land of Edw'd Beachum & pt'ly the land of John Tompkins deceased & on other side by the land of Peas formerly but now in possession of Caleb Buffum & one end of sd five acres bounded by some land of Robert Stones & other end bounded upon a ten acre lott which was Thomas Spooners deceased but now in possession of Thomas Ruck. *Signed*: Benjamin Gerish. *Release of Dower*: Hanah wife doe yield up dower. *Date*: 9 March 1682:3. *Witnesses*: Hilliard Veren; Daniell King Jun'r. *Acknowledged*: none. *Recorded*: 3:Aprill:1684.

NICHOLAS HOLT SEN'R to ROBERT GRAY – (6:722) Nicholas Holt sen'r of Andever gave to son in law Robert Gray of Andever for good causes & mature considerations but in especiall my reall love & affection unto son in law Robert Gray five acres of land in Andever which by estimation ought so to be as by towne apoynted out layes Nathan Parkers manuscript of the same as p' under sd Parkers hand butting to the southward on the land of my son Nicholas Holt which he bought of the towne at the southeast corner with a marked white oake on southwest corner bounded with a black oake marked bounded at northwest with a heap of rocks by fence bounded at northeast corner with black oake marked & which five acres of land is part of what was laid out to me for streete division, these signifies that sd Robert Gray is to pay to the minister in consideration of land abovesd one shilling by the yeare during the way of rating. *Signed*: Nicholas Holt [mark]. *Date*: 10 March 1679:80. *Witnesses*: Richard Barker; William Chandler sen'r. *Acknowledged*: none: *Recorded*: 4:Aprill:1684.

JOHN ORNE to SIMOND ORNE – (6:725) John Orne of Salem (carpenter) for divers good causes & considerations especially for love & naturall affection unto son Simond Orne of Salem (cordwinder) have given all that new end of my dwelling house in Salem where I now live that is to say the north end of sd dwelling house with the sellar under it & the lentos on the back side of house all soe farr as the parting of the chimnies of that north end & the south end of sd house where his brother Benjamin Orne dwells with the ground it stands upon with one third part of my ground or oarchard behinde or on back side of housing to east that third part through east that lies on north side next Widdow Ropes land alsoe with free liberty of passing to & fro from time to time with a cart or otherwise upon occasion betweene by sonn Benjamin's south end of the house & my sonn Joseph's dwelling house from the streete through y^t way into his owne ground behinde the house without any lett, deniall or disturbances from his brother Joseph or Benjamin or either of them alsoe one third part of my lott or land at great cove in the north neck in bounds of Salem that part viz: the neck caled Mr. Peeters neck all of said neck except a slip of marsh that runs along one side of neck viz: the easterly side next to Goodells lott, alsoe ten pounds of that pay which will be due to me from Capt. Price after my decease.

Memorandum there being a great part of the two & twentieth line on middle of blotted out & the words betweene 23d & 24th line viz: (from time of my decease) interlined, & all by consent of parties before signing & sealing of these pr'sents & the words (the time of my decease) also interlined betweene 28th & 29th lines before signing. *Signed*: John Orne sen'r [mark]. *Date*: 25 May 1681. *Witnesses*: Mary Mackmallen [mark]; Hilliard Veren sen'r. *Acknowledged*: 27 February 1683:4. *Recorded*: 5 Aprill:1684.

SIMOND ORNE and BENJAMIN ORNE – (6:728) Whereas our father John Orne sen'r in the settlement & distribution of his estate amongst his children by his will hath given to us underwriten to each of us one third part of his land & orchard where he has for a long time past dwelt with the housing upon the said two thirds, viz: to Simond Orne north end of said house & to Benjamin Orne southerly end thereof & of w'ch our said father hath possessed us, of each his pt & our father having alsoe in his said will given unto Simond Orne the privilidge of a highwaye betweene house of Benjamin Orne & Joseph Orne through the ground of sd Benjamin unto land of Simond aforesd & also the sd Benjamin since his part has been in his possession hath pulled downe his part of the ould building erected a new dwelling house which is sett about halfe a foot on upon the land of Simonds part according to a true division: and alsoe that Benjamin Orne by a former gift of his father hath a claim unto the upper part of the porch that joins to Simonds part of house: now considering it is our duty to endeavor to maintaine peace & mutual concord between ourselves & to remove all ocasions of quarel & disagreement it is now mutually agreed for ourselves our heires, executors, administrators & assigns first: that Simond Orne shall have free liberty of egress & regress unto his land in the said highwaye between Benjamin & Joseph Orne's house for the space of three yeares from date hereof without lett, deniall or molestation of sd Benjamin or any of his & from thence forward the said Simond Orne doth forever release quitclaime all his right title & interest in and unto aforesd privilidge of the highway unto Benjamin Orne aforesd to have & to hold same forever: & in consideration of twenty shilllings money in hand paid or secured in law by Benjamin Orne unto Simond Orne aforesd the sd Simond Orne doth alsoe by these pr'sents release & forever quitclaime unto Benjamin aforesd all right, title interest & claime in or unto any part of sd Benjamin's part of land: as allready sett out unto & possessed by him, the aforesd twenty shillings being in full sattisfaction for what said sd Benjamins house hath taken in of Simonds part & the sd Benjamin to have & to hold the same: & the sd Benjamin Orne doth by these pr'sents release & quitclaim unto sd Simond Orne all his right, title & interest or claime of & into the porch & chimny adjoining unto the dwelling house of sd Simond given by his father John Orne: the sd Simond to have & to hold the same to him forever. ***Signed***: Simond Orne; Benjamin Orne. ***Date***: 1 Aprill 1684. ***Witnesses***: Gershom Bowne; William Gedney. ***Acknowledged***: none. ***Recorded***: 7 Aprill:1684.

JOHN GARDNER – (6:731) I John Gardner sen'r some time of Salem have made, ordained, constituted & put my loving cowzen Mr. Samuel Gardner Jun'r of Salem my true & lawfull aturney for me & in my name to act & doe in any matter or business that do, or any maner of waies may belong unto me, in any case whatsoever and in perticuler in the respect of the estate of my father Grafton deceased & by virtue of administration thereof unto me granted hereby giving & granting unto my said aturney full power & lawfull authority in & about the premisses & any other business dew or may belong unto me as fully & amply as I might or could doe being personally present hereby holding stable & firme & ratifying & confirming w^t soever my sd aturney shall legally doe or cause to be don in or about premisses or any other matter or business whatsoever. *Signed*: John Gardner. *Date*: 21 July 1682. *Witnesses*: John Browne; John Buttolph. *Acknowledged*: 21 July 1682. *Recorded*: 12 June:1684.

SAMUELL ARCHARD and HANAH ARCHARD to LEIFT. JOHN PICKERING – (6:732) Samuell Archard of Salem (carpenter) sold to Leift. John Pickering of Salem for consideration thirty two pounds in hand paid, a certaine p'cell of land containing ten acres or thereabouts lying in south field in Salem & bounded on west end with the salt marsh over against Castle hill & butting easterly against the south harbour & bounded on southerly side with some land of John Horne & the northerly side with land of Paule Mansfield. *Signed*: Samuell Arch[ard line through and er written above]; Hanah Arch[ard line through and er written above]. *Release of Dower*: Hanah wife doe yield up dower. *Date*: 9 November 1680. *Witnesses*: Hilliard Veren; Resolved White. *Acknowledged*: 28 August 1682. Hanah released right of dower & acknowledged before me Barth. Gedney Assist 2 May 1684. *Recorded*: 2 May:84.

JONATHAN PICKERING – (6:734) I Jonathan Pickering have received full sattisfaction from my brother John Pickering for my pt & portion given by my father's will & for myself, heires, executors & administrators of & from the same doe hereby acquit & discharge my sd brother his heires, executors & administrators forever & doe hereby alsoe putt an end to all the diferences betwixt us about the same, wherein alsoe is included my pt of what was given my mother in my fathers sd will: & the bounds of the land betwixt us to stand according to devission of the feilds now laid out. *Signed*: Jonathan Pickering [mark]. *Date*: 18 May 1671. *Witnesses*: Henry Bartholmew; Phillip Cromwell; Eleazer Hathorne. *Acknowledged*: 5 May 1684. *Recorded*: 5:May:1684.

FRANCIS SCERRY to JOHN PICKERING – (6:735) Francis Scerry of Salem (yeoman) sold to John Pickering of Salem (yeoman) for consideration nine pounds paid, a certaine p'cell of land containing seaven score & tenn rod or pole of ground, that is to say, one acre wanting ten rod of ground: which p'cell of land I had lately delivered me by execution upon a judgment granted me at county court against Nicholas Maning & was laid out & bounded as in the returne of the execution may appear & is as followeth the sd parcell of land is lying in that feild of land sometimes bought by sd Manning of William Lord deceased & is lying in Salem betwene land of sd John Pickering & land of Major William Hathorne the sd parcell now sold being in bredth next common or highway fower pole or rod & soe to run downe southerly the same bredth next adjoining to p'cell of land of Mr. Resolved White's also lately recovered by execution of said Nicholas Maning & being the same bredth of fower poles to the making up of the full quantity of one acre less ten pole according as the stakes were sett down by the Marshall & the aprisers & soe is bound south & west by land of said Maning east by land of sd White & north by sd common or highwaye, provided & it is further agreed upon that in case sd Maning or the heires or successors of Robert Gray deceased should molest & trouble sd John Pickering forever heareafter in the peaceable injoyment of bargained pr'misses I sd Francis will not be ingaged to make good my right in sd p'cell of land by cource of law in my owne person but shall & do by these pr'sents ingage & promise that said John Pickering shall have the just right & interest in sd judgment against sd Maning for his further security against sd Maning or successors of sd Gray whereby sd Pickering or assignes may not be justly damnified for time to come. *Signed*: Francis Scerry. *Date*: 4 August 1676. *Witnesses*: Hilliard Veren sen'r; Bartholmew Gedney. *Acknowledged*: 5 October 1681. *Recorded*: 2 May 1684.

MARY GEDNEY to THOMAS MAULE – (6:738) Mary Gedney the relict, widdow & administratrix of Eleazer Gedney late deceased of Salem sold to Thomas Maule of Salem (marchant) for consideration forty five pounds currant money which was owing & the estate of Eleazer Gedney was justly indebted unto Thomas Maule sd Mary Gedney as administratrix in order to the paying of soe much debt, a certaine p'cell of land containing by estimation fifteene acres as it now lies & is bounded lying in northfeild belonging to Salem & is bounded southerly with north river westerly by some land formerly Richard Bishop's deceased in pt & by some of Robert Buffum deceased formerly northerly bounded p'tly by some land that was formerly Thomas Golthrites late deceased & partly by some land of Francis Scerry & easterly by some land formerly of Thomas Cole deceased now the land of Jonathan Curwin. *Signed*: Mary Gedney. *Date*: 3 August 1683. *Witnesses*: John Marston; Eleazer Gedney. *Acknowledged*: 3 May 1684. *Recorded*: 3 May:1684.

John Gedney sen'r Bartholmew Gedney Esq. & Eleazer Gedney son of sd Eleazer Gedney deceased in consideration that estate of sd Eleazer being in debt to sd Maule the sum abovesd in money & the estate being in no waies in capacity to pay same do judge it best & meetest way for the good & security of the rest of the estate to make sale of sd p'cell of land as abovesd & therefore do consent to & alow of the sale of the same as abovesd by sd Mary administratrix: day & yeare abovesd. *Signed*: Bartholmew Gedney; Eleazer Gedney.

ROBERT BURGES to HENRY ROADES – (6:741) Robert Burges of Linn with consent of Sarah wife in reference to her surrending up thirds sold to Henry Roades of Linn (yeoman) for consideration eleaven pounds ten shillings in moneys paid, two acres and one quarter of salt marsh ground lying in the lower devission in Rumly marsh in township of Linn which is the remaining part of a five acre lott which sd Robert Burges had sould unto sd Henry Roades before, the whole five acres being bounded easterly with marsh of Andrew Mansfeild & the marsh lately Samuel Mansfeilds lately deceased & westerly with an other devission of lotts abutting upon marsh of Goodman Bread northerly & upon an other devission of lotts southerly. *Signed*: Robert Burges [mark]. *Date*: 10 May 1683. *Witnesses*: Josiah Roades [mark]; Ann Roades [mark]. *Acknowledged*: 21 Aprill 1684. *Recorded*: 5 May 1684.

MARGARET BENNIT to MARY DOWNING – (6:744) I Margaret Bennit give unto my daughter Mary Downing all my estate for & in consideration of her dayly love & care towards me & considering how chargable I have ben to my daughter and though the former desiers of my hart hath bin towards Joane my grandchilde yet now for many good reasons doe cut her short of anything ordered her formerly finding & being sensable of my grandchildes crossing of my expectations now she is growne up & therefore doe declare that she shall not share in anything that is mine & on the contrary doe for the causes above specified do set to my daughter Mary Downing in all that estate left me by my former husband & doe declare that this is my full minde concerning pr'misses: my daughter Mary & her husband maintaining me & looking after me so long as I shall continue in this fraile life & my mind is y^t my daughter Mary Downing shall injoy all my estate whether it doth consist in house & land or moveables for & in consideration of my daughters care & charge they have binn out about me, I doe sett over & confirme to my daughter my house and land in Marblehead with all my moveables without dores or within. *Signed*: Margaret Benet [mark]. *Date*: 13 March 1676:7. *Witnesses*: Eleazer Eaton; Humphry Deverix. *Acknowledged*: by Eleazer Eaton & Humphry Deverix 29:4 mo:1677. *Recorded*: 10 May:1684.

RICHARD ADDAMS and SUSANA ADAMS to LEIFT. JOHN PICKERING – (6:745) Richard Addams of Salem (mason) sold to Leift. John Pickering of Salem (yeoman) for consideration one hundred fifty pounds to me secured in law to be paid, all that my dwelling house, outhouses with all the land they stand upon & is adjoining and belonging thereto containing about fower or five acres containing arable land, pasture or mowing land, oarchard & garden with the yards, being all within fence & most pt stone wall lying in Salem at the westerne end of the towne, over against Major Hathornes & is bounded with the street southerly & a lane or streete easterly & a highway or comon land ptly westerly & the land formerly of William Flint deceased now the land of Edward & Thomas Flint northerly. *Signed*: Richard Adams [mark]; Susana Adams [mark]. *Date*: 30 Aprill 1679. *Witnesses*: with seizin & possession of the pr'misses given according to law Richard Prytherch; Hilliard Veren sen'r. *Acknowledged*: by both 16 May 1684. *Recorded*: 6 May:1684.

SAMUELL PRINCE to JOHN CRUMWELL – (6:749) Samuell Prince of Salem (taylor) sold to John Crumwell of Salem (slautherer) for consideration fourteen pounds in hand paid, a certaine peece or parcell of land lying in southfeild in the pr'cincts of Salem being by estimation three acres & halfe & is the land which was given unto me by my father Richard Prince deceased bounded on the highway that goes through the sd southfeild on east, with land w'ch Stephen Daniell hath now in possession on south, runing the length of it with the land of Joseph Hardy sen'r on the north of it runing the length of sd land & the Deacon's marsh on the west. *Signed*: Samuell Prince. *Date*: 15 February 1682:3. *Witnesses*: Simond Willard; Richard Croade. *Acknowledged*: 14 December 1683. *Recorded*: 20 May 1684.

JOHN GILES to VSALL WARDALL – (6:752) John Giles of Salem (yeoman) sold to Vsall Wardall of Ipswich (house carpenter) for consideration one hundred fifty pounds in hand paid, my dwelling house with all the outhouses, barne, cornhouses, with all land they stand upon & all land adjoining & belonging thereto, with all fences, pastures, inclosures, oarchards, gardens & appurtenances thereto belonging, the sd messuage of tenement or p'cell of land containes by estimation nine or ten acres of land in the whole which sd messuage or tenement is lying within township of Salem and now in possession & occupation of sd John Giles & is bounded southwesterly with comon land west northerly by land of Samuell Very as fence runs by a circumference line northerly by some land of John King & easterly by land of Eleazer Giles. *Signed*: John Giles. *Date*: 18 April 1679. *Witnesses*: Hilliard Veren Jun'r; Hilliard Veren sen'r. *Acknowledged*: Bridgett Giles mother of said John Giles & executrix or administratrix of Edm'd Giles deceased doe give consent & give up all right therein. John Giles achnowledged 18 April 1684. *Recorded*: 23 May 1684.

VZALL WARDALL and GRACE WARDALL to WILLIAM BROWNE JUN'R – (6:756) Vzall Wardall of Salem (housewright) & Grace Wardall wife sold to William Browne Jun'r of Salem (marchant) for consideration ninety pounds currant mony or other pay equivalent to theire full pay & sattisfaction, all their messuage tenement or dwelling house with all yards garden orchard pastures inclosures & land whatsoever on which sd tenement standeth & is thereunto adjoining & belonging containing by estimation nine or ten acres in the whole lying within township of Salem which they formerly purchased of John Giles of Salem & is bounded southwestery with comon land west northerly by land of Samuell Very as the fence runs by a circumference line northerly by land of John King & easterly by land of Eleazer Giles or however otherwise bounded together with the barne, cornhouse, outhousing, edefices, buildings, fences, wood, trees, timber & stones upon sd land or any pt thereof. *Signed*: Vzall Wardall; Grace Wardall. *Date*: 21 April 1684. *Witnesses*: Benjamin Browne; William Addams; Robert Gibbs. *Acknowledged*: 25 April:84 by both. *Recorded*: 23 May:1684.

THOMAS JEGGELLS and ABIGALL JEGGELLS to WILLIAM BROWNE – (6:760) Thomas Jeggells of Salem (marriner) sold to William Browne of Salem (Esq.) for consideration thirty pounds in hand paid, a certaine p'cell of land containing by estimation about halfe an acre of land or betweene or neere about seaventy or eighty rod lying in Salem neere to township & is bounded southerly with house & land of Peter Cheevers westly with some land of Peter Ardlee the land of Nathaniell Sharp northerly & the streete easterly where the sd land is in bredth about three rod next or abutting against streete & soe runs as the garden fence of Nathaniell Sharp stands untill it comes to the wester end of his garden fence, & then runs northerly behinde his garden fence one pole or thereabouts & carps that bredth (being there neere aboute fower pole) to aforesd land of sd Peter Ardlee. *Signed*: Thomas Jeggels; Abigall Jeggells [mark]. *Date*: 21 December 1682. *Witnesses*: Hilliard Veren; Benjamin Browne. *Acknowledged*: 2 Mary 1684 by Thomas and Abigall. *Recorded*: 27 May:1684.

CAPT. THOMAS MARSHALL – (6:762) Capt. Thomas Marshall aged about 67 yeares do testifie that about 38 yeares since the ould water mill at Linn which was an under shott mill was by Mr. Howell comitted to him or before the sd time and about 38 yeares since, the building of an over shott mill was moved to the town of Linn & for incuragement to go on with sd worke they then of the towne of Linn granted their pr'vilidges of water & water courses to sd mill & that the water mill & this sd water mill is now in possession Henry Roades. *Signed*: Thomas Marshall. *Date*: 12 May 1683. *Recorded*: 3 Jun 1684.
Swore 15 May 1683 before me Bartholmew Gedney Assistant. This above written evedence refers to a deed recorded in booke 4th folio 88.

WILLIAM BROWNE to NICHOLAS NOYCE – (6:763) William Browne of Salem (merchant) sold to Nicholas Noyce of Salem (clericus) for consideration twenty fower pounds in hand paid, a certaine parcell of land containing by estimation about half an acre of land or between or neere seventy or eighty rods & lying in town of Salem neere to the towne house & is bounded southerly with house & ground of said Noyce westerly with some land of Peter Ardlee with land of Nathaniell Sharp northerly & the streete easterly, where the sd land is in bredth about three rods next or abutting against sd streete, & soe runs as the garden fence of Nathaniel Sharp stands untill it comes to wester end of his garden fence & then runs northerly behind his garden fence one pole or thereabouts & carries that bredth (being theire neere aboute fower poles) to aforesd land of aforesd Ardlee. *Signed*: William Browne. *Date*: 15 Aprill 1684. *Witnesses*: Daniell Epes Jun'r; William Redford *Acknowledged*: by William Browne Esq. 22 May 1684. *Recorded*: 27 May:1684.

NATHANIELL SHARP to NICHOLAS NOYCE – (6:766) Nathaniell Sharp of Salem (mariner) being administrator to estate of Samuell & Alice Sharp, formerly of Salem, now deceased have delivered to Nicholas Noice of Salem the pr'sent owner of that tract of land which by agreement with my sisters fell to my sister Abigall Giggells scituate and lying between land of sd Noyces & said Sharp 3 poles in bredth next the main cast st for ten rods then only at west end of sd 10 rods wanting 5½ foot then to run out in bredth northerly behinde sd Sharps garden so much as makes whole bredth fower rods & eight foot & soe to containe that bredth twelve rods & a halfe to the west or thereabouts as it lyes stated out by sd Sharp & Noyce being bounded on west by land of Peter Ardlee containing in all eighty two poles or theire abouts. *Signed*: Nathaniell Sharp. *Date*: 22 May 1684. *Witnesses*: Daniell Eppes Jun'r; Martha Eppes. *Acknowledged*: none. *Recorded*: 27 May:1684.

THOMAS CHEEVER to NICHOLAS NOYCE – (6:767) Thomas Cheever of Maulden (clericus) sold to Nicholas Noyce of Salem (clericus) for consideration one hundred twenty pounds in hand paid, a considerable parcell of land with a dwelling house, bake house & stable standing upon sd land which parcell of land containes about half an acre being scituate in Salem bounded by the street on east by some land of Joshua Ray on west by land formerly of Thomas Jeggells now belonging to Mr. William Browne on north by house & land of Mr. Edward Norrice on south. *Signed*: Thomas Cheever. *Date*: 14 April 1684. *Witnesses*: Samuell Chever; Daniell Epes Jun'r. *Acknowledged*: 14 April 1684 and Boston 28:3:1685 by Sarah Cheevers to be done & sealed by her husband Mr. Thomas Cheevers with her consent. *Recorded*: 27 May:1684.

JOHN MARSHALL to JOHN NILSON – (6:769) John Marshall of County of Essex (merchant) & Hannah his wife mortgaged to John Nilson of Boston (merchant) for consideration forty and two pounds eight shillings in hand paid, theire messuage or tenement lying within township of Salem with all land belonging to the same, containing about halfe an acre bounded westerly with land of late William Robinson deceased eastward by highway & northerly land of John Pease sen'r alsoe three acres of ground in north feild belonging to Salem bounded easterly & partly northerly upon land formerly belonging to Thomas Spooner deceased and by land of John Pease sen'r north south & westerly together with all houses edefices buildings shops profits pr'viliges right comodities hereditaments & appurtenances provided that if abovenamed John Marshall do pay or cause to be paid unto sd John Nelson the full & just sum of forty two pounds 8 s, of currant money on or before eleaventh of January 1684 then this pr'sent sale be voyde & of none effect. *Signed*: John Marshall. *Date*: 11 January 1683. *Witnesses*: Elizabeth Barden; James Loyton. *Acknowledged*: in Boston 15 January 1683. *Recorded*: 28 May:1684.

RICHARD MORE SEN'R to SAMUEL DUTCH – (6:773) Richard More sen'r of Salem to Samuel Dutch of Salem (mariner) for natural afection unto well beloved son in law Samuel Dutch as alsoe for other good causes more especially in consideration of marriage betwixt him & my daughter Susannah his now wife have given Samuel Dutch & the heires of his body lawfully begotten of my daughter Susannah, a quantity of land lying in Salem upon part of which land Samuell Dutch his house now standeth & alsoe a highway through part of my oarchard to said land: the house lott or quantity of land is about a quarter of an acre as it is now fenced in, length of land is north & south buting on north with Mr. Richard More sen'r upon my oarchard & on south with river bredth of the land is fower poles two foot and is bounded on west with Mr. Geo. Keiser his land & on north with Richard More sen'r my land the highwaye is in length north & south ten poles & a halfe bounded with Mr. George Keiser & Thomas Mould theire land & in bredth east & west sixteene foot bounded on east with Mr. Richard More sen'r west with Mr. George Keiser & Thomas Mould with all apple trees that is now thereupon.
Memo: before signing & sealing hereof it is to be understood that haw tree in oarchard is the north end of highway & soe to runn east 16 foot.
Signed: Richard More. *Date*: 4 June 1684. *Witnesses*: Jeames Collins; Richard More Jun'r; Frances Neale sen'r. *Acknowledged*: by Capt. Rich'd More 6 June 1684. *Recorded*: 10 June:1684.

GARTRUDE POPE to JOSHUA BUFFUM and CALEB BUFFUM – (6:776) Gartrude Pope of Salem (widow) sold to two sonns in law Joshua Buffum & Caleb Buffum both of Salem for consideration valuable summ in hand already paid, a certaine p'cell of land which for some yeares since I bought of Edward Flint of Salem containing twenty eight rodd or pole of ground lying in Salem on westerly side of bridge street neere over against the houses of sd Joshua and Caleb Buffum the sd p'cell of land bounded northwesterly with som land of John Mccarter which he bought of the sd Edward Flint north easterly with streete or lane & southeasterly and southwesterly with land of sd Edward Flint the sd parcel of land containing in bredth next the streete five pole & three foot & soe to carry the same breadth backward so farr as to make up the full quantity of twenty eight pole as now enclosed & according to bill of sale given me pr Edward Flint for sd parcel of land: but they sd Joshua & Caleb are by these pr'sents bound to acquit exonerate free & discharge me sd Gartrude of & from my covenant & engagement to & with aforesd Edward Flint with respect to the keeping up & maintaining fences in & about sd p'cel of land in equall halves between them in ths manner unto sd Joshua one halfe part of pr'misses both for the front next to the street & soe backward northerly & the other halfe part to sd Caleb which is the south eastern pt of abovesd penn or parcell of ground. *Signed*: Gartrude Pope. *Date*: 6 June 1684. *Witnesses*: John Macarter [mark]; Richard Croade. *Acknowledged*: 11 June 1684. *Recorded*: 11:June:1684.

JOSHUA GRAFTON to GARTRUDE POPE – (6:779) Joshua Grafton of Salem (marriner) sold to Gartrude Pope of Salem for consideration valuable sum of mony in hard paid, a parcell of land containing about twenty pole lying in Salem buting upon land of Joseph Hardy Jun'r north north west & upon the east northeast side upon land of Mrs. Elizabeth Turner widow to Mr. John Turner deceased & south southeast upon land of Mr. Joshua Grafton marriner & so buting upon a lane laid out which runs betweene my uncle John Grafton's land & mine the aforesd land of Joshua Grafton fronting to the abovesd lane ninety foot & ninety foot back by Mrs. Turner's fence as it now lyeth. *Signed*: Joshua Grafton. *Date*: 2 June 1684. *Witnesses*: Samuell Gardner Jun'r; John Buttolph Jun'r. *Acknowledged*: 2 June 1684. *Recorded*: 12 June:1684.

WILLIAM HASCALL to THOMAS CHUB SEN'R – (6:781) William Hascall of Gloster sold to Thomas Chub sen'r for full satisfaction, a certaine parcell of upland ground lying in towne of Beverly being bounded easterly by land formerly pertaining to Roger Hascall sen'r southerly by land formerly pertaining to John Crover westerly by land of Mark Hascall northerly by land of Mark alsoe containing three acres. *Signed*: William

Hascall [mark]. *Date*: 21 June 1682. *Witnesses*: Samuell Hardie; Josiah Hascall. *Acknowledged*: 26 June 1683. *Recorded*: 23 June:1684.

JOHN GROVER to THO. CHUB SEN'R – (6:783) John Grover of Beverly (husbandman) sold to Tho. Chub sen'r of Beverly (carpenter) for consideration valuable sum in hand paid, three acres of upland ground lying in Beverly and is bounded easterly with the highwaye or comon roade southerly with the land of John Trask sen'r westerly with land of Mark Hascal northerly with land of sd Thomas Chub. *Signed*: John Grover. *Date*: 29 June 1678. *Witnesses*: John Benet; David Perkins. *Acknowledged*: 1 May 1682 and Sarah wife did release dower. *Recorded*: 23 June:1684.

JOHN GATCHELL and WIBERA GATCHELL to JEREMIAH GATCHELL & HIS CHILDREN – (6:784) John Gatchell of Marblehead with consent of wife Wibera gifted to Jeremiah Gatchell & his children for consideration divers good causes, one parcel of ground being ten acres of land being in Marblehead butting & bounding on the west side joining to Robert Bartletts land & towards southeast butting to Mr. John Devoreux farme & northwest butting home to Salem river to low water marke & the east side joyning to the sd Gatchell's land. *Signed*: John Gatchel; ~~Wilbra Gatchel~~. *Date*: 17 Aprill 1680. *Witnesses*: Robert Bartlett; Thomas Posland [mark]; Edw. Humphry sen'r. *Acknowledged*: 14 December 1682. *Recorded*: July:12:1684.

JOHN GATCHEL SEN'R to JEREMIAH GATCHEL – (6:787) John Gatchel sen'r of Marblehead with consent of wife Wibera sold to Jeremiah Gatchel sen'r son of Marblehead for consideration valuable sum of money in hand paid, a small tract of land lying together in township of Marblehead & is by estimation ten acres bounded southeastward with Mr. John Deveroux his land where it is to be sixteene poles in breadth northwest with the river caled Forrest river eastward with or upon a ten acre lott now belonging to me John Gatchel westerly with a ten acres lot I John Gatchel formerly gave to him Jeremiah Gatchel provided I John Gatchel for my own use am for pasturidge for cattle & timber for my own use to make use of what I have ocasion of unless fenced in by Jeremiah Gatchel & manured w'ch use I am in my perticuler concerns to make use of till such time as Jeremiah Gatchell shall pay unto me full & just sum of twenty pounds in silver according to tenour of former bills bearing date of these presents. *Signed*: John Gatchel. *Date*: 1 May 1682. *Witnesses*: Francis Neale sen'r; Joseph Gatchel. *Acknowledged*: 14 December 1682. *Recorded*: July 12:1684.

JOHN GATCHELL and WILBOROUGH GATCHEL to JEREMIAH GATCHEL – (6:790) John Gatchell of Marblehead (planter) & Wilborough wife sold to Jeremiah Gatchel of Marblehead (wheelwright) for consideration twenty five pounds, sixteene pound ten shillings being in hand paid by our son Jeremiah Gatchel & the remainder of sd sum being eight pounds ten shillings secured by an obligation made to us by our son, a tract of land lying in Marblehead by estimation ten acres bounded at the head on southeast with Mr. John Devereux his land where it is to be sixteene poles in bredth, on northwest with Forrest river, on eastward with land of Geo. Bonfeild to which it is adjoin & come home on westward with his own ten acre lott formerly sold unto him by us. It is agreed before signing that sd John Gatchel out of the pr'misses reserves a liberty for himselfe & wife to cut off his necessary firewood for his & her proper use during their naturall lives. *Signed*: John Gatchel [mark]; Wilborough Gatchel [mark]. *Date*: 8 February 1682. *Witnesses*: Samuel Cheever; Mary Waymouth. *Acknowledged*: 27 August 1683. *Recorded*: July 12:1684.

JOHN ORNE SEN'R to JOSEPH ORNE – (6:792) John Orne sen'r of Salem (house carpenter) sold to Joseph Orne of Salem (cordwinder) for divers good causes and considerations especially for love and natural affection unto son Joseph Orne, house he now liveth in with one third pt of all my land lying betweene Widow Ropes & Capt. John Price their land together with a small strip of land his house now standeth on bounded with the land of Capt. Price and Capt. Corwin on the south side & on north with land of son Benjamin Orne as itt is now devided y^t is to say the whole of the land his house stands upon besides his third pt as fully as it is mentioned in the will: alsoe a third part of my lott or ground y^t lyeth neere great cove viz: y^t pt which was Mr. Higginsons lott which adjoines to Gov Symonds his lott southwardly with a piece of meddow adjoining to itt bounded with brooke eastwardly and northwardly with land of Mr. Berth. Gedney & alsoe a knowle of land lying by Goodale's spring bounded on west with lott of my son Benjamin which was comonly called Normans Lott, only it is to be understood my daughter Harvey is to live in that part of my son Joseph Orne his house during tyme of my natural life. *Signed*: Joseph Orne sen'r [mark]. *Date*: 1684. *Witnesses*: Jno. Norman; Benjamin Orne. *Acknowledged*: 17 July 1684 by Deacon Joseph Orne. *Recorded*: July:17:1684.

ABRAHAM COLE and SARAH COLE to STEVEN SEWALL – (6:795) Abraham Cole of Salem sold to Steven Sewall of Salem for consideration fifteene pounds in hand paid, a certain p'cell of land containing about nineteen rodd or pole lying in towne of Salem & is bounded within land of Thomas Walter northerly with land of Joshua

Buffum easterly with land of Joshua Swazey Jun'r southwardly & with lane or highwaye westwardly. ***Signed***: Abraham Cole; Sarah Cole. ***Date***: 30 May 1684. ***Witnesses***: & seizin & possession given of pr'misses Richard Croade; Robert Kitchin. ***Acknowledged***: 25 July:84. ***Recorded***: July:26:1684.

ROBERT BARTLETT and RICHARD CROAD – (6:798) These are to certifie unto whomsoever itt maye concerne y^t Robert Bartlett aged about forty six years att pr'sent an inhabitant in Marblehead owning himselfe to be sone of William Bartlett of towne of Frampton County of Dorset in old England, came personally before me seaventeenth of July 1684 & did affirm upon his corporall oathe y^t Richard Croade now an inhabitant in Salem likewise before mee pr'sent living & in health was & is the reputed sone of Richard Croad of Frampton aforesd borne unto him by Anstice his wife: & y^t this Richard Croad now before me, the sd Robert Bartlett testifieth y^t he hath well known whilest in his youth in Frampton & ever since untill now, & y^t he well knew this Richard Croad now before me to have a tenement in maner of Frampton aforesd whereof Mr. Thomas Browne was late Lord.

Sworne before me John Hathorne one of his Majesties justices of the peace in Salem seaventeenth July 1684.

The testimony of Magdalen Bartlett is recorded in the book of the County Court. ***Date***: Aprill 17:84.

RALPH KING and ELIZABETH KING to WILLIAM BROWN ESQ'R. – (6:799) Ralph King of Lyn & Elizabeth his wife mortgaged to William Brown Esq'r of Salem for consideration three hundred pounds in hand paid, all my farme given me by my father Daniell King deceased being twelve hundred acres of upland & meadow lying in township of Lin comonly caled by name of Swapscot: butted & bounded with sea at westerly end of long pond lying along by sea side & so upon a straite line over quite to a little red oake standing upon a brow of a hill on southerly side of a path going to my farme or to farme where George Darlin did live wh'ch tree is marked with a (D & a K) on northerly side & an (R & a K) on westerly side & soe this line to runn to a line between Lyn & my farme & be to runn all along between Lynn & my farme to a running brooke at the southerly end of John Farr's & Edward Richards lott & over Swapscott pond to a litle walnutt tree on westerly side of pond marked with (R.K.) on the northerly side with (N.E.) & so to runn westerly to an other wallnut tree marked with (RK) on side & (NE) on northerly and is bounded on northerly side with land of Ezekiell Needham & soe all along upon the brow of a hill westerly & soe to highwaye to Lynn to a stake & a heap of stones & from thence downe to sea against highwaye & itt is agreed in case within named

Ralph & Elizabeth King pay or cause to be paid unto William Brown at his dwelling house in Salem the full sume of sixty eight pounds in currant money of New England on or before twenty eighth of July 1685: & sixty five pounds in currant money on or before twenty eighth July 86 & sixty two pounds in currant money on or before twenty eighth 87 & fifty nine pounds currant money on or before twenty eighth July 88 & fifty six pounds currant money on or before twenty eighth July 89 & fifty three pounds currant money on or before 28 July 1690 then above written deed to be voide & of none effect. *Signed*: Ralph King; Elizabeth King. *Date*: 28 July 1684. *Witnesses*: Benjamin Brown; William Redford. *Acknowledged*: 28 July 1684 by Ralph & Elizabeth & she delivered up right of dowry. *Recorded*: August 4:1684.

CHRISTOPHER CODNER and JOHN DEVORIX SEN'R and RICHARD KNOTT – (6:803) Then I received full possession of my house & land in Marblehead & then delivered unto mee by John Devorix sen'r & Richard Knott according to a Court order within specified as witness my hand the day and year above written. *Signed*: Christopher Codner. *Date*: 15 August 1679. *Witnesses*: Samuell Morgan; Jno. Legg. *Acknowledged*: 30 July 1684. *Recorded*: no date.

GEORGE BONFEILD and REBECKA BONFEILD to ROBERT BENNIT – (6:804) George Bonfeild of Marblehead (fisherman) sold to Robert Bennit of Marblehead for consideration a certaine sum of money in hand received, one p'cell of land being one acre in Marblehead bounds being to west side of my dwelling house & joining to Gatchells ground towards southwest & lying within my land excepting great oake trees yt stands in sd land which shall be reserved for my owne use provided if said Robert Bennit should be constrained by reason of poverty or sickness to sell sd land he shall not sell itt till suche tymes as I or my heires shall first have the refuse of itt. Itt is to be understood sd Robert Bennit is to have privilidge of a waye to go to his ground by our house the same waye as we have. *Signed*: George Bonfeild [mark]; Rebecka Bonfeild [mark]. *Release of Dower:* Rebecka Bonfeild did yield right in land 29 July 1684. *Date*: 19 January 1682. *Witnesses*: Edw. Humphries; Elizabeth Gatchell. *Acknowledged*: 20 March 1683 4. *Recorded*: 27 August:84.

WILLIAM BEALE SEN'R and ELIZABETH BEALE to ROBERT BENNIT – (6:806) William Beale sen'r of Marblehead (husbandman) with consent of wife Elizabeth sold to Robert Bennit of Marblehead for considerable value paid, one acre fresh meadow in bounds of Marblehead having other meadow of sd Beales joyning to east George Bonfeilds land to west mill brooke to south a ditch cast up and other lands of sd Beales to north as alsoe itt is to be understood Robert Bennitt is engaged from time to time and at all times to maintaine in good reparation suficient the north ditch betwixt Beales land and Bennits meadow and in case any disturbance about damage betwixt them Bennit is to make & maintaine a suffitient fence on east bounds betwixt them. *Signed*: William Beale; Elizabeth Beale [mark]; Robert Bennit [mark]. *Date*: 28 August 1682. *Witnesses*: Rebecka Bonfeild [mark]; Moses Beales [mark]. *Acknowledged*: by William Beales; Robert Bennit 29 July 1684. *Recorded*: 27 August:1684.

JNO. BENNIT to JACOB KNIGHT – (6:808) Jno. Bennit of Boston (sonne of Mr. Samuell Bennit of Boston) sold to Jacob Knight of Lyn (mason) for consideration: a judgment of Court of eighteene pounds graunted aforesaid Jacob Knight against aforesd Samuell Bennit natturall father of sd John Bennit together with twenty shillings charges about serving an execution upon sd Samuell for obtaining of the same whereby sd Samuell Bennit is imprisoned for his namely sd Sam'll Bennit sitting at liberty & his full payment of abovesd nineteene pounds unto sd Jacob Knight as full satisfaction for same, two acres salte marsh ground being in township of Boston being part of farme which lately sd Samuell lived upon adjoining westerly one wide brooke as country highwaye lyeth from Lyn to Boston: sd two acres lyeth in salt marsh below now barne standing on sd farme & is bounded eastwardly with salt marsh of sd John Bennit on a straite line neere a little cricke westwardly on marsh of said John Bennit northerly on upland of sd Bennit & southwardly with marsh of sd Bennit together with free liberty of an highwaye through land of sd John Bennit whereby sd Jacob Knight may make improvement of sd two acres of marsh. *Signed*: John Benit. *Date*: 27 January 1674. *Witnesses*: Thomas Newall; Theophylus Baylee. *Acknowledged*: 25:11 mo:1675. *Recorded*: 27 August:1684.
These witnesseth that Jacob Knight of Lyn in consideration of nine pounds in money paid by John Newall of Lyn hath assigned and made over unto John Newall within mentioned deed as witness his hand 25 January 1676. Jacob Knight owned this to be his act & deed 25:11 mo:1675.

JUDETH COOKE to ELISHA KEBBEE – (6:810) Judeth Cooke of Salem relict of Henry Cooke of Salem (slautherer) sold to Elisha Kebbee for good causes and considerations & most especially my love and affections unto my sone in law Elisha Kebee & Rachell my daughter his wife, my p'cel of land in Salem on part whereof now stands dwelling house of sd Elisha & which together with all sd parcell of land hath with my free consent bene long since in tenure, use & possession of sd Elisha conteining in whole tract twenty acres by estimation bounded att north end upon land of my son Isaac Cooke, westerly upon land of Jno. Hill upon land of Robt.

Follet southwardly & eastwardly upon land of Jno. Small: alsoe a parcel of fresh meadow by estimation six acres lying in pr'cints & township of Salem & bounded eastwardly upon brook comonly caled Mr. Norrice brook westerly upon upland called Pope's upland northerly upon meddow caled Henery Rennol's meddow & southwardly by meddow of Isaac Cooke, being my daughter Rachell's portion with sd Elisha Kebee. *Signed*: Judeth Cooke [mark]. *Date*: 29 December 1680. *Witnesses*: Joseph Foster; Jno. Pudnye; Rich'd Croade. *Acknowledged*: Judeth Cooke acknowledged writing with proviso the land bee not sould or alienated from children of Elisha Kebbee by daughter Rachell unless itt bee to pay for purchase of land to like value wherein sd children shall have an estate inheritance 22 November 1681. *Recorded*: 9 September 1684.

Judeth Cooke acknowledged deed of gift & cleerly freely & positively without any condition or limitation as exspressed in former acknowledgment or intaile but to be at his sole and absolute disposal 26 September 1684.

NICHOLAS HOULT SEN'R and MARTHA HOULT to NICHOLAS HOULT – (6:814) Nicholas Hoult sen'r of Andevor (dishturner) with consent of wife Martha gifted to Nicholas Hoult of Andevor for naturall love and afection to third sone Nicholas Hould & other good causes and considerations, one third pt of farme where he now dwells, upland & arable ground being bounded on northwest with a maple tree marked standing at end of pine swamp & soe bounded with highwaye on west and southwest & on southeast with heape of stones & from thence bounded with highwaye on east side yt comes up to the house & from northeast corner of house yt now is running on a straite line to the swamp or run of water & from the run of water easterly to a greate rock on south side of path from rocke running over swamp northerly to a white oake marked & from thence to a white oake marked standing by the path side yt goes from James Holts house to great meddow & soe running on the path side to another white oake marked yt is standing bounds of land of James Hoult & on north end of his land & soe bounded with heape of stones that is on brooke by old well & on northwest with stake and heape of stones & from thence to another stake & heape of stones & from thence to first principle bounds of land of James Hould & att south end of his land by sd Nicholas Hoult his heirs executors administrators & assigns forever shall leave a highway betwixt land of Jno. Hoult & sd Nicholas Hoult's land on east side of his land this way shall be left fower rods wide full length thereof: alsoe one third pt of my great medow being within bounds of Andever & on south side of meadow bounded on norwest with a stake standing by ditch w'ch is bound of meadow of James Hoult & from thence running & adjoining to meadow of James Hoult bounded with a stake standing by a ditch on northeast & soe adjoining on south side of ditch & running to a black ash tree marked & northerly with a white oake & soe bounded east & south with upland unto a maple tree marked standing by side of meadow & from maple tree to a stake westerly which is standing bound betwixt aforesd meadow & meadow of Jno. Hoult & from thence to bounds of James Hoults meadow; another piece of meadow bounded round with upland & with black oake tree marked standing by spring: alsoe two parcells of meadow being about place where old house stood as is usually soe called & bounded round with upland: alsoe two p'cells of meddow being a little distance from aforesd farme & neere to Sutton's bridge or att place where the bridge was, these two p'cels of meadow are bounded & compassed about with upland; my dwelling house yt now is together with cellar, roomes & leantowe & other conveniences of house, also the well & oarchard to wit: all apple trees & all other fruite trees already planted & growing upon aforesd ground moreover barne with leantowe together with all other housing for cattle already builded & standing upon this land. three acres of comon pr'viledge or comonage according to my graunt of towne sd Nicholas paying yearly tenn shillings in leue of all rates & charges both to towne & church of Andever so long as inhabitants of Andever shall continue this waye of ratinge by house lotts: & in consideration of father's gift Nicholas Hoult doe promise & engage to pay yearly to father for his maintenance sume of three pounds money only accepted this sume shall be paid to father soe long as he liveth: moreover Nicholas am hereby engaged after the death of my father to pay yearly unto my mother in law Martha Hoult wife of father Nicholas Hoult to pay unto her sume of fortye shillings money yearely only accepted for her maintenance soe long as she shall remain a widow & if she marry to any other man then aforesd engagement shall be voide & said Nicholas & Martha doe give up all our right in aforesd land meadow & comonages to our son Nicholas Hoult. *Signed*: Nicholas Hoult [mark]; Martha Hoult [mark]. *Date*: no date. *Witnesses*: Dudly Bradstreet; Henery Hoult. *Acknowledged*: June 16:1682. *Recorded*: 9 September 1684.

DANIEL CHACE and MARTHA CHACE to ROBT. RUSELL – (6:819) Daniel Chace of Nuburye (weaver) and Martha wife sold to Robt. Rusell of Andevor (weaver) for consideration twenty five pounds in hand paid & surety given, twenty acres of upland in towne of Andever lying betweene land of Robert Russell and Samuell & Henry Hoult being part of great division of Nicholas Hoult sen'r graunted by towne of Andevor and by him to Roger Marks & by him sould to John Chase & by him sould to Daniell Chace being bounded on southwest corner with a great pine marked, on southeast corner with a white oake tree marked, on northeast corner with stake & stones, on northwest with maple marked lyinge for twenty acres. *Signed*: Daniell Chace. *Date*: 30 April 1684. *Witnesses*:

Henery Hoult; John Chace. *Acknowledged*: 13 September 1684. *Recorded*: no date.

JOSIAH SOUTHERICK to ELISHA KEBBEE – (6:821)   Josiah Sotherick of Salem (yeoman) with full consent of wife Mary sold to Elisha Kebbee of Salem for consideration twenty five shillings in money, certaine parcell of fresh medow ground in pr'cincts of Salem containing by estimation an acre & halfe bounded northerly upon line & upon land of Robert Goodale westerly upon Garthred Pope southerly upon land of sd Elisha Kebbee easterly on brooke called Norrice his brooke furthermore it is agreed between parties notwithstanding what is exspressed in deed of sale Elisha Kebee shall have an acre & halfe of medow as abovesd in place mentioned yett it is to be understood yt sd Elisha shall have but sd Josiah's share in that plott as above bounded. *Signed*: Josiah Southericke. *Date*: 18 November 1681. *Witnesses*: Isaack Cooke; Steven Smale. *Acknowledged*: 20 November 1681. *Recorded*: no date.

THOMAS BAKER – (6:824)   I Thomas Baker of Winter harbour fisherman appoint Jno. Polin of Ipswich to be lawfull attorney to dispose or sell ten acres of land bounded in Beaverly according to tenour exspressed in bill of sale. *Signed*: Thomas Baker. *Date*: 1 June 1680. *Witnesses*: Marke Rounde [mark], Jno. Tookies. *Acknowledged*: Hannah wife of Thomas Baker testified on oath yt above written is act and deed of her husband Thomas Baker [no date]. *Recorded*: no date.

(6:824)
    Essex Registry Deeds. Southern District, Salem Mass. January 1 1877. The foregoing copy of the Sixth Book of Deeds for Salem & vicinity was made in 1855 under the direction of the County Commissioners. It has now been examined & corrected and is a true copy of the original.
             Attest
                    Ephr. Brown Regr.

ABBETT/ABBOTT/ABBUT
  James, 29
  John, 107, 132
ADAMS/ADDAMS
  George, 76, 126
  Richard, 138, 139
  Susana, 138, 139
  Thomas, 58, 79
  Walter, 65
  William, 140
ADDINGTON/ADDINTON
  Isa, 68
  Isaac, 78
AGER
  Jonathan, 114
ALCOCKE
  John, 121
ALDERMAN
  John, 126
ALFORD
  Charity (Dike), 75
  John, 75
ALLEN
  Jacob, 109
  William, 35
ANDREW/ANDREWES/ ANDREWS
  Daniell, 86, 87
  Nicholas, 86
  William, 56, 64, 83, 99
APLETON/APPLETON
  Elizabeth, 115
  Samuell, 111, 115
ARCHARD/ARCHER
  Hanah (___), 136
  Samuell, 23, 136
ARDLEE
  Peter, 140, 141
ARINGTON see also **ERRINGTON**
  Thomas, 47
ARMITAGE
  Joseph, 57, 95, 127
ATWATER
  John, 37, 38, 67, 83

BABADGE/BABAGE/ BABBADGE/BABBIDDGE
  Christopher, 45, 52, 118
  Sarah, 124
BACHELER/BACHELLER/ BACHELOR
  John, 28, 60, 77, 80
  Joseph, 77
  Mark, 60
  Mary (___), 77
  Miriam, 77
  Sara (Goodell), 28
  Sarah (___), 60
BACON
  Daniell, 23, 116
  Isaac/Isaack, 89
BAILES/BAILIES
  ___, Mrs., 87
BAILEY /BAILY
  James, 12, 13,43
BAKER
  Cornelius, 132
  Edward, 27
  Hannah (___), 151
  Thomas, 40, 151
BALCH
  Benjamin, 46, 132, 133
  Free, 105
  John, 46
BALLARD
  John, 23, 24
  Nathaniel/Nathaniell, 22-24
  William, 23
BANCROFT
  Thomas, 102
BARBER, 82
BARDEN
  Elizabeth, 142
BARKER
  Richard, 134
BARNES, 82
BARNY
  Jacob, 46
BARTHOLMEW/ BARTHOLOMEW/ BATHOLMEW
  Henry, 18, 35, 71, 72, 136
  Sarah, 71
  William, 5, 6
BARTLETT
  Magdalen, 146
  Nicholas, 116
  Robert, 144, 146
  Thomas, 18
  William, 146
BARTOLL
  William, 107
BARTON
  J., 72
  John, 38, 64, 74
  Lidea, 38

Mathew, 83, 84
BASSETT
   William, 29, 41, 61, 109
BATTER
   ___, Mr., 89
   Edmond/Edmund, 43, 45, 64, 75, 85, 86, 88, 116, 121, 123
   Mary (___), 43
BAXTER
   John, 33
BAYLEE
   Theophylus, 148
BEACHUM
   ___, Goodman, 92
   Edward/Edw'd, 89, 133
BEADLE
   Hanna/Hannah (___), 24, 32
   Sam'll/Samuel/Samuell, 21, 24, 25, 32, 33, 74
BEALE/BEALES
   Elizabeth (___), 147, 148
   Moses, 148
   William, 147, 148
BECKET/ BECKETT
   John, 29, 55, 58
   Margarett (___), 29
BEEBE
   John, 71
BELINGHAM see BELLINGHAM
BELKNAP/ BELKNAPP/BELNAP, 42
   Hanah, 114
   Joseph, 60, 95, 96, 114
   Samuel, 114
BELLINGHAM/BELINGHAM/ BILLINGHAM
   ___, Gov., 130, 132
   Rich'd, 1
BELNAP see BELKNAP
BENET/ BENETT/ BENIT/ BENNETT/ BENNETT/ BENNIT/ BENNITT, 109
   Aron, 111
   Elizabeth (Goodell), 73
   Henry, 73
   John, 23, 24, 47, 63, 144, 148
   Jno., 148
   Margaret (___), 138
   Samuell, 20, 56, 65, 148
   Sarah (___), 20
   Robert, 147, 148
BERRY
   Betterice, 101
   Edward, 103
   Thomas, 54
BETTS
   John, 120
BILLINGHAM see BELLINGHAM
BISHOP
   ___, Mrs., 129
   Edward, 59, 132, 133
   Margaret (___), 104
   Richard/Rich'd, 7, 14, 15, 28, 30, 89, 137
   Samuell, 104
   Thomas, 28, 30. 104
BLACK
   John, 37, 43, 44
BLACKFORD
   Thomas, 103
BLAKE
   John, 132
BLY
   Benjamin, 82
BONFEILD/ BONFELD
   Geo./George, 145, 147
   Rebecka, 148
   Rebecka (___), 147
BOOTEMAN
   Jeremiah, 29, 30
BOULDS, 115
BOWDITCH
   William/Wm., 21, 22, 29
BOYLES
   Jonathan, 69
BOYNTON, 120
BRACKENBURY
   John, 69
   Richard, 69
BRACKETT
   Peter, 114
   Thomas, 94
BRADSTREET/ BRADSTREETE
   Ann (___), 100
   Dudly, 150
   Mercy, 99, 100
   Mercy (___), 99
   S., 100
   Samuell, 99, 100
   Simond/Simonds/Simon/Symon, 40, 97-100, 111
BREAD/BREADE
   ___, Goodman, 138
   Allan/Allen, 7, 8, 23, 24, 68
   Elizabeth, 24
   Elizabeth (___), 22, 23
   John, 23, 46, 47

BREWER
  Crispus, 100
BRIDGES
  ___, Capt., 56
  Edmond/Edmund, 10, 30, 55, 56,
    58, 59, 85, 91
  Elizabeth (Croade), 58
  Robert, 127
BRIMBLECORNE
  Phillip, 65
BRIMSDON
  Rebecka (___), 98, 99
  Robert, 98, 99
BRISCO
  Joseph, 68
BRONSDON
  Robert, 107
BROWNBROWNE
  Abigaile, 52, 111
  Abraham, 47
  Benja/Benjamin, 37-39, 45, 83, 140,
    147
  Ephr., 151
  Gershom, 135
  Hannah (___), 78
  James, 21, 78
  John, 7, 72, 74, 76, 87, 88, 136
  Richard, 128
  Sarah (___), 110
  Thomas, 146
  William/Wm., 5, 21, 39, 42, 45,
    57, 66, 68, 74, 75, 83, 91, 106,
    110, 111, 117, 126, 139, 140,
    141, 146, 147
BROWNING
  Thomas, 44, 50
BUCKLEY/BUCKLY
  Sarah (___), 115
  Wm/William, 115
BUFAM/BUFFUM
  Caleb, 13, 16, 77, 92, 126, 133, 143
  Joshua, 78, 143, 146
  Robert, 137
BULLOCK
  John, 16, 77, 125, 126
BURCHAM/BURCHUM
  Edw'd/Edward, 65, 120
  Edmund, 56
BURGES/BURGESS
  Robert, 2, 3, 138
  Sarah (___), 2, 138
BURNAP
  Elizabeth (___), 89
  Isaack/Issac, 88, 89

BURRELL/BURRELLS
  John, 61, 97, 109
BURT
  Betterice, 101
BURTON
  Isaack, 133
  John, 94, 126
BUSH
  Edward, 114
BUTLER
  Lewis, 120
BUTTOLPH
  John, 136, 143
BYRBE
  Joseph, 85

CALLY/KALLY
  John, 85
CANTLEBURY
  William, 9
CARD
  John, 63
CARRELL/CARRILL
  John, 77
  Náthaniell, 75
CASH
  William/Wm., 33, 103, 104, 116,
    127
CAUELL/CAUILL/CAUVILL
  Nathaniel, 71
CAVE
  Thomas, 131, 132
CHACE see also CHASE
  Daniel, 150
  John, 151
  Martha (___), 150
CHADWELL see also CHATWELL
  Benjamin, 8, 23, 24
  Elizabeth (___), 24
  Thomas, 60, 119, 120
CHAMBERLAIN
  Richard, 55
CHANDLER
  William, 132, 134
CHASE see also CHACE
  John, 150
CHATWELL see also CHADWELL
  Elizabeth, 7, 8
CHEAS
  John, 48
CHEEVER/CHEEVERS/CHEVER
  ___, 87
  Ellen (___), 36, 37
  Ezekiel/Ezekiell, 34-37, 128, 129

155

Peter, 126, 140
Samuel/Samuell, 65, 68, 70, 106, 141, 145
Sarah (___), 141
Thomas, 34, 36, 37, 128, 141
CHIN
John, 67
CHUB
Tho./Thomas, 143, 144
CLAP/CLAPP
Edward, 114
Susanna (___), 114
CLEARK/CLEARKE
Daniell, 85
Mathew, 67
Samuell, 24
Thomas, 55
CLIFFORD
John, 45, 109
CLOYCE
Peeter, 85
COALE, 52
John, 20, 51
COATES
John, 82
COBBETT/COBBITT
Samuell, 61, 109
COBOURNE
Robert, 34
COCKERELL
Elizabeth (___), 114
CODMEN, 54
CODNER
Christopher, 110, 147
COFFIN
Tristnam, 128
COLDFOX
Venus, 17
COLDUM
Clement, 56
COLE
Abraham, 58, 78, 79, 145, 146
Alexander, 107
Bethia (Pickman), 107
John, 26, 51
Sarah, 78, 79, 145, 146
Thomas, 78, 137
COLENS/COLLENS/COLLINS
Frances, 1, 84, 114
Hanna, 114
Hannah (___), 1
Henry, 102, 120
Hester (___), 95
James/Jeames, 17, 142

John, 63
Robert/Robt., 95, 96
COMBES
Michaell, 29
CONANT
Exercise, 59, 130
Lott, 132, 133
Roger, 1, 130
COOK/COOKE
Henry, 10, 148
Isaac/Isaack/Isaak, 10, 31, 126, 148, 149, 151
John, 10, 122
Judeth, 149
Judeth (___), 148
COOMES
Humphrey, 38
COREE/COREY
Giles, 129
Mary (___), 129
CORNING
Samuell, 99
CORNISH
___, 37
CORWIN
___, Capt., 145
Eliza, 99
Elizabeth, 99
George, 90, 99
John, 22, 45, 73, 84-86
Jonathan, 87, 88
Margarett, 5
COTLE, 92
COTTER, 118
COX
Phillip, 130
COY
Frances, 92
CRAFT
William, 8
CRANIFURE
Elizabeth, 118
CRESY
John, 77
CROAD/CROADE
___, Mr., 14
Anstice (___), 101, 146
Elizabeth, 16, 58, 59
Frances, 16, 31
Hanna/Hannah, 15, 16
John, 15, 16, 49, 66, 81, 82, 92
Judith, 59
Richard/Richerd/Rich'd, 7, 9, 10, 14-17, 21-23, 26, 28-31, 42 45,

51, 58, 59, 63, 78, 82-84, 95,
101, 104, 121, 139, 143, 146,
149
CROFTS
William, 95
CROMWELL/ CRUMWELL, 100
Hannah (___), 90
John, 10, 11, 22, 23 29, 30, 42, 90,
91, 93, 104, 130, 139
Mary (___), 30, 42, 45, 46, 127
Philip/Phillip, 10, 17, 21-23 26, 29,
30, 42, 43, 45, 46, 58, 88, 90, 99,
103, 110, 111, 123, 126, 127,
130, 136
Tho./Thomas, 29, 36, 110
CRYNES
Nathaniel/Nathaniell, 15, 16
CURTICE
Alce (Rumboll), 77
William, 77, 78
Zacheus, 80
CURWIN
Jonathan, 137
CURWITHIES, 45
CUTLER
Thomas, 126
CUWIN
George., 132

DABY
Thomas, 59
DAMMER
___, Goodwife, 101
DANIELL
Steephen/Stephen, 52, 139
DARBY
Roger, 14, 28, 30
DARLIN/DARLING
George, 26, 146
John, 14, 28, 30, 31, 70
Mary, 28, 30, 69, 70
Mary (___), 14
Mary (Bishop), 30
DAVENPORT
___, Leift., 87, 95
DAVIS
John, 95
DAVY
Humphrey, 35
DEAN/DEANE
George, 7, 14, 15, 17, 59, 82, 83
DENISON
Daniel/Daniell, 39-41, 98
Patience, 22

Patience (___), 40, 41
DENNES
James, 86
**DEVEREUX/DEVERIX/
DEVEROUX/DEVOREUX/
DEVORIX**
Ann (___), 11
Humphry, 138
John, 11, 144, 145, 147
DIKE
Anthony, 75, 79
Charity, 75
DIVIN
Hestor (___), 127
John, 127
Mary, 127
DIXE/DIXIE/DIXY
___, Capt., 48
William/Wm., 11, 43, 105, 130
DODG/DODGE/DOGE
Edward, 132
John, 59
Joseph, 46, 132
William, 37, 46, 130, 132
DORY
Philip, 55
DOUNTON
William, 43, 86
DOVE/DOWE
Hannah (___), 66
Mathew, 66
DOWLETTEL
John, 7
DOWNING
___, Mr., 89
Joane, 138
Mary (___), 138
DRIVER
Phebe, 95
Phebe (___), 94
Robert, 68, 94, 95
DUE
Elizabeth, 29
DUMMER, 120
DUTCH
Osmond, 63
Samuel, 142
Susannah (More), 142
EATON
Eleazer, 138
EBORNE
Samuel/Samuell, 10, 31, 47, 77, 126
EDMONDS/EDMUNDS
John, 26

Joseph, 34, 97
Samuell, 34, 97
William/Wm., 7, 61
EDWARDS
Elizabeth (Price), 119
George, 72
Griffen/Griffin, 29, 41, 61, 109
John, 119
William, 47
EGER
Jonathan, 66
ELETHORPE
John, 70
ELIOTT/ELLIOT/ELLIOTT
Andrew, 46, 59, 130
ELLERLY/ELLERY
William, 63
ELLWELL/ ELWELL
Jane (___), 109
John, 109
Joseph, 63
ENDECOT/ENDECOTT/ ENDICOTT
Elizabeth, 2
Elizabeth (___), 2, 12, 66
Elizabeth C. (___), 5
John, 2, 5, 48, 65, 66
Jon., 9
Zarabbabell/Zarobabell/Zarubabell/ Zerobabell/Zarubbabell, 5, 12, 44, 64-66
ENGLISH
Phillip, 45, 84
EPES/EPPES/EPPS
Daniel/Daniell, 64, 65, 71, 141
Martha, 141
ERRINGTON see also ARINGTON
Thomas, 47
ESTES
Mathew, 59
EVERTON
William, 35, 36

FAIREFEILD
Walter, 43
FARLY
Michael/Michaell, 52-55
Mischeck, 53
FARR
Benjamin, 61, 109
John, 146
FARRER
Thomas, 7

FARRINGTON, 65
Edmond, 57
Edward, 108, 109
John, 108
Mathew, 57, 60, 108, 109
Sarah, 60
FELTON
Benjamin, 36, 86, 121, 123
John, 9
Nathaniel/Nathaniell, 9, 31, 44, 48, 80, 85
FERRY
Samuel, 39
FLINDER/FLINDERS
Richard, 55, 58, 94
FLINT
Edward, 16, 129, 139, 143
Thomas/Tho., 16, 28, 60, 74, 122, 129, 139
William, 126, 139
FLOYD
John, 7
FOGG
Ralph, 88
Susana, 88
FOLLET/FOLLETT
Robert/Robt., 4, 39, 75, 149
FOOT/FOOTT
Pasco, 22, 35
FOSTER
John, 24, 25
Joseph, 149
Mary, 80
Mary (___), 25
FOWLE
John, 115
Peter, 115
FOWLER
Joseph, 71
FOX
Elizabeth (___), 105, 106
Nicholas, 105
FOYE
___, Mr., 54
FULGIM
Niklis, 113
FULLER
Benjamin, 70
John, 56, 60, 109
Mary (Darling), 69, 70
Robert, 30, 66
Thomas, 44, 128-130
FURBUSH
John, 105, 107

FURNEAX/FURNEUX
William, 4, 5

GALE
Ambros/Ambrose/Ambross/
  Ambrosse, 67, 70, 71, 79
Edmund, 11, 130
Edward, 59
GANSON
Benjamin, 23
GARDNER
Ann (___), 97, 98
Ebenezer, 82
John, 38, 117, 135, 136
Jonathan, 116
Joseph, 126
Samll/Samuel/Samuell, 19, 33, 35,
  72, 76, 77, 90, 92, 107, 103, 117,
  135, 143
Thomas, 89
GASKIN
Edward, 38, 42, 89
Samuell, 77, 126
GATCHEL/GATCHELL, 147
Elizabeth, 147
Jeremiah, 144, 145
John, 4, 5, 110, 144, 145
Jonathan, 4, 5
Joseph, 144
Samuell, 110
Wibera/Wibra/Wibrah/Wibro/
  Wiborough (___), 4, 110, 144,
  145
GEDNEY/GEDNIE/GENDY
___, Mr., 4
Amos, 40
Barth.Barthlomew/Bartho./Ba-hol./
  Bartholomew/ Berth., 10, 49, 55,
  87, 88, 101, 136, 137, 140, 145
Eleazer, 13, 14, 17, 43, 137
John, 45, 74, 137,
Mary (___), 137
William, 129, 135
GEDRY
___, Mr., 3
GEERISH see GERISH
GEORGE
Richard, 6, 65
**GERISH/GEERISH/GERRIS/
GERRISH**
Benjamin, 92, 116, 118, 127, 133
Hanah/Hannah (___), 92, 118, 133
Moses, 128

GIBBS
Robert, 140
GIDDING
Samuel, 55
GIGGELLS see also JEGGELLS
Abigail (___), 141
GILBER
William, 96
GILES
Bridgett (___), 139
Edm'd/Edmond, 95, 139
Eleazer, 19, 139, 140
John, 46, 139, 140
GILLOW
John, 8, 61, 68
GILLOWAY
John, 20
GINGEN
John, 1
GLANFEILD
Liddea/Lidia (___), 75, 76
Robert, 75, 76
GLASS/GLASSE
Elizabeth (___), 105, 106
Richard/Rich'd, 105, 106
GODSOE, 52
William/Wm., 73, 116, 117
GOFFE
John, 103
GOLD
John, 85
**GOLTHRITE/GOLTHWAITE/
GOLTHWITE/
GOLTHWRIGHT**
Rachell, 48, 95
Samuell, 95
Thomas, 89, 95, 137
GOODALE/GOODELL, 24, 25, 60,
  91, 134, 145
Elizabeth, 73
Isaac/Isaack/Isaacke, 28, 60, 73, 80,
  91
Jacob, 9
Margarett, 73, 74
Robert, 8, 9, 28, 60, 73, 74, 80, 151
Sara, 28
Zachariah, 74, 80
GOODRIDGE
Joseph, 120
GOOLD see also GOULD
John, 80
Thomas, 3
GOTT
Daniell, 56, 60, 97

GOULD see also GOOLD
　John, 39, 40, 121
　Sarah (___), 40, 121
GOURDING
　Elizabeth (___), 74
　Lott, 21, 72, 74
GRAFTON, 135
　Jno./John, 117, 118, 143
　Joseph, 17, 108, 117, 118, 123
　Joshua, 117, 118, 143
GRAIES see also GRAY
　Samuell, 72
GRAVES
　Elizabeth (___), 108, 109
　Hanah (___), 76
　Mark, 108
　Thomas, 76
GRAY/GRAYE see also GRAIES
　Elizabeth, 118
　Mary, 72
　Robert, 7, 72, 74, 133, 134, 137
　Samuel/Samuell, 73, 117
GREELY
　Phillip, 98
GREEN/GREENE
　Jacob, 6
　John, 6, 46, 62, 77, 105
　Mary (___), 6, 46, 77
　Thomas, 93
　William, 129
GREENSLADE
　John, 1
GRIGGS
　William, 42
GROVE
　___, Mr., 18
　Edward, 18, 38, 42, 76, 94
GROVER
　Edmond, 59
　John, 143, 144
　Nehemiah, 59
　Sarah (___), 144
GUPPE
　John, 116
GUTCH
　Robert, 29
HADLOCK, 48
　James, 87
HAINES see also HAYNES
　Richard, 12, 13
　Thomas, 12, 13, 16, 48
HALE
　John, 11, 69

HALEY/HALLEY
　Joanna (___), 107
　Richard, 107
HALL see also HALLS
　Joseph, 24
HALLEY see HALEY
HALLS see also HALL
　Joseph, 109
HAMMOND
　Laurance, 111
HARDIE/HARDIE/HARDY
　Mary, 70
　Joseph, 14, 113, 117, 130, 139, 143
　Sam./Samuel/Samuell, 36, 69, 70, 77, 96, 105, 130, 144
HARRIS
　Joseph, 94
　Richard, 66, 125
HART/HARTE
　Jonathan, 38
　Samuel/Samuell, 8, 23, 24
HARVEY/HARVI
　___ (Orne), 145
　Peter, 122
HARWOOD
　___, Goodman, 29
　Henry, 43
HASCAL/HASCALL
　Josiah, 144
　Mark, 143, 144
　Roger, 59, 143
　William, 143, 144
HASKETT
　Steephen/Stephen, 20, 51
HASKINS
　Roger, 96
HATHAILIE
　___, Goodwife, 101
HATHORNE, 132
　___, Maj., 28, 139
　Ebenezer, 47
　Eleazer, 136
　Elizabeth, 44
　John, 20, 21, 36, 42, 43, 47, 61, 64-66, 72, 87, 88, 108, 116, 146
　Sarah, 124
　William, 28, 44, 47, 88, 136
HAVEN
　Richard, 6, 34, 92, 93, 97
HAWKES/HAWKS
　John, 46, 47, 111
　Sarah (___), 47
HAYMAN
　Nathan, 111

Samuell, 111
HAYNES see also HAINES
  Thomas, 17, 67
HAYWARD
  John, 42, 96
  Nathaniell, 38
  Nicholas, 38, 39, 77
HEALY
  Sarah (___), 47
  William, 47
HENFEILD
  Edmond, 17
HENLY
  Elias, 11
HERRICK
  Henry, 132
  Joseph, 62
HESELTINE
  John, 70
  Robert, 70
HEWET
  William, 67
HIBBERT/HIBBURT
  John, 9
  Robert, 132
HICHINS see HITCHIN
HICKES/HICKS
  Dorcas, 122
  Timothy, 94
HIDE
  John, 119, 120
  Richard, 114
HIGGENSON/HIGGINSON
  ___, Mr., 145
  Henry, 73
  John, 107, 108
  Sarah (Savage), 108
HILL
  Abigaile (___), 46
  Jno./John, 25, 26, 39, 46. 89, 104, 148
  Zebulon/Zubelon, 15, 16, 104
HILYARD
  Edward, 123
HINES
  William, 65
HIRST
  William, 38, 42, 75, 76
HITCHIN/HITCHINS/HICHINS see also HUCHINS
  Daniel/Daniell, 6, 56, 111
  Ellenor (___), 6
HOARE
  William, 96

HODG/HODGE/HODGES
  George, 33, 35, 127
  Robert, 83, 116
  Sarah (___), 33
HOEMAN
  Ann (___), 107
  Edward, 107
HOLEMAN
  Edward, 65, 67, 68
  Richard (___), 65
HOLEUP
  Thomas, 11
HOLIOAK/HOLYOCK
  Edward, 8, 120
HOLLINGSWORT/ HOLLINGWORTH
  ___, Mr., 109
  Elenor/Ellenor/Ellinor (___), 45, 84
  William, 21, 45
HOLT see also HOULD/HOULT
  James, 149
  Nicholas, 133, 134
HOLTON see also HOULTON
  Joseph, 19, 47
  Sarah, 48
HOLYOCK see HOLIOAK
HOOD
  Mary (___), 60, 61
  Richard, 60, 61
HOOPER
  Elizabeth (___), 67, 68
  John, 11
  Robert, 65, 67, 68
HORNE
  ___, Deac., 24, 25
  Benjamin, 64
  John, 62, 66, 136
  Joseph, 64
HOULD/ HOULT see also HOLT
  Henery/Henry, 150, 151
  James, 149, 150
  Jno., 149, 150
  Martha (___), 149, 150
  Nicholas, 149, 150
  Samuell, 150
HOULTON see also HOLTON
  Joseph, 13, 14, 47, 48
HOW
  John, 40, 85
HOWARD
  William, 57
HOWELL
  ___, Mr., 140

HUCHENSON/HUCHINSON see also HUTCHENSON/ HUTCHINSON
Joseph, 13, 44, 48, 115
Rich'd, 46
HUCHINS see HUTCHINS
HUCHINSON see HUCHENSON
HUDD
Richard, 41, 109
HUDSON
Jonathan, 61
HULL
John, 2
HUMPHERY/HUMPHREY/ HUMPHREYS/HUMPHRIES/ HUMPHRIS/HUMPHRY/ HUMPHRYES/HUMPHRYS/ HUNPHRYES
___, Mr., 113
Ann (___), 29, 109
Edm., 67
Edw./Edward, 4, 11, 79, 107, 110, 115, 144, 147
John, 29, 41, 42, 61, 93, 109
HUNN
Priscilla, 78
HUNPHRYES see HUMPHERY
HURD
John, 55
HUTCHENSON/HUTCHINSON see also HUCHENSON/ HUCHINSON, 87
Hadlock, 48
Joseph, 19, 48
Richard, 23
HUTCHINS/HUCHINS see also HITCHIN/HITCHINS/HICHINS
Daniell, 6, 93
Elinor (___), 6
HUTCHINSON see HUTCHENSON

INDIAN
Job, 23, 24
Kate, 23, 24
Mary, 23, 24
Will, 23, 24
INGALLS see also INGOLLS
Robert, 41
Samuell, 104
INGERSOLL
John, 19
Nathaniel, 115
Richard, 66

INGERSON
Nathaniell, 12, 13, 48
INGOLLS see also INGALLS
Eleazar, 67
Francis, 120
Henry, 120
IRELAND
John, 47
William, 1

JACKSON
John, 43, 44
JAMES
Thomas, 75
JAMISON
Sarah (Price), 119
William, 118, 119
JEANEVERIN/ JEANVERIN
Daniell, 20, 21
JEGGELLS see also GIGGELLS
Abigail, 140
Thomas, 140, 141
JENSON
Benjamin, 109
JEWETT
Elizabeth (___), 8
John, 8
Nehemiah, 36
JOALES/ JOALESI, 54
JOANES
Ephraim, 111
Hugh, 29
Mary, 111
JOHNSON
___, Mr., 4
Daniell, 61, 109
Elizabeth (___), 131
Frances, 39, 75
Samuell, 8, 29
Stephen, 130, 131

KALLY see CALLY
KEASER see also KEISER
Elizur, 69
George, 22, 60, 68, 69
KEBBE/KEBBEE/KEBBY/KEBE/ KEBEE
Elisha, 32, 39, 148, 149, 151
Rachell (___), 148, 149
KEISER see also KEASER
Geo/George., 142
KELAND/KELLAND
Thomas, 84

KEMBLE
  Thomas, 99, 103
KENESTONE, 87
KENNY/KENY
  Henry, 12, 61, 62
KILLICUPP
  William, 6
KILLUM
  Lott, 28, 31, 32, 60, 80
KING
  Daniell, 81, 93, 112, 113, 120, 133, 146
  Elizabeth (___), 146, 147
  John, 139, 140
  Katheren (___), 88
  Ralfe/Ralph, 8, 29, 113, 146, 147
  Richard, 81
  William, 15, 79, 88, 89
KITCHEN/KITCHIN/KITCHING/ KITCHINS
  Elizabeth (___), 7
  John, 7, 9, 15, 82, 89
  Joseph, 27
  Robert/Robt., 32, 63, 71, 92, 118, 146
KNIGHT/KNIGHTS
  Jacob, 41, 148
  Job, 109
  Jonathan, 130-132
  Margaret (___), 131
  Phillip, 130-132
  Robert, 107
  Ruth (___), 130, 131
  William, 22
KNOTT
  Richard, 15, 43, 93, 147
KNOWLES/KNOWLS
  ___, Mr., 120
  John, 8

LAIGHTON see also LAUGHTON
  ___, Mr., 56
  Sarah (Rednap), 100
  Tho./Thomas, 8, 100
LAKE
  Margarett (___), 71
LAMBERT
  Daniell, 115, 125
  John, 96, 122, 123
LASKIN
  Timothy, 18
LATTAMORE
  ___, Mr., 67
  Christopher, 65, 68, 110

  Mary (___), 65
LAUGHTON see also LAIGHTON
  Thomas, 105, 114
LAWES
  Frances, 44, 57, 121, 124
LAWTHROP
  ___, Capt., 128
LAZENBY
  Margaret/Margarett, 8, 9
LEACH
  Elizabeth (___), 48
  John, 9, 38, 46, 48, 62, 63, 86
  Laurance, 48
  Mary (___), 62, 63
  Richard/Rich'd, 9, 10, 48
  Samuell, 91, 92, 111
  Sarah (___), 9
LEGG
  Jno./John, 105, 106, 147
LEMEN/LEMIN
  John, 18
  Solomon, 18
LEONARD
  Henry, 39, 40
LEWIS
  Abraham, 113
  John, 2, 41
LILLINGTON
  Allexander, 71
  James, 71
LINDALL
  Timothy, 18, 69
LINSEY
  Eleazer/Eliezer, 82, 114
LOIS
  Abraham, 114
LORD
  Abigail (___), 20, 117
  Margaret, 117
  Robert, 122
  William, 4, 20, 51, 52, 57, 72, 73, 89, 117, 121, 122, 136
LOTHROP
  ___, Capt., 23
  Tho./Thomas, 34, 36, 37, 99
LOVEJOY
  John, 132
LOVETT
  John, 69, 96
LOYTON
  James, 142

MABEE
  Richard, 99

MACARTER
John, 143
MACKMALLEN
Mary, 134
**MACKMANING/
MACKMANNING**
Alexander, 32, 33
MAHEW
George, 119
MAINE
Henry, 110
Richard, 36
MAKCALLON
Calliam, 80
MALE/MALL see also MAULE
Thomas, 27, 82, 83
MANING/MANNING
Elizabeth (___), 72
Nicholas, 24, 26, 72-74, 136, 137
MANSFEILD/MANSFIELD
Andrew, 2, 3, 56, 76, 102, 124, 127, 138
Damarice/Damaris (___), 82
Mary (___), 124, 125
Paul/Paule, 18, 19, 82, 114, 136
Robert/Robt., 56, 65
Samuel/Samuell, 3, 138
MARKS
Roger, 150
MARSHALL
Hannah (___), 142
John, 66, 76, 77, 142
Mary, 115
Rebecka (___), 26, 27
Ruth, 115
Tho./Thomas, 8, 26, 27, 29, 34, 56, 57, 99, 100, 127, 140
MARSTON/MARSTONE
Benjamin/Benjamine, 27, 93, 117, 118, 123, 125, 128, 129
John, 137
Manasseth/Mannasseth/Mammasett, 36, 72, 92, 107, 108
Marcy (___), 108
MARTIN
William, 20
MASCOLL/MASKOLL
John, 43, 123
MASON
___, Wid., 104
Elias, 13, 16, 114
John, 1, 116, 122
Sarah, 89

MASSEY, 12
Jeffery, 90
John, 17, 21, 90
Sarah (___), 90
MASTER/MASTERS
Nathaniell, 96
MAULE see also MALE/MALL
Naomy, 122
Naomy (___), 28
Tho./Thomas, 14, 15, 17, 27, 28, 31, 42, 59, 60, 68, 70, 118, 122, 126, 127, 137
MAVERICK
___, Mr, 86
Elias, 1
Eunice (___), 70, 71, 79
Moses, 70, 71, 79
Paul, 1
MAXEE
Alexander, 68
MAYO
Joseph, 117
MCCARTER
John, 143
MEACHUM
___, Goodman, 66
Isaac, 49, 50, 52, 66
MERRIAM see also MIRRIAM
William, 97
MERRIOTT
John, 70
MICHELL
Jonathan, 104
MIGHILL
___, Wid., 70
MILBURNE
Israel, 2
MILES see also MYLES
Ann (___), 41, 61, 109
John, 41, 61, 109
Joseph, 119
MIRRIAM see also MERRIAM
William, 7, 34
MOLD
Mary (___), 69
Thomas, 69
MOODY
Eliezur, 96
MORE
___, Capt., 83, 117
Richard, 68, 97, 142
Susannah, 142
MORGAINE/MORGAN
Elizabeth (___), 67

Samuell, 67, 147
MORRELL
Samuell, 100
MORRLE
Edward, 21, 39
MOULD
Mary (___), 68
Thomas, 50, 52, 68, 142
MOULE
Edward, 109
MOUNJOY/MOUNTJOY/ MUNJOY
Elizabeth (___), 19
Martha (Walton), 86
Walter, 19
MUDGETT
Thomas, 20
MUNJOY see MOUNJOY
MURRAY/MURRY
William, 21, 57
MYLES see also MILES
Ann (___), 29, 41, 42, 61
John, 29, 41, 42, 61

NEALE
An, 57
Ann (___), 45, 79, 101, 102
Frances/Francis, 2, 14, 66, 80, 119, 125, 142, 144
Jeremiah, 21, 24-28, 31, 38, 42, 45, 51, 57, 70, 79, 80, 102, 104, 116
John, 7, 24, 25, 39, 44, 45, 50, 57, 79, 101, 122, 124
Jonathan, 27, 50, 51, 57, 58, 115, 116, 124, 125
Joseph, 21, 27, 28, 31, 50, 51, 95
Mary (___), 21, 79, 80, 124, 125
NEALS
Francis, 119
NEALY
Ann (___), 45
NEEDHAM
Anthony, 55, 74
Daniell, 109
Ezekiell, 112, 113, 146
Sarah (___), 112, 113
NELSON
John, 142
NEVERS
Richard, 70
NEWALL/NEWELL/NEWHALL
Anthony, 61
John, 24, 61, 65, 148
Samuel, 54

Thomas, 20, 56, 57, 112, 113, 148
NEWMAN
Antipas, 2
John, 2, 105
NEWMARSH
John, 40
NICHOLLS/NICOLLS/NICOLS, 128
Edmond, 55
John, 133
William, 133
NICKES
William, 93
NICOLE
Francis, 116
NICOLLS/NICOLS see NICHOLLS
NILSON
John, 142
NOICE see NOYCE
NORMAN
___, 145
Arabella (___), 91
Jno/John., 23, 86, 91, 92, 102, 145
Joseph, 91, 92
Richard, 63
NORRICE/NORRIS, 151
___, Mr., 28, 31, 80, 94, 123, 149
Edmond, 117
Edw./Edward, 19, 62, 86, 89, 99, 133, 141
NORTHEY/NORTHY
John, 93
NOYCE /NOICE
Joseph, 47
Nicholas, 141
NURSE/NURSSE
John, 4

OLIVER
Bridgett (___), 64, 66
Tho./Thomas, 64, 74
ORNE
Benjamin, 134, 135, 145
John, 134, 135, 145
Joseph, 134, 135, 145
Simond, 134, 135
OSBOURNE/OSBURN/OSBURNE
Allexander, 12
William, 31, 42, 77, 126, 133
OSGOOD
Christopher, 132
Thomas, 132

PALME
　Jonathan, 27
PALMER
　___, Maj., 71
PARKER
　Nathan, 133
PARKES
　Thomas, 103
PARKMAN/PARKMON
　Deliverance, 14, 15, 17, 25, 52, 81, 93, 94
　Sara, 4
PARMITER
　Benjamin, 35
PASCO
　Hugh, 76, 123
PATCH
　John, 69, 99
PEALE
　Malachy/Mallachy, 81, 82
PEARCE
　Elizabeth (___), 90, 91
　Richard, 90
　William, 90, 91
PEAS/PEASE, 133
　Abigail (___), 126
　Ann (___), 31
　John, 31, 60, 66, 76, 77, 91, 92, 126, 142
　Margarett (___), 66
　Robert, 24, 25, 31, 76, 77, 126
PEETERS see PETERS
PERKINS
　David, 144
　Thomas, 85, 132
PETERS/PEETERS
　___, Mr., 24, 25, 134
PETHERICK
　John, 110
　Miriam (___), 110
PHELPS, 108
　Christopher, 19
　Edward, 126
　Henry, 126
　John, 107
　Nicholas, 126
PHILLIPS
　Charles, 16
PHIPPEN
　Samuell, 44
PICKAD
　John, 46
PICKERING
　Jane (___), 103

　John, 5, 21, 92, 94, 136-138
　Jonathan/Jonathen, 27, 50, 51, 102, 103, 136
PICKMAN
　Bethia, 106, 107
　John, 22, 117
　Nathaniell/Nath'll, 26, 75, 106, 107
　Samuell, 21, 22
PICKWORTH
　___, Wid., 111
　Samuell, 83
PILGRIM
　Elizabeth (Bartholomew), 18
　John, 18
PINSON
　William, 16, 32, 109
PITT
　William, 35, 36, 115
POATE
　William, 105
POLIN
　Jno., 151
POOLE
　John, 68
POPE, 149
　___, Wid., 13, 16, 31
　Banjamin, 47
　Garthred/Gartrude, 143, 151
PORR
　William, 63, 64
PORTER
　Benjamin, 46, 84, 133
　Israell, 12, 19
　John, 23, 122
　Joseph, 48, 68
POSLAND
　Thomas, 144
POTTER
　Nicholas, 24, 25
　Robert, 20, 61, 95
POWLAND
　James, 17
PRAY
　Mary, 111
PREIST
　John, 66, 74
PRESCOTT
　Peter, 131
PRICE see also PRISE
　___, Capt., 134
　Elizabeth, 119, 122
　Elizabeth (___), 116, 119
　Jno./John, 21, 81, 82, 116, 122, 128, 129, 145

Mathew, 119
Sarah, 119
Sarah (___), 116
Walter, 108, 116, 122, 124
PRICHET
John, 121
PRIDE
John, 37
PRINCE
Jonathan, 14, 15, 17, 59, 60 126, 127
Joseph, 89
Mary (___), 59, 60, 126
Richard, 2, 126, 139
Robert, 12, 44, 61, 62
Samuell, 126, 139
PRISE see also PRICE
Elizabeth (___), 118, 122
Mathew, 118
Walter, 122
PRITHARRCH see PRYTHERCH
PROCTER/PROCTOR
John, 55
Joseph, 55
Martha (___), 55
PRYTHERCH /PRITHARRCH
Richard, 33, 139
PUDDEATER/PUDEATER
Ann (___), 2
Jacob, 1, 2, 45, 57, 98
PUDNEY/PUDNYE
Jno./John, 93, 149
PURCHAS/PURCHASE/PURCHIS
Oliver, 6, 93, 105, 113
PUTNAM
Ann, 131
John, 11, 12, 23, 62, 86-88, 128, 129, 133
Jonathan, 133
Nathaniel/Nathaniell, 11-13, 23 43, 44, 46, 48, 86-88
Rebecca/Rebeccah (___), 128
Tho./Thomas, 5, 11, 43, 44, 87 128, 131, 132

QUINSEY
Daniell, 24

RAIES see RAYES
RAIMENT see RAYMENT
RAINSBERY
___, Maj., 113
RAMDELL
Elizabeth (___), 80

John, 80
RAND
Robert, 76, 120
RAVE
Samuell, 18
RAWSON
Edward, 8
RAY
Joshua, 132, 141
RAYES/RAIES
___, Goodman, 48
Daniel, 88
RAYMENT/RAIMENT
Thomas, 85
William, 59, 129, 130
REA
Joshua, 13, 14, 17, 19, 84
REDFORD
Charles, 45, 57
William, 141, 147
REDKNAP/REDNAP
Abraham, 114
Benj./Benjamin, 105, 114
Joseph, 100, 114
Samuel, 114
Sarah, 100
REED
Thomas, 94
REEVE/REEVES, 92, 118
John, 7, 82, 126
REINOLDS see RENOLD
REITH
Richard, 79
REIVES see REEVE
RENNOL/RENOLDS/RENOLS/ REINOLDS
Henry, 12, 31, 121, 149
REVES/REVESES/REVIS see REEVE
RICH
Margarett, 75
RICHARDS
Edward, 8, 146
John, 11
RIDDAN
___, Mr., 79
Thaddeus, 71
ROADES/ROADS
Ann, 2, 138
Henry, 2, 3, 97, 111, 115, 138, 140
John, 105, 110
Joseph, 2
Josiah, 97, 138
ROAPES see ROPES

ROBBINS
 Mary (___), 16
 Thos./Thomas, 7, 14-17, 21, 28, 31, 32, 60, 82, 88, 129
ROBBINSON see ROBINSON
ROBERTS
 Richard, 33
ROBINSON
 Ellen, 89
 John, 76, 85, 121, 133
 Thomas, 111
 William, 66, 142
ROGERS
 Jeremiah, 28, 36
 Johabad, 55
ROLFE
 Ezra, 95
ROOTE
 Thomas, 35
ROOTEN/ROOTON
 ___, Wid., 95, 100, 114
 Richard, 119, 120
ROOTES/ROOTS
 Joseph, 42
 Josiah, 59, 104, 130, 132
 Richard, 104
 Thomas, 33, 35, 104, 127
ROOTON see ROOTEN
ROOTS see ROOTES
ROPES/ROAPES/ROPPS
 ___, Wid., 92, 134, 145
 John, 39, 82, 84
ROSE
 Richard, 19
ROUNDE
 Marke, 151
ROWLAND
 Richard/Rich'd, 86
RUCK
 ___, Mr., 128
 John, 23, 40, 41, 81, 92, 122, 123, 132
 Sarah (___), 122, 123
 Thomas, 92, 133
RUMBOLL
 Alce, 77
 Daniell, 77, 78
RUSELL/RUSSELL
 Robt/Robert., 150
 Roger, 68

SALMON
 Remember, 93
SALTONSTALL
 Richard, 52, 53, 55, 104
SANDER/SANDERS see also SAUNDERS
 John, 26, 38, 106, 107
SANDIN
 Ephraim, 79
SANDY
 Samuell, 71
SAUNDERS see also SANDERS
 John, 8
SAVAGE
 Ebenezer, 108
 Ephraim, 108
 Perez, 108
 Thomas, 108
SCERRY see SKERRY
SEARLE
 John, 110
 Thomas, 44, 45
SEAWELL see SEWALL
 Henry, 23
SEVERNIE
 John, 27
SEWALL/SEWELL /SEAWELL
 Hanah (___), 120
 Henry, 23, 120, 121, 128
 Jane (___), 120
 John, 120
 Samuel, 121
 Steephen/Stephen/Steven, 43, 120, 128, 145
SHADDUCK/SHADOCK see SHATTOCK
SHAFLIN
 Michaell, 89
SHARP/SHARPP
 Alice, 141
 Charles, 85
 Nathaniell, 140, 141
 Samuell, 141
SHATTOCK/SHADDUCK/ SHADOCK
 Samuell, 51, 52, 57, 60, 115, 125
SHAW
 Roger, 119, 120
 Susannah (___), 120
 Wm., 75
SHEPPARD
 Jeremiah, 104
 John, 87
SHOANE
 Priscilla, 65

SHRIMPTON
  Samuell, 78
SIBLY
  William, 12
SILSBY
  Bethia (Pickman), 106, 107
SIMES
  Abraham C., 7
SIMMONDS/SIMMONS/
SIMONDS/SIMONS/SYMONDS
  ___, Gov., 145
  Hanna/Hannah (___), 83, 84
  Harlackendine, 71
  Richard, 44, 83, 84
  Samuel, 40
  William, 71
SKERRY/SCERRY
  ___, Marshall/Marchall, 28, 116
  Bridgett (___), 90
  Frances/Francis, 21, 39, 89, 90, 136, 137
  Henry, 17, 24, 74, 110
SMALE/SMALL
  Benjamin, 32, 42
  Jno./John, 39, 48, 75, 94, 149
  Steephen/Stephen/Steven, 32, 151
SMITH
  Elizabeth (Goodell), 73
  John, 41, 73, 80, 91, 116
  Rebecka, 40
  Samuell, 68
  Thomas, 68
  William, 76
SOLLAS
  Thomas, 29
SOTHWICK/SOUTHERICK/
SOUTHERICKE/SOUTHWICK
  Daniell, 89
  Isaac, 10
  John, 10
  Josiah, 13, 16, 31, 76, 151
  Lawrance, 126
  Mary (___), 151
  Samuell, 10
SOWDEN
  Thomas, 106
SPENCER
  ___, Col., 81
  Garrard, 120
  N., 81
SPOONER
  ___, Wid., 28, 30, 73, 92
  Thomas, 66, 92, 133, 142

STACKHOUSE
  Richard, 11
STACY
  Benjamin, 131
  John, 106
STANDISH
  James, 11, 35, 36
STANLLY
  Mathew, 121
STANY
  Mathew, 44
STARLING see STERLING
STARR
  Richard, 84
  Robert, 84
  Susanna, 84
STERLING/STARLING
  William/Wm., 101, 102
STILEMAN
  Elias, 20, 51, 88, 111, 117
STILSON
  Vinson, 11
STOCKER
  Thomas, 27
STONE
  John, 59
  Nathaniell, 99
  Robert, 31, 77, 88, 89, 92, 133
STORR
  Robert, 45
STOUGHTEN/STOUGHTON
  William/Wm., 53, 54
STRATTON
  ___, Mr.,, 29
SUTTON
  ___, 150
SWASYE/SWAZEY
  Joseph, 84
  Joshua, 146
SWEATLAND/SWETLAND
  Will/William, 10, 11
SWINERTON/SWINTERTON
  Hannah (___), 78
  Job, 11, 24, 25, 28, 80, 126
  John, 62, 78
SYMONDS see SIMMONDS

TALMADGE
  Thomas, 47
TAPLY
  Gilbert, 123
TARBOX
  Samuell, 100, 105

TAULY/TAWLEY
John, 49, 52
TAYLER/TAYLOR
George, 56
Joseph, 117
THING
Jonathan, 71
THISTLE
Richard, 38
THORNDIKE/THORNEDIKE
___, Mr., 37, 59
Paule, 36, 69
THORNE
Israell, 97
THORNEDIKE see THORNDIKE
TILTON
Susanna (___), 120
William, 120
TOMLINS
Edmond, 56
Edward, 27
TOMPKINS
___, Goodman, 92
John, 133
TOMSON
George, 108
TOOKIES
Jno., 151
TOWNSEND
Thomas, 56
TRASK
___, Capt., 89
Henry, 31
John, 13, 16, 144
Osmond, 132
William, 16
TRUSLER
Thomas, 126
TUCK
Joane (___), 42, 43, 94
John, 42
Thomas, 1, 42, 43, 94
TUCKER
Andrew, 110
TURLAND
Joshua, 1
TURNER
___, Wid., 117, 130
Elizabeth (___), 55, 63, 83, 143
John, 63, 83, 117, 143
TURRELL
Daniel, 26

VEREN/VERIN/VERON/VIREN
___, Mr., 94
Dorcas, 85, 86
Dorcas (___), 121
Hana/Hannah (___), 83, 124
Hiliard/Hilliard, 1, 4-6, 12, 14, 15, 17, 18, 20, 21, 24-29, 31, 33, 36, 42, 45, 49, 50-52, 60, 66, 70, 72-75, 77, 81, 82, 84-94, 97, 102-107, 109, 110, 116-118, 121-124, 126-129, 133, 134, 136, 137, 139, 140
Mary, 128, 129
Phillip, 121
Sara, 85, 86
William, 21
VERRY/VERY
Samuel/Samuell, 3, 4, 75, 139, 140
VIALL
John, 99
VINNING
John, 29
VIREN see VEREN
VOEDEN/VOEDON
Mary, 52
Mary (___), 49

WADE
___, Mr., 54
WADLEY
Robert, 71
WAKEFIELD
Samuel/Samuell, 58, 115, 124, 125
WALCUTT
Jonathan, 12, 13, 80
WALDRON
John, 86
WALKER
Richard, 93
WALLER
Christopher, 9
WALLIS
Nath., 63
WALLTIN see WALTON
WALTER
Thomas, 72, 78, 145
WALTIN see WALTON
Jno./John, 113
WALTON/WALLTIN/WALTIN
Elizabeth (___), 86
John, 114
Nathaniell, 67, 86
William, 86

WARD
  Samuell, 71
WARDALL
  Grace (___), 139, 140
  Vsall/Vzall, 139, 140
WARREN/WARRIN
  Abraham, 77
  Thomas, 44
WASTON
  John, 70
WATERMAN
  Richard, 87
WATERS
  William, 107
WATSON/WATTSON
  ___, Goodman, 1
  Thomas, 57, 98
WATTELL
  William, 107
WATTSON see WATSON
WAYE
  Aron, 1
  Joane (___), 1
  Richard, 103
  William, 1
WAYMOUTH
  Mary, 145
WEBB
  Daniel/Daniell, 57, 83, 84
WELD
  ___, Mr., 123
  Daniell, 43
WENBORNE
  John, 6, 111
WENMAR
  Thomas, 80
WEST
  Henry, 43, 49, 94, 123
  John, 85
  Thomas, 46, 85, 92
  William, 44, 83, 84
WESTGATE
  Adam, 19
WESTON
  John, 78
WHARTON
  Edward, 51
  George, 51
  Richard/Richerd, 2, 100
WHEELER
  Joseph, 8
  Thomas, 56

WHITE
  Abigail/Abigaile (___), 20, 72, 73, 117
  Margarett, 29
  Resolved, 72, 73, 136, 137
WHITING
  John, 99
WHITNEY
  Richard, 8
WHITTYEARE
  Abraham, 35
WIDDESGIN
  ___, 24
WILKINS
  Bray, 1
WILLARD
  Simond, 139
WILLIAMS
  Isaack, 11, 30
  Jenckin, 36
  Jno./John, 95, 98, 105, 116
  Joseph, 44
  Sam'l/Samuell, 81, 128, 129
WILLIS
  ___, Mr., 56
WILLOUGHBY/WILLOWBY
  Nehamiah, 18, 78
WILSON
  Joseph, 127
WING
  John, 120
WINTHROP
  John, 85
WISWALL
  John, 108
WOLCOTT
  Jos., 111
WOLLAN/WOLLAND see WOOLAND
WOOD
  William, 105
WOODBERRY/WOODBERRYE/ WOODBERY/WOODBERYE/ WOODBURY
  Andrew, 114
  Hugh, 11, 43
  Humphrey, 37
  Isaack, 37, 99
  John, 46
  Mary, 114
  Nicholas, 36, 132
  Peter/Peeter, 46, 132
  Tho./Thomas, 36-38, 69

WOODCOCK
William, 20
WOODMAN
Edward, 70
WOODWELL
Mathew, 62
**WOOLAND/WOLLAN/
WOLLAND/WOOLEN/
WOOLLAN/WOOLLEN**
Edward/Edw'd, 17, 44, 45, 84, 123, 130
Margery, 123
Martha, 83

www.ingramcontent.com/pod-product-compliance
Lightning Source LLC
Chambersburg PA
CBHW050814160426
43192CB00010B/1758